ASCD YEAR BOOK

1998

LEARNING WITH TECHNOLOGY

EDITED BY CHRIS DEDE

ASSOCIATION FOR SUPERVISION AND CURRICULUM DEVELOPMENT
ALEXANDRIA, VIRGINIA USA

Association for Supervision and Curriculum Development
1250 N. Pitt Street • Alexandria, Virginia 22314-1453 USA
Telephone: 1-800-933-2723 or 703-549-9110 • Fax: 703-299-8631
Web site: http://www.ascd.org • E-mail: member@ascd.org

Gene R. Carter, *Executive Director*
Michelle Terry, *Assistant Executive Director, Program Development*
Nancy Modrak, *Director, Publishing*
John O'Neil, *Acquisitions Editor*
Mark Goldberg, *Development Editor*
Julie Houtz, *Managing Editor of Books*
Kathie Felix, *Associate Editor*
Jo Ann Irick Jones, *Copy Editor*
Ginger O'Neil, *Copy Editor*
Gary Bloom, *Director, Editorial, Design, and Production Services*
Karen Monaco, *Senior Designer*
Tracey A. Smith, *Production Manager*
Dina Murray, *Production Coordinator*
John Franklin, *Production Coordinator*
Valerie Sprague, *Desktop Publisher*

Printed in the United States of America.

January 1998 member book (pc). ASCD Premium, Comprehensive, and Regular members periodically receive ASCD books as part of their membership benefits. No. FY98-4.

ASCD Stock No. 198000
ASCD member price: $15.95   nonmember price: $18.95

ISSN: 1042-9018

ISBN: 0-87120-298-0

03 02 01 00 99 98   10 9 8 7 6 5 4 3 2 1

1998 Yearbook

Introduction

CHRIS DEDE, EDITOR

"Learning" intentionally comes before "technology" in the title of this Yearbook. The authors and editor of this volume see technology as a means, not an end in itself. These chapters were created by people who have worked very hard to develop new media as tools in the service of richer curricula, enhanced pedagogies, more effective organizational structures in schools, stronger links between schools and society, and the empowerment of disenfranchised learners. We believe that properly designed and implemented computing and communications have the potential to revolutionize education and improve learning as profoundly as information technology has transformed medicine, finance, manufacturing, and numerous other sectors of society. None of us see technology as a "vitamin" whose mere presence in schools can catalyze better educational outcomes. We also reject the idea that technology is simply another subject in the curriculum, suited primarily for teaching students to use tools they may encounter as adults.

This Yearbook focuses on exemplary projects with the potential to reconceptualize schooling; it does not examine technological applications that automate typical practice. Here the important issue is using new media to provide an effective means of reaching 21st century educational objectives through distributed partnerships for learning. The technology-driven evolution of a global knowledge-based economy requires more than "drill and skill" preparation for work and citizenship. Just as medical practice has shifted dramatically with antibiotics, anesthetics, and immunizations, so the skills and knowledge required of educators are rapidly changing, as computers and communications enable a broader range of students to master more complex subjects via rich interactions, both with teachers and with resources outside of classroom walls.

As educators, our task is to prepare our children to function in a future civilization created by the biggest leap in technology since the Industrial Revolution two centuries ago. The key to meeting this challenge centers on facilitating students' mastery of sophisticated knowledge. Our authors are designers/developers/researchers focused on learning, individuals who work with technology because they find computers and communications a powerful means to improve educational outcomes for all students. They are the busiest people I know and I am grateful for their participation.

You, the audience for this Yearbook, are the reason we put forward our ideas. The opportunity to share visions, successes, and lessons learned with more than 100,000 practitioners was irresistible. Systemic educational reform based on learning with technology is a complex task requiring literally millions of people working together to aid tens of millions of students. We want to scale-up our islands of innovation, improving their design and implementation in the process, and need your help to accomplish this.

As editor, I have focused on one crucial theme within technology-based innovations: helping all students master complex skills and content to prepare them for 21st century society. I see this as the most important challenge facing schools today. The chapters that follow provide numerous illustrations of exemplary projects using technology to improve education. My only regret is that space constraints made it impossible to include all of the efforts worthy of attention.

This Yearbook is organized into five sections. The three chapters in the section "Empowering Learning Communities" describe computer-based tools and curricula that help students to master complex content and skills. This theme is expanded by the three chapters in the "Extending Learning Communities" section that emphasize how suites of interrelated technologies can enable large-scale educational reform. Two chapters serve as "bookends" for these sections on current exemplary projects, presenting visions of learning with technology in a decade or two, depicting huge shifts in the practice and organization of schooling by extending today's innovations with more powerful technologies coming via the entertainment and information services industries. In contrast, the closing chapter delineates "tomorrow morning" issues in implementing technology and gives advice on some of the tough questions now facing educators. Readers can skip around in the Yearbook as they choose; every chapter is written so that its ideas are relatively self-contained. Each set of authors also provides Web sites and other sources of information to enable additional exploration and follow-through.

Many of the projects presented here focus on educational technology as a means of learning science and mathematics. Of course, these are not the only subjects that can benefit from computers and communications; information technology is a powerful medium for teaching the social sciences, the humanities, the arts, and the professions. However, because the National Science Foundation is currently the primary source of funding for exemplary research on educational technology, most of the studies underway today tend to emphasize technical subjects. In addition, this volume stresses K-12 instruction because the vast majority of ASCD members work in that arena. Nonetheless, the chapters' underlying ideas about pedagogy, equity, and linkages between schools and community can generalize and transfer across the curriculum and across a range of students' developmental levels.

After the Introduction, Kozma and Schank present a vision of the way technology may support educational reform in the 21st century. They depict vignettes of students learning in school settings quite different than today's classrooms and link these educational advances to shifts in the nature of work and society likely to occur over the next generation.

Krajcik, Soloway, Blumenfeld, and Marx open the "Empowering Learning Communities" section by describing two learning tools created as part of a larger initiative to improve science education. Model-It aids students in science inquiry by helping them build models of complex systems, such as stream ecosystems. PIViT provides teachers with support for designing and implementing instructional plans that enable project-based science education.

Guzdial extends this discussion about orchestrating project-based learning by presenting a five-stage model for project progression. He discusses tools designed to aid each stage, shows how similar technological supports can be modified to support learners at different stages of expertise, and describes outcomes from a range of classroom settings where these tools are used.

Behrmann concludes the "Empowering Learning Communities" section by discussing a range of assistive technologies that can improve learning for children with various types of abilities. He outlines the evolution of these tools and indicates how each type of technological advance may compensate for a particular need. This array of technologies provides a repertoire of devices teachers can use to aid in mainstreaming students with disabilities and developing classroom environments that empower all learners to succeed.

To begin the "Extending Learning Communities" section of the Yearbook, the Cognition and Technology Group at Vanderbilt University describes the Schools for Thought project currently underway in a number of settings across the United States. This initiative uses technology to restructure curriculum, assessment, professional development, and community participation in education. Here, tools developed by several different research groups are integrated into a coherent strategy for technology-based educational reform.

Honey, Hawkins, and Carrigg continue this section, describing the ways they have used technology to empower a comprehensive program of educational reform in an urban New Jersey school system. Their project, Union City Online, employs advanced telecommunications to integrate Internet resources into the district's curriculum, aid in teachers' professional development, enable students in creating World Wide Web resources for the community, and facilitate parental involvement in children's education. This project has been designed to generalize many of its results to other educational settings using networked technologies as tools for learning, teaching, and community involvement.

Concluding the "Extended Learning Communities" section, Lento, O'Neill, and Gomez describe a range of methods for integrating Internet services into school communities. They illustrate their strategies by describing the evolution of CoVis, a project that uses Internet resources to aid science instruction by forming virtual communities based on collaboration among teachers, students, and scientists. This project illustrates the philosophy that, to prepare students for the future, learning environments in school settings should mirror the processes and tools of emerging workplace settings.

To complement Kozma and Schank's vision in Chapter 1, Riel describes another possible future for learning and teaching in educational communities. This scenario centers on teacher learning and continuous professional development as elements crucial to student success. She describes technology-based strategies for organizing the collaborative learning of students and educators in ways quite different than those found in schools today.

The final chapter shifts the focus from the future to what to do "tomorrow morning" in implementing the types of ideas described in this Yearbook. Here, the emphasis is on how to scale up the scattered, successful "islands of innovation" empowered by instructional technology into universal improvements in schooling enabled by major shifts in standard educational practices. Six questions that school boards, tax-payers, educators, business groups, politicians, and parents are asking about implementing large-scale, technology-based educational innovations are examined. The answers outline a strategy for scaling-up, leveraging the power of technology, while minimizing its intrinsic challenges.

Common themes pervade the disparate applications that all of our authors have developed for learning with technology. These include:

- guided, reflective inquiry through extended projects that inculcate sophisticated concepts and skills and generate complex products,
- standards-based curricula centered on authentic problems and real world settings,
- modeling and visualization as powerful means of bridging between experience and abstraction,
- students' collaborative construction of meaning via different perspectives on shared experiences,
- mixtures of face-to-face and virtual learning communities, using advanced tools similar to those in today's high-tech workplace,
- students as partners in developing learning experiences and generating knowledge, and
- success for all students through special measures to aid the disabled and the disenfranchised.

To make this model of learning affordable and sustainable, our authors emphasize:

1. reconceptualizing educators' roles, knowledge, and skills;
2. building partnerships among teachers, parents, workers, experts, and the community; and
3. encouraging systemic reform that simultaneously alters curricula, pedagogy, assessment, incentives, and the organization and management of schooling.

Such an approach to innovation underscores that the greatest barriers to actualizing these visions of educational technology are psychological, organizational, political, and cultural—not technical or economic, even though these are significant obstacles.

The authors and editor hope that this Yearbook will stimulate an extended dialogue among ASCD members about improving the visions illustrated here, implementing and extending powerful ways of learning with technology, scaling-up isolated innovations into shifts in standard educational practices, and helping all students master complex skills and content to prepare them for 21st century society.

Part I

Education in the 21st Century: One Vision

1

Connecting with the 21st Century:

Technology in Support of Educational Reform

ROBERT KOZMA AND PATRICIA SCHANK

INTRODUCTION

During the past decade, a number of deficiencies have been recognized in our current approach to schooling in the United States, deficiencies that must be addressed if our students are to be prepared for work and life in the next century (Resnick 1987). In this chapter, we present a vision for 21st century education that addresses these perceived shortcomings. Our vision includes an image of what schools could be like and a set of interlocking social, pedagogical, and technological changes that could transform the entire educational enterprise.

Currently, the emphasis in U.S. schools is on individual learning and performance—what students can do by themselves without the aid of other students or external supports such as books, notes, calculators, and computers. From time to time, students get to use computers in the back of the classroom and, occasionally, group activities are under-

3

taken. But, when it comes down to it, students ultimately are judged on their solo performances on tests and assignments. Schools stress the learning of specific facts and generalized principles outside of the context of their use in the real world and apart from the value, needs, or interests that children may bring with them to the classroom. And, American schools are organized in assembly-line fashion with the curriculum divided neatly into subjects, taught in predictable units of time, arranged sequentially by grade, and controlled by standardized tests.

This approach to schooling served us well when our production economy demanded a large number of graduates who could read, write, perform simple computations and, most of all, take direction from supervisors. But the 21st century promises to make very different demands on our students and schools. Economists (Reich 1991) see a dramatic shift in jobs away from those engaging individuals in production services, moving workers instead toward the role of "symbolic analysts." Symbolic analysts are problem identifiers, problem solvers, and strategic brokers. They have job titles such as research scientist, engineer, public relations executive, lawyer, consultant, art director, cinematographer, writer, musician, and television producer. Symbolic analysts use a variety of tools and resources, including computers and scientific and creative instruments, to generate and examine words, numbers, and images. They often have partners and associates and work in small teams. Their work schedules may vary, depending on a particular project. Their work products range from plans, designs, sketches, and scripts to reports, models, and multimedia productions that are judged on such criteria as originality, cleverness, and the degree to which they solve a problem.

To meet these new demands, students will need to acquire a new set of skills. They will need to be able to use a variety of tools to search and sort vast amounts of information, generate new data, analyze them, interpret their meaning, and transform them into something new. They must have the ability to see how their work fits into the larger picture, to understand how the pieces work together, and to assess the consequences of any changes. They must develop the capacity to work with others to develop plans, broker consensus, communicate ideas, seek and accept criticism, give credit to others, solicit help, and generate joint products.

Change of this magnitude cannot depend on the skills and efforts of teachers alone; the entire community must elevate the importance of education in everyday life by developing a strong social commitment to the educational endeavor shared by students, teachers, parents, businesses, and community leaders.

Schools, homes, and workplaces today function separately—connected always by geography and circumstance, but only infrequently by common purpose and collaborative action. In our vision of communities of understanding, digital technologies are used to interweave schools, homes, workplaces, libraries, museums, and social services to reintegrate education into the fabric of the community. Learning is no longer encapsulated by time, place, and age, but has become a pervasive activity and attitude that continues throughout life and is supported by all segments of society. Teaching is no longer defined as the transfer of information; learning is no longer defined as the retention of facts. Rather, teachers challenge students to achieve deeper levels of understanding and guide students in the collaborative construction and application of knowledge in the context of real-world problems, situations, and tasks. Education is no longer the exclusive responsibility of teachers; it benefits from the participation and collaboration of parents, business people, scientists, seniors, and students across age groups.

How can technology support this transformation? First, the Internet is connecting schools with one another and with homes, businesses, libraries, museums, and community resources. This connection between school and home will help students extend their academic day, allow teachers to draw on significant experiences from students' everyday lives, and enable parents to become more involved in the education of their children and find extended educational opportunities for themselves. Connections between school and work will allow students to learn in the context of real-life problems and will allow teachers to draw on the resources of other teachers, a range of professional development providers, and technical and business experts. Connections among schools, homes, and the rest of the community will enable students to relate what is happening in the world outside to what is happening in school, will allow teachers to coordinate formal education with informal learning, and will allow the community to reintegrate education into daily life.

As important as digital information technology is to our vision of the future, we have deliberately avoided the temptation to become speculative about cutting-edge developments. We have chosen to be conservative and limit our chapter to technologies likely to be in wide use early in the next century. We focus instead on the collateral social and educational reform that must occur for this transformation to be realized. We have been daring, however, in developing a vision that addresses the reform issues in systemic and positive ways. When advanced technologies are integrated into a broad effort for school reform, educators, students, parents, and communities will have a powerful combination that can bring necessary, positive change to the U.S. educational system (Means and Olson 1995).

We present a vision, not a prediction, of the way education might be transformed when technology is coordinated with significant social and pedagogical change. We do not assert that this will happen, only that it can and should occur.

With that introduction, let's look at what schools might be like in the 21st century.

A VISION FOR 21ST CENTURY EDUCATION

CHARACTERS (IN ORDER OF APPEARANCE):

> Carmela Zamora (age 15) and Steve Early (age 14), Falcon learning team members.
> Nelson, Carmela's 17-year-old electronic pen pal. The two met the previous summer at a Science Camp not far from Nelson's home town.
> Valerie Spring, a senior teacher with a degree in biology who lives in the western U.S., a member of TeachNet.
> Sharon Gomez, a mathematics teacher.
> George Shepherd, an apprentice first year language arts teacher.
> Noriko Miyake, a science teacher on the east coast, a member of TeachNet.
> Christopher Lindsay, a school-work coordinator.
> Ms. Lucero, an engineer at Earth Systems, Inc.
> Mr. and Ms. Early, Steve's parents, owners of a small pet store.
> Other children, schools, parents, and community members.

SETTING

Most of the events take place in the McAuliffe Learning Center in Lone Tree, Nevada, the physical locus for formal learning, community activities, and social services. McAuliffe is divided into a variety of spaces designed for technology-supported learning. The facilities include learning team pods with a workstation and project resources, small-group meeting rooms with collaborative technologies and personal interaction devices, and a large multimedia auditorium and performance center. These resources are used by students and teachers during the day and are open to community members at other times. The students and teachers form "learning teams" around various cross disciplinary projects. The teams generally are comprised of four to eight students and coached by at least two teachers with complementary areas of expertise (e.g., math and language arts).

SCENE ONE

As she does every morning, Carmela Zamora eats breakfast in front of the telecommunications computer (TC). While she watches a news program in one window, her personal communication service relays a video message in another window from her friend, Nelson, who lives in a neighboring state. Nelson's vid-message is about a train derailment on a river upstream from the science camp where their school groups stayed.

"The train caused a hazardous fuel spill and now endangers the ecosystem along the river," Nelson explains. "I am afraid it will poison the water and hurt the animals."

Also concerned, Carmela works at the keyboard to construct an information seeking program, an online "scout" agent, that can electronically search for news clips about the accident, sort them chronologically, and store them on the school server. As she finishes her breakfast, Carmela and her parents watch the video retrieved by the scout agent.

At school, Carmela meets Steve and three other members of their Falcon learning team at the playground. This morning they must present a project idea to their teaching team. Steve also heard about the spill, and he and Carmela tell the others about it.

"I want to find out what can be done to save the animals along the river and keep the campground safe," Steve says. "Let's ask the teachers if we can figure out how to stop hazardous spills from hurting the environment."

The other students agree.

In the project planning room, teachers Valerie Spring, Sharon Gomez, George Shepherd, and the five students of the Falcon learning team gather around the computer and open a project planning software program. This software walks them through the design and management of their project, from goals and timelines to individual student tasks.

Ms. Spring starts off, "OK, let's fill in the goals for the project. What do you have in mind?"

The students chime in with their ideas.

"Your ideas sound interesting," Ms. Spring responds, "but what specifically would you like to accomplish with your project?"

"I think we should come up with ways to clean up the mess," says Carmela.

"One report said the scientists are trying to figure out normal conditions for the river to help them know how serious it is," another student offers. "Do you think they could use the data we collected at camp? Like water temperature and pH?"

"Good idea," says Ms. Gomez. Always looking for a way to bring math into the conversation, she adds, "Suppose the scientists know how much spilled. How would you calculate the concentration of the fuel in the river, and determine if the concentration is safe?"

Steve puzzles for a moment and then offers, "If you knew the volume of the river you could calculate it. You could test the water to be sure."

"Yeah, it might help to look at temperature and pH before and after the spill, too," Carmela says. "My mom was a summer science camp volunteer, so she has names of other students who were at the camp and would also have data. Maybe she could even be a mentor on our project."

"Let's e-mail those kids! And the counselors who have lists from other summers! We can collect our observations, notes, and pictures from our nature walks and offer them to the scientists!" Steve shouts. "Maybe they'll tell us more about the damage and we can figure out ways to clean up the mess together."

"Great idea," says Ms. Spring. "First, let's plan the project in more detail. "Carmela, would you like to contact your mother to see if she'd like to work with us on this?"

Carmela contacts her mother on the telecommunications computer, and she agrees to help.

Using the planning software, the team and Ms. Zamora work together to develop the project's organization, timeline, and goals, as well as each student's learning objectives and tasks. As the discussion progresses, the teachers check the goals the students suggest against those listed in the curriculum. The software lets them see the skills, activities, and subject matter that past projects have emphasized, as well as each student's learning history profile. The teachers suggest activities that will help the students gain the skills, knowledge, and experiences identified as absent from their profiles.

With the planning software, Ms. Gomez is able to indicate that the new project will help the students strengthen certain mathematical skills and concepts, including measurement of concentrations, graphing number relationships, and making mathematical connections to real-world problems. She can also list scientific models, skills, and concepts appropriate to the project, including thinking critically about the relationships between evidence and explanations, and understanding ecosystems and organisms. Like most of her colleagues, Ms. Gomez has become adept at thinking in terms of the broad, ambitious goal statements established by her school and district and converting these to specific student activities.

The students decide to begin by immediately contacting the other schools affiliated with the camp and the scientists studying the river. They decide to ask Nelson and his schoolmates to collaborate by gathering video and other information about the accident, and to assess the spill's impact and various cleaning methods. They want to obtain the data as soon as possible and make an interactive multimedia report as their final product.

"You need to think about your audience for the report," comments Mr. Shepherd, their language arts teacher, "and what they would want to know about your topic."

The students decide to store their multimedia report on the community video server, make it available through the community access cable television channel, and send it to all of the scientists and schools contributing data. At its conclusion, the report will take viewers to the Environment Chat Room on the GlobalNet, where they can talk to scientists, environmentalists, and others about the problem and potential solutions.

Each student has an assignment and downloads the project plan into a hand-held computer, or personal digital assistant (PDA), loaded with a beginning set of pointers to key resources.

"I think we could really help here," Carmela says. "I can't wait to tell Nelson."

SOCIAL PERSPECTIVE

CONNECTING LEARNING TO HOME AND PARENTS

The National Education Commission on Time and Learning (NECTL 1994) identified time constraints on learning as a major impediment to educational reform. While efforts to extend time in school are important, another key factor in creating more time for learning is the extension of learning environments to include students' homes and parents.

In the United States, children between the ages of two and 11 spend an average of 28 hours per week in front of the television and teenagers spend about 23½ hours weekly watching tv (Comstock 1991). But only 29% of U.S. students spend 14 or more hours per week doing homework (NECTL 1994). Time spent at home represents a significant resource for student learning, and can be particularly valuable if parents are involved.

When parents are involved with children's learning—especially parents of students from low-income families and ethnic minorities—students earn higher grades and score better on tests. Involved parents have higher expectations for their children and their schools and, consequently, schools perform better when parents are involved. It is estimated that a school as a whole begins to improve when as few as a third of the parents become actively involved (Henderson and Berla 1994). In this case, the performance of all students tends to improve, not just that of the children whose parents are participating. Ultimately, the highest level of student achievement occurs when families, schools, and community organizations work together.

The increased pervasiveness and connectivity of technology in the home can increase parent involvement and student interest in out-of-school learning. Easy access to technology and rich educational content can make learning easier, more convenient, more interesting, and more productive. Connections between school and home can put a student's out-of-school technology use into the context of school learning. Parents can find increased involvement easier as time constraints dissolve and education-related interactions can occur in the comfortable, familiar context of home.

In Scene One, the ready access to computing and its integration with television supported Carmela's use of her morning "telecommunication" as the origin of a learning project. In Scenes One and Three, con-

10

nections between school and home allow Carmela's mother and Steve's father to mentor the students' project without attending the school meetings. In Scene Three, technology also allows Steve to bring his project work home in a form that connects to digital data from his father's store. Behind the scenes, technology supports other activities and services, including videotext services and dedicated school video channels that provide continual updates of school activities, video-mail messages that explain student assignments and provide tips for parent help, computer-based assignments, educational projects, and multi-player games that parents can experience with their children.

CONNECTING LEARNING TO THE WORKPLACE AND THE COMMUNITY

Society is recognizing that students must be prepared for productive jobs within the competitive world market and that the skills and knowledge for these jobs could be obtained if academic work more closely resembled authentic work. Reports such as *America's Choice: High Skills or Low Wages!* (National Center on Education and the Economy 1990) rang the alarm that the United States is not providing an education that prepares young people for productive careers in a technology-dependent and highly competitive 21st century work environment.

Work-related learning should expose students to both the practical contexts and the meaningful tasks of adult work, as well as the conceptual knowledge and generalizable skills normally associated with formal learning (Schlager, Poirier, and Means 1996). Teachers play the important role of guiding the transfer of knowledge between school and the workplace. At the same time, community members more experienced in the practical applications of these skills and knowledge can help students understand how they can be used to solve real-world problems.

An important motivation for learning comes from relating events that happen in the workplace and larger community to things that happen in the student's world. The need to understand these events and do something about them can create a context for learning. Connecting the needs, problems, and experiences of the outside world with the formal learning of the classroom makes the acquired knowledge more useful and the world outside more comprehensible.

With this work-related approach, students should be challenged by tasks that:

11

- Have analogs in adult work, but also reflect students' interests.
- Are complex and open-ended, requiring students to work through the definition of the problem and regulate their own performance.
- Relate to practical situations so that experiences from work and daily living provide important information, strategies, and insights.
- Can be accomplished in multiple ways, typically with more than one good answer or outcome.
- Are performed by student teams, with different students taking on different specialized roles.
- Are performed with the same information and the same types of technology tools used by professionals.
- Result in a product that allows students to feel they are making a contribution to the larger community.

Networked communications and collaborative software can be used to support new relationships among the school, the workplace, and the rest of the community. As reflected in our scenario, teachers, volunteers, and experts from various professions can jointly design realistic activities based on authentic tasks that motivate the learning of generalizable skills and concepts. Within this context, teachers provide an overall structure, assess student work, create ways for student self-assessment, and point out linkages between project activities and the concepts under study. Outside mentors and experts can work with students on specific tasks, providing guidance and assistance not associated with the grading process, helping students when they reach an impasse, and modeling the way practitioners in the field solve problems.

A Vision for 21st Century Education: Scene Two

Over lunch, Valerie Spring logs into TeachNet, a nationwide on-line professional development institute for teachers, and enters her virtual office. After reading the messages and flyers stuffed in the mailbox on the office door, she files in her "public" filing cabinet a position paper that she wrote for an accreditation workshop on teaching environmental awareness.

Using a diagram of the floor plan for the virtual institute, Valerie moves into the common area, a large space with a community directory, an announcement board, and an event calendar. She consults the community directory to look for a fellow middle school science teacher,

Noriko Miyake. Valerie knows that Noriko usually logs in after school and it's about that time on the east coast. Noriko had mentioned working on a hazardous materials project with her students last year, and she may have some helpful suggestions for the Falcon team.

After scrolling through several screens of login names ("There must be another brown-bag lunch seminar going on in the conference room!" Valerie thinks.), she identifies Noriko's online location. After paging Noriko, Valerie joins her in the Planetary Projects Room.

"Hi, Noriko." Valerie says over the audio channel. "Do you have a few moments to chat?"

"Sure," Noriko replies.

Valerie describes the Falcon team's project. After a short conversation, Noriko suggests that they look at EnvironModel, a virtual reality simulation environment she has used with her classes. The simulation was designed by Earth Systems Inc. to be used collaboratively by engineers in a corporate office and environmentalists in the field to plan quick responses to hazardous spills. A modified version had been developed for classroom use. With EnvironModel, students can "walk through" and experience a virtual spill site—an unsafe experience in real life.

Valerie and Noriko move to the Curriculum Resources Room to preview a demonstration version of the EnvironModel software. They launch the simulation in shared mode and it appears on both of their screens simultaneously. Noriko opens a sample environment and a 3-D rendering of a coastline fuel spill appears on their screens. Norika selects one of the sampling tools and demonstrates how to collect a sample at a particular spot and depth.

"This is an important skill because deciding where and how to sample can vary depending on the type of spill, the environment, and other things. Students learn this by comparing the results they get when they sample in different ways," Noriko explains.

"Once you've assessed the damage, you can select one or a combination of several cleanup methods, like fuel-munching microbes, jellies, or photocatalyst-coated microspheres. Where and how to apply them may depend on additional factors including how to minimally disturb the surrounding wildlife during the process," Noriko adds. "They have some nice support modules and resource materials on GlobalNet that go with this software. Earth Systems also has a resident engineer on their Internet site who is available to work with teachers and their classes. It's really a nice service."

"This is great! My students are particularly interested in a recent spill on a river that goes by their science camp. Are there example river scenarios, or can we create our own?" Valerie asks.

"Sure, the software lets you customize environments," Noriko says. She shows Valerie how to select one of several kinds of environments, chemicals, and sampling tools from a design palette.

"Sample environments are provided with the software and also are contributed by other teachers, so you may find what you need without creating your own, unless you want to," Noriko points out. "Environments contributed by teachers are kept here in the Example Environments folder. Feel free to try some and contribute your own."

Valerie's lunch period is almost over. She asks Noriko to meet again later in the week for more discussion after she has had a chance to explore the simulation and some of the sample environments on her own.

Valerie next moves to the TeachNet Library to copy a list of environmental project resources for her students. The GlobalNet Science Topic Kiosks, constructed and kept current by TeachNet members, are valuable resources for teachers like Valerie. Here she can find more resources that are both teacher-tested and mapped onto various state curriculum standards. If she needs information that is not in the library, she can consult the librarian or colleagues with more experience in the area in question.

The class bell rings and Valerie logs off to teach her 6th period class.

PEDAGOGICAL PERSPECTIVE

PROJECT-BASED LEARNING

In recent years, consensus has evolved around a set of national education goals (National Goals Panel 1994) to improve student learning. By the turn of the millennium, individual states and local school systems are likely to implement these goals into an extended set of standards used as a focal point for the design of learning environments and activities. Prominent among the national goals is the objective of increasing student ability to solve problems and demonstrate competency over challenging subject matter, particularly in mathematics and science. In our vision of the future outlined here, the "learning project" is used to meet these goals.

Project-based learning involves students in the identification of a problem or goal of personal or group interest and the generation of activities and products designed to solve the problem or meet the goal (Blumenfeld et al. 1991). Within this framework, students pursue solutions to nontrivial problems, ask and refine questions, debate ideas, design plans and artifacts, collect and analyze data, draw conclusions, and communicate findings to others. Because they work with problems from their own real-world situations, students are more motivated to pursue a deep understanding of a cluster of topics across related domains. This approach contrasts with the current practice of superficial coverage of many topics in a single domain.

The project also serves to value and integrate knowledge from multiple perspectives and disciplines. Using this approach, naturally occurring problems are not compartmentalized into subject areas such as mathematics, science, and language arts. Furthermore, solutions to problems benefit from the diverse expertise, perspectives, and modes of expression that come from multiple members of teams of students and teachers. No one person is likely to have the solution to complex, real-world problems and, as a result, differences among students in terms of expertise and experience are valued.

Project-based learning, particularly in terms of projects that emerge from student-identified interests, increases the complexity of planning and accountability. For teachers, the challenge of working with student-generated interests focuses on project development and efforts to make certain that students are challenged to accomplish important educational objectives within the curriculum. Teachers must build on individual strengths and accommodate the individual needs of students within the group. In addition, they must work with students to generate productive activities and provide access to useful resources.

Technology can help teachers and students manage the complexities of project-based learning. In Scene One, the teachers and students use project software to help them identify goals, make plans, and track progress. At the same time, the teachers use curriculum software to see what students have already accomplished, identify individual student needs, and ensure that the curriculum goals are embedded in the project. While developing their projects, students use real-world software tools. And teachers and students use technology to share experiences and resources.

SCAFFOLDING

"Scaffolds" are external aids that provide cognitive and social support for people new to a task or knowledge domain, much as scaffolds on a construction site support workers and materials while a building is erected. These external aids may be questions, prompts, or procedures provided to students that more knowledgeable people have internalized and provide for themselves. By providing this support, scaffolding allows students to manage tasks that are more challenging than those they are able to handle alone (Vygotsky 1978). When these aids are a normal part of the classroom discourse, students begin to model new skills for each other and seek assistance from the teacher and others in the group (Brown and Palincsar 1989). As students refine and internalize the new skills, the supports gradually can be withdrawn and students can perform more of the task on their own.

Problem solving and critical thinking are particularly challenging curricular goals for young students. They must learn to analyze problems and specify goals, identify information and plan problem-solving, identify work products and specify evaluation criteria, and work with a team to accomplish their goals. The use of scaffolding helps young students work through these cognitive and social processes. By using these processes repeatedly across projects, students begin to generalize them and apply them to problem solving outside of the classroom.

In our view of the future, students use a combination of technological and social supports to scaffold problem solving. In working on the fuel spill, the students use a computer-based tool for project design and management. This tool and the team of teachers scaffold student work by walking students through the planning process, asking them to define their goals, prompting them to select activities to accomplish these goals, guiding them to resources, and structuring their assessments. Students begin to use the scaffolded prompts socially with each other and, ultimately, the skills become internalized and used automatically. While students work on a project, the tool keeps their goals and plans visible as they get deeply involved in their activities.

A VISION FOR 21ST CENTURY EDUCATION: SCENE THREE

After speaking with Noriko, Valerie spent several weeks creating a model of the fuel spill, working with her students, her colleagues at McAuliffe, and Ms. Lucero, the engineer who works with schools using

EnvironModel. Earth Systems' Western office was grateful for the student collected data, which sped up the analysis and cleanup process. In return, Ms. Lucero is working with the Falcons to assess cleanup methods. For this part of the project, the students are coached by their biology teacher Valerie Spring, school-work coordinator Chris Lindsay, and math teacher Sharon Gomez.

Chris connects the Falcons' telecommunications computer to Ms. Lucero's computer at Earth Systems. The students are using the school version of EnvironModel, a package that has the basic features of the professional version and runs on less powerful and less expensive computers than the one in Ms. Lucero's office. With the linking technology, the fuel spill simulation appears on both computers simultaneously and can be altered by the students and Ms. Lucero. The students are wearing special glasses that enhance the 3-D lifelike effect of the environment.

The students can see Ms. Lucero's image onscreen, broadcast in a small window next to the larger screen displaying the fuel spill model. In her office, Ms. Lucero also can see an image of the students. She uses a stylus to select some photocatalyst-covered microspheres from the cleanup palette and sprinkle them on the spill. She speeds up the program's clock and the students see the spheres rapidly become coated with the fuel and convert it to carbon dioxide and water. A graph shows the length of time it takes to clean up varying amounts of fuel.

"How does this compare to other methods you've tried?" Ms. Lucero asks. "Your report should compare methods in terms of disturbance to the wildlife, speed and thoroughness of cleanup, cost, and ease. You might find that a combination of methods is best."

The student team discusses these and other issues with Ms. Lucero and the teaching team. At the end of the session, each student uses a hand-held personal digital assistant (PDA) to record information and a reflection on the day's activities in a "learning log." Meanwhile, as they work with each learning team, the teachers use their PDAs to track new skills the students have demonstrated and their impressions of how well the exercise fosters collaborative skills.

"OK, team," Ms. Gomez announces, "everyone please make a note in your PDA to show your parents the model and get their comments on relevant factors and anything we may have overlooked. Remember, part of the scientific process is presenting a coherent argument to your audience and incorporating their input."

"You will present your report in two weeks, so you should choose an approach by the end of the week," Mr. Lindsay reminds them. "Remember, we've invited communities near the spill site and schools and families who contributed to the project to watch the report. Ms. Lucero will also be joining us, so you need to be sharp."

That evening, Steve shows his parents the model.

"I'd like to know more about the animals in the area to help me weigh cost versus thoroughness," Mr. Early says. "You've shown me information on the kinds of animals, but not on the food chain. If some plants and insects die, could that cause seemingly unaffected animals to die indirectly by starvation?"

Ms. Early reaches for the family PDA and calls up the animal diet database used at their pet store. "Let's link these data to your classroom database, like this, too."

They look over the data and sketch out a food web that Steve can show his class tomorrow and incorporate into their report.

"Dad, will you mentor our next project?" Steve asks. "The kids want to learn about reptiles and raise one, and you work with reptiles at the pet store."

"Sure, let's send e-mail to your teachers asking how I can help," he says.

TECHNOLOGICAL PERSPECTIVE

A broad range of technological tools will be available in the next decade to support learning and connect it to the experiences, resources, and people outside of the classroom. For this discussion, we have focused on three selected areas—integrated personal communication services and agents, simulation and virtual reality, and virtual places and collaboration.

INTEGRATED PERSONAL COMMUNICATION SERVICES AND AGENTS

Current approaches for exchanging electronic documents and accessing the Internet assume that users send, receive, and store documents via a single service provider (America Online, Bell Atlantic, InternetMCI, etc.). These electronic services are separate from voice and other information services, creating difficulties and barriers for users.

Several trends suggest significant changes that will integrate these services and make them easier to use. Telephone companies are increasing infrastructure capabilities to transmit text and high-quality audio and digital video. Cable providers will likely offer similar services and access to the kinds of databases currently carried by information utilities. These companies are developing the infrastructure to provide video-on-demand and interactive home shopping, as well as building the video servers and set top boxes necessary to support these initiatives. Powerful, wireless information appliances such as the previously-mentioned PDAs will bring computer processing and communications to situations anytime and anywhere, allowing learners to work on projects opportunistically, regardless of their location. Support for the integration of all of these services and devices will be provided by networks of fiber, coaxial cables, and wireless communication connecting schools, homes, and offices to each other and to other networks around the world via satellite and microwave.

In Scene One, when Carmela checks the personal communication service on her television for vid-messages, she does not leave the television experience and go to a desktop computer to enter a communications mode in a different medium (that is, text). In addition, she doesn't have to interrupt her train of thought to log on to an information utility. She can access all of the needed information in one medium, using a single piece of equipment. Similarly, the students use their PDAs as needed, to update their "learning log" with information as varied as voice annotations, reflections, and pointers to new information from discussions in school and at home. The teachers use their PDAs to track student skills as they are demonstrated. This convenient integration of services frees the cognitive capacity normally used to operate different systems and allows for a deeper engagement with the ideas contained in the documents.

As a result of this type of service integration, the amount of information and the number of people available on electronic networks will increase dramatically. Tools will be needed to make this explosion of resources useful. Programmable, information-seeking programs—often called agents—will decrease the difficulty of finding and using resources. Collaborating with the user and with other agents, these programs will automatically perform functions such as searching, collecting, organizing, and distributing information to specific people at specific times. The agents will be instructed directly or trained by example. In training by example, a software agent monitors a user performing a task, forms a model of the task, and carries out the action in the future when it is "confident" that it "understands" the process (Maes 1994).

In Scene One, Carmela constructs an agent to find and organize information on the GlobalNet about the train derailment and fuel spill. In this case, the construction of an agent would be easy; the agent would recognize these as the information tasks that Carmela normally requests.

SIMULATION AND VIRTUAL REALITY

The opportunity to model a phenomenon offers students a significant new way to represent and operate on their understanding of the world. By manipulating and explaining dynamic models, students come to understand system relationships and uncover strengths and weaknesses in their understanding. Emerging advances in simulation technology and computational power will enable new types of teaching and learning, such as situated learning via immersive virtual reality (VR) and distributed simulations that create an illusion of three-dimensional space.

Computational power and speed has been quadrupling every three years while prices have been dropping by half, suggesting that classroom computers will have enough power to render and manipulate the detailed graphics such simulations require at speeds greater than those afforded by today's dedicated graphics workstations. Advances in virtual reality devices (e.g., special glasses, displays, and hand-held wands) will enhance the lifelike effect of the environment and let learners collaboratively interact with the simulation. Using such immersive, multisensory virtual realities, students and teachers will be able to conduct activities in, and construct new understandings of, a range of systems impossible (or unsafe) to experience in the real world––from studying virtual spill sites to reconfiguring virtual DNA molecules and exploring virtual galaxies (Salzman, Dede, and Loftin 1996).

In our scenario, the students and teachers create a virtual spill site using "smart objects" from a "design palette" that *know* how to interconnect and *know* about properties of the world in which they operate. The students "walk through" the fuel spill site to assess the damage and collect and analyze samples, and apply and evaluate cleanup methods. Here, the technologies that support modeling create a learning environment that involves students in a systematic process of recursive design—a process that requires the construction of a grounded understanding of science and math and the simultaneous development of a mental model of systematic inquiry.

VIRTUAL PLACES AND COLLABORATION

Currently, researchers are focusing a great deal of attention on work group computing, also known as computer-supported collaborative work environments. These are hardware and software environments that connect people, some at different sites, to work on shared tasks. These environments scaffold collaborative problem solving and design by allowing users to exchange and work on shared multimedia documents, in synchronous or asynchronous modes. Computer-supported cooperative learning environments are just beginning to spin out of these technological developments (Cockburn and Greenberg 1995, Pea 1994).

Developers of next generation collaborative work technologies are employing a particular technology called graphical multi-user virtual environments (MUVEs) (Roseman and Greenberg 1996, Harrison and Dourish 1996). These "place-based" environments employ a spatial or building/room metaphor to organize and enable social relationships and interactions in a distributed environment. Text-based professional and educational MUVEs have existed for years (Bruckman and Resnick 1993), but emerging technologies are adding audio, video, shared applications, and shared gesturing to these environments.

In Scene Two, Valerie Spring works via TeachNet with a distant colleague who introduces and demonstrates a modeling environment useful to the Falcon team's project. On this network, she can also attend formal events (such as inservice workshops) and informal ongoing activities (such as teacher collaboratives) in the environment, and access standards-based resources used by her TeachNet peers. In this way, teachers can employ collaborative environments to sustain and enrich professional discourse, while gaining access to greater numbers of educators.

Similarly, the students collaborate with an expert, Ms. Lucero, who can see and manipulate the virtual spill site they are exploring. The students can hear Ms. Lucero, see what she is doing, and work with her to develop the virtual spill site. In addition, Ms. Lucero can see and hear the students. She collaborates with them to solve special problems their teachers do not have the expertise to tackle, and collaborates with their teachers to create an authentic task and experience for the students. These capabilities enable new kinds of relationships, new levels of participation, and new activities that support learning.

MOVING TOWARD THE VISION

If the vision that we present here is to be realized, a number of corollary social changes must take place along with the development of advanced technology. Education must become a more central focus of the community and innovative pedagogical practices must become commonplace. These changes will both support and be supported by technological resources as they become widely available. Two additional concerns are even more immediate: teacher training and equity of access to technology. Addressing these concerns is the necessary first step toward a vision of technology and education reform in the 21st century.

CONNECTING TEACHER TRAINING TO A COMMUNITY OF PRACTICE

To fulfill our vision, teachers would need to learn not only to use the various technologies described in our scenarios, but also to design, structure, guide, and assess learning progress centered around student projects. They would also need to help students design projects that incorporate important content and overcome work impasses without dominating the group process. For this process, teachers must become comfortable letting students move into domains of knowledge where they themselves lack expertise and they must be able to model their own learning process when they encounter phenomena they do not understand or questions they cannot answer. And teachers will need to continue to work with colleagues and other professionals to coordinate resources and services. Finally, teachers will need to be creative in finding ways to embed measures of student understanding within group projects—no easy task when multiple groups are working concurrently and different students assume different roles within the groups.

This new role for teachers is challenging and requires a very different approach to teacher professional development. New approaches posit that to support significant change, teachers must engage in sustained training and create membership in a broader community of professional practice (Little 1993). Typical summer institutes for teachers do little to alter the isolated and isolating character of classroom teaching. Too often, teachers returning from these experiences have little opportunity to implement what they have learned to make significant changes in established practices in their home schools. Ongoing, collaborative approaches to professional development help establish a professional culture that creates self-expectations among teachers that they will be studying some aspect of practice, comparing notes on implementation, seeking new ideas, and helping each other.

As collaborative technologies become more available, they will support this culture of sharing and continuous professional development. In Scene Two, Valerie finds a valuable resource in her colleague, Noriko, who is not the teacher next door (although these teachers are also collaborators in Valerie's work). Noriko is on the east coast; Valerie is in the western United States. The collaborative environment of virtual "places" allows the two teachers separated by distance to meet at a mutually convenient time, access rich resources, and work together with the same materials.

EQUITY AND ACCESS

The biggest assumption in our scenario is that students and their families will have near-universal access to high-end technologies. As technology connects learning environments and homes, it becomes increasingly important that differences in socioeconomic status not create an electronic form of school segregation between the technological haves and have-nots. Government and school programs and regulations will need to ensure the accessibility and affordability of at least a minimum form of network service for all homes.

Although the number of computers and video-based technologies in schools has grown exponentially (Office of Technology Assessment 1995), the number of hours per week that individual students have access to technology in most schools is still very low. Moreover, schools serving children from economically disadvantaged homes have less access to technology than those serving more affluent communities and, when they do have access to computers, are less likely to use them in ways other than drill and practice (DeVillar and Faltis 1991). In some states, school budgets are stretched so tightly that students must share basic texts; under such circumstances, teachers have a hard time building enthusiasm for learning to use new technologies.

There are positive signs, however, that the issue of equity is getting more attention. School financing mechanisms that leave low property value areas with limited per-pupil educational funding are being challenged successfully in many states. Federal programs are supporting the acquisition of technology and the implementation of parent involvement programs as part of the effort to improve the educational prospects for children at risk of school failure. Corporate support for education programs, particularly programs that incorporate technology, is at an all-time high and is likely to continue. The business community has become much more aware of its dependence on a well-educated workforce and of the changing cultural, gender, and ethnic composition of that workforce. Many corporations are making a particular effort to reach out to schools serving large numbers of children from less affluent homes where computer technology is usually absent.

The concentration of resources for technology in schools serving larger proportions of children from low-income homes will not bring real equal opportunity, of course, if the students do not have the same kinds of home resources used by other students and their caregivers. Without something approaching universal access and perhaps special rates for low-income households, we will not see the kind of across-the-board parental participation described in our scenario. One way to make technology accessible to all parents is to make school equipment and services available during non-school hours. The McAuliffe Learning Center described here, for example, has a technologically and socially rich community center. This central location of community groups, social services, and educational programs increases the effects of these services and their efficiency. Making these resources available to parents and students during non-school hours can increase opportunity and reinforce educational goals. As a place where parents and children come together to engage in learning activities, the learning center (or school) can become the center for building communities that learn together.

PLANNING FOR THE FUTURE

While the technologies discussed in this chapter are not currently available to most educators, schools can prepare for the future that we have envisioned here. The following are some general guidelines that can put schools on the path to applications of 21st century technology in the classroom:

- Train teachers to use technology and integrate it into the curriculum. Teacher training and technical support will be at least as important as establishing the technology infrastructure. Consequently, both should be major components of a school district's technology plan.
- Hire a technology person or teacher to provide ongoing technical support to the school.

- Encourage teachers and students to start using the Internet to become familiar with the technology. Provide Internet access in each classroom or, at the least, in as many classrooms as possible.
- Provide e-mail accounts for teachers and, if possible, for students. Provide teachers with Internet service accounts so that they can browse the Web from home.
- Establish a Web server at the school that teachers and students can use to store documents and create Web pages.
- Make equipment (e.g., Powerbooks, WebTV boxes, etc.) available for teachers to check out and take home to prepare lessons or to just get familiar with the technology. In addition, districts can establish programs to help teachers purchase computers.
- Install the highest speed Internet connections you can afford (T1 or T3 lines if possible, otherwise ISDN or whatever is the latest and fastest). The interactive simulations discussed in this chapter have high bandwidth requirements. Installing a low bandwidth network may save money in the short term, but may be costly in the long run when it must be replaced.
- Consider installing a wireless local area network to support access to services (e.g., Internet, voice, etc.) for hand-held, wearable, laptop, and even desktop devices. The wireless approach may be the easiest way to provide Internet access to all classrooms, especially in old buildings.
- "Play" with advanced technology at every opportunity, including exhibits, museums, and Web sites such as SRI's TAPPED IN.

  The Teacher Professional Development Institute, or TAPPED IN, is a project of the Center for Technology and Learning at SRI International (Schlager and Schank in press). This project includes the development of a synchronous multi-user environment for teacher development, similar to the TeachNet experience featured in Scene Two. Experience TAPPED IN at http://www.tappedin.sri.com/

REFERENCES

Blumenfeld, P.C., E. Soloway, R.W. Marx, J.S. Krajcik, M. Guzdial, and A. Palincsar. (1991). "Motivating Project-Based Learning: Sustaining the Doing, Supporting the Learning." *Educational Psychologist* 26, 3: 369-398.

Brown, A., and A. Palincsar. (1989). "Guided, Cooperative Learning and Individual Knowledge Acquisition." In *Knowing, Learning, and Instruction*, edited by L. Resnick. (pp. 393-452). Hillsdale, N.J.: Lawrence Erlbaum Associates.

Bruckman, A., and M. Resnick. (May 1993). "Virtual Professional Community, Results from the MediaMOO Project." Presented at the *Third International Conference on Cyberspace* in Austin, Texas. Available FTP: Hostname: media.mit.edu Directory: pub/asb/papers/ File: MediaMOO-3cyberconf.txt.

Cockburn, A., and S. Greenberg. (October 1995). "TurboTurtle: a Collaborative Microworld for Exploring Newtonian Physics." *Proceedings of the First International Conference on Computer Supported Cooperative Learning (CSCW 95).* (pp. 62-66). Hillsdale, N.J.: Lawrence Erlbaum Associates.

Comstock, G. (1991). *Television and the American Child.* San Diego, Calif.: Academic Press.

DeVillar, R.A., and C.J. Faltis. (1991). *Computers and Cultural Diversity: Restructuring for School Success.* Albany, N.Y.: State University of New York Press.

Harrison, S., and P. Dourish. (1996). "Re-place-ing Space: The Roles of Place and Space in Collaborative Systems." In *Proceedings of the Conference on Computer-Supported Cooperative Work.* (pp. 67-76). New York: Association for Computing Machinery.

Henderson, A.T., and N. Berla. (1994). *A New Generation of Evidence. The Family is Critical to Student Achievement.* Washington, D.C.: National Committee for Citizens in Education.

Little, J. (1993). "Teachers' Professional Development in a Climate of Educational Reform." *Educational Evaluation and Policy Analysis* 15, 2: 129-151.

Maes, P. (1994). "Agents that Reduce Work and Information Overload." *Communications of the Association for Computing Machinery* 37, 7: 31-40.

Means, B., and K. Olson. (1995). *Technology's Role in Education Reform.* Menlo Park, Calif.: SRI International.

National Center on Education and the Economy. (1990). *America's Choice: High Skills or Low Wages!* The Report of the Commission on the Skills of the American Workforce. Rochester, N.Y.: Author.

National Education Commission on Time and Learning (NECTL). (1994). *Prisoners of Time.* Washington, D.C.: U.S. Government Printing Office.

National Goals Panel. (1994). *The National Education Goals Report.* Washington, D.C.: U.S. Government Printing Office.

Office of Technology Assessment. (1995). *Teachers and Technology: Making the Connection.* Washington, D.C.: U.S. Government Printing Office.

Pea, R. (1994). "Seeing What We Build Together: Distributed Multimedia Learning Environments." *The Journal of the Learning Sciences* 3, 3: 285-299.

Reich, R. (1991). *The Work of Nations: Preparing Ourselves for 21st-Century Capitalism.* New York: Alfred Knopf.

Resnick, L. (1987). "Learning in School and Out." *Educational Researcher* 16, 9: 13-20.

Roseman, M., and S. Greenberg. (1996). "TeamRooms: Groupware for Shared Electronic Spaces." In *Human Factors in Computing Systems CHI '96 Confer-*

ence Companion. (pp. 275-276). New York: Association for Computing Machinery.

Salzman, M.C., C. Dede, and B. Loftin. (1996). "ScienceSpace: Virtual Realities for Learning Complex and Abstract Scientific Concepts." In *Proceedings of IEEE Virtual Reality Annual International Symposium*. (pp. 246-253). New York: IEEE Press.

Schlager, M., C. Poirier, and B. Means. (1996). "Mentors in the Classroom: Bringing the World Outside In." In *Situated Learning Perspectives*, edited by H. McLellan. (pp. 243-261). Englewood Cliffs, N.J.: Educational Technology Publications.

Schlager, M.S., and P.K. Schank. (in press). "TAPPED IN: A New Online Teacher Community Concept for the Next Generation of Internet Technology." To appear in *Proceedings of Computer Support for Collaborative Learning (CSCL) '97*. Hillsdale, N.J.: Lawrence Erlbaum Associates.

Vygotsky, L. (1978). *Mind in Society. The Development of Higher Psychological Processes*. Cambridge, Mass.: Harvard University Press.

Part II

Empowering Learning Communities

Scaffolded Technology Tools to Promote Teaching and Learning in Science

Joseph Krajcik, Elliot Soloway, Phyllis Blumenfeld,
and Ronald Marx

Abstract

Technology can provide new opportunities to deal with age-old challenges in learning and teaching. In this chapter, we report on two pieces of software that we have developed and tested extensively in classrooms. We hope these software projects provide examples of the way technology can be used effectively in education to support inquiry learning and teaching. Our program, Model-It, scaffolds students as they engage in science inquiry and build models for complex systems (e.g., stream ecosystems, predator-prey systems, etc.). The Project Integration Visualization Tool (PIViT), a flexible design program, scaffolds teachers as they design and employ instructional plans for project-based science education. In addition to classroom evidence about the effectiveness of Model-It and PIViT, we also present an underlying rationale for their design.

Introduction

Inquiry is a central component of effective science teaching and learning (Lunetta 1997, Roth 1995). New constructivist and social constructivist approaches to science instruction feature inquiry as essential for student learning. Both approaches assume that students need opportunities to find solutions to real problems by asking and refining questions, designing and conducting investigations, gathering and analyzing information and data, making interpretations, drawing conclusions, and reporting findings. Congruent with recommendations by the American Association for the Advancement of Science (1993), the National Research Council (1996) urges "a de-emphasis on didactic instruction focusing on memorizing decontextualized scientific facts, and . . . new emphasis placed on inquiry-based learning focusing on having students develop a deep understanding of science embedded in the everyday world."

Constructivist conceptions of teaching and learning assign primary importance to the way learners attempt to make sense of what they are learning, rather than the way they receive information. In this view of learning, students actively construct knowledge by working with and using ideas (Brown, Collins, and Duguid 1989; Newman, Griffin, and Cole 1989; Resnick 1987). Drawing analogies from everyday learning, researchers point out that knowledge is contextualized and that learners solve real (complex and ambiguous) problems in situations where they use cognitive strategies, tools, and other individuals as resources. Integrated and usable knowledge is possible when learners develop multiple representations of ideas and, through their work in school and beyond, are engaged in activities that require the use of this knowledge. Cognitive tools that can extend and amplify learners' cognitive processes, such as computers and accompanying software programs, can help learners solve complex and ambiguous problems by providing access to information and data and opportunities to collaborate, investigate, and create artifacts (Salomon, Perkins, and Globerson 1991). Moreover, learning occurs in a social context; learners interact with and internalize modes of knowing and thinking represented and practiced in a community and draw on group members' expertise. Recent reform efforts from the American Association for the

Advancement of Science (AAAS) and the National Research Council (NRC) are consistent with these views, recommending that science be taught in a way that is authentic and engages students in inquiry and collaboration around real-life problems to help build a rich understanding.

The constructivist notions are not unique to science learning. Similar calls for an inquiry pedagogy have come from other core academic areas: language arts, social studies, and mathematics. Integrating across the disciplines is a natural outcome of a constructivist pedagogy. In focusing on authentic activities, students may well need to bring in content from a range of disciplines to make sense of those activities. In our work, we integrate the sciences into inquiry projects at the middle school and high school levels. We also integrate science with language arts in middle schools. Our approach and technology are effective in these multidisciplinary/interdisciplinary situations. And, our programs can cross disciplines. In this chapter, for example, Model-It is used in science instruction, but it is also effective for the social studies teacher working with complex social systems.

In our work in science classrooms, we help create learning environments that are consistent with constructivist ideas about teaching and learning (Blumenfeld, Soloway, Marx, Krajcik, Guzdial, and Palincsar 1991). Project-based instruction is one of several attempts by researchers in several fields to carry out constructivist theory in classrooms (Bransford and the Cognition and Technology Group 1990, Brown 1992, Linn 1997). Features of project-based learning associated with the premises of constructivist theory are presented here to help focus collaborative teacher discussion that grounds theory in the language of classroom practice (Figure 2.1).

The features of project-based science (Krajcik, Blumenfeld, Marx, and Soloway 1994) include:

1. a driving question, encompassing worthwhile content that is meaningful and anchored in a real-world problem/question;
2. investigations that allow students to ask and refine questions, debate ideas, make predictions, design plans and/or experiments, gather information, collect and analyze data, draw conclusions, and communicate their ideas and findings to others;
3. artifacts that allow students to learn concepts, apply information, and represent knowledge in a variety of ways as they address the question/problem;
4. collaboration among students, teachers, and others in the community; and

5. technology that supports students in data gathering, data analysis, communicating and document preparation (Salomon, Perkins, and Globerson 1991).

FIGURE 2.1

Framework of Project-based Science and the Challenges Teachers Face

Learning Theory	Project-based Science Feature	Challenges for Teachers

Authentic Problem
  Contextualized
  Important
  Complex
  Meaningful
    interesting
    valuable
	Driving Question
	  Real-world
	  Nontrivial
	  Worthwhile
	    science content
	  Feasible
		Question versus Topics
		    How can a teacher focus instruction on a
		    driving question rather than on specific
		    topics?
		Link concepts and activities
		    How can the driving question be used to
		    link concepts and diverse activities?
		Select/create
		    How can teachers select/create authentic
		    questions?
		Ownership
		    How can a teacher encourage students to
		    see the problem as authentic and take
		    ownership of the problem?
		Worthwhile science content
		    How can the driving question be used to
		    help students develop science
		    understanding?

Understanding
  Active
    construction
  Multiple
    representations
  Applying
    information
  Situated
  Using strategic
    thinking
	Investigation
	  Artifact
	    development
		Investigate
		    How does a teacher help students to
		    design, carry out, analyze, and interpret
		    investigations?
		Artifact development
		  Select
		    How can teachers select artifacts around
		    the driving question that are rich and
		    feasible so students can develop
		    meaningful understandings?
		  Create
		    In the process of creating artifacts, how
		    can a teacher help students share,
		    critique, and revise?
		  Assess
		    How can a teacher use artifacts to assess
		    student understanding?

FIGURE 2.1—*(continued)*		
Learning Theory	**Project-based Science Feature**	**Challenges for Teachers**
Community of Learners Collaboration Social context Negotiated meaning Distributed expertise	Collaboration Establish norms Sustain focus Hold students accountable	How can a teacher help students respect each other's opinions and ideas so that students will listen, share, and take risks as they explore ideas related to the driving question?
Cognitive tools	Technology Collaborate, investigate, and develop artifacts	Teacher use: Proficiency in instruction How can a teacher develop the skills to use the technology in the service of instruction? Student use: Investigation, collaboration, and artifact development How can a teacher help students use the technology for investigation, collaboration, and artifact development?

The changes in methodology that we advocate are consistent with the calls from national organizations for a new science pedagogy; the AAAS (American Association for the Advancement of Science 1993) and the NRC (National Research Council 1996) argue that K-12 science education needs to move beyond didactic instruction where students engage in activities and learn *about* science, to a more constructivist, inquiry-based pedagogy, where students actually engage in authentic, long-term, science investigations. If we are going to ask students to carry out serious science investigations, however, we need to provide them with tools that can scaffold and support these investigations. Teachers, too, need tools to support them in their work.

Fortunately, computers and communications technologies have progressed to the point where they can be crafted to meet the unique needs of learners. In collaboration with local science teachers, the Center for Highly-Interactive Computing in Education at the University of Michigan has developed a suite of six software programs, ScienceWare, that supports students as they investigate driving questions such as "Is

Traver Creek, behind our school, safe?" Constructed using learner-centered design guidelines (Soloway, Guzdial, and Hay 1994), ScienceWare tools support all phases of an investigation: data gathering (RiverBank); data visualization (Viz-It); modeling (Model-It); project planning for students (PlanIt-Out); publishing findings on the Internet (Web-It); and project planning for teachers (PIViT).

In this chapter, we explore the way technology can be designed and used to promote learning for students and teachers by examining two ScienceWare programs: Model-It and PIViT. Both are currently available for Macintosh computers; Java versions are in development.

- Model-It, a Macintosh-based modeling and simulation program, has been used by hundreds of high school and middle school students in suburban and urban settings. Originally a university project, Model-It is now a commercial product available from Cognito Learning Media in New York, http://www.cogitomedia.com/.
- PIViT (Project Integration Visualization Tool), a Macintosh-based design program, has been used by hundreds of classroom teachers throughout North America to develop project plans. PIViT can be downloaded at no charge from http://www.umich.edu/~pbsgroup/psnet/.

Supporting Students in Model Building: Model-It

Modeling is at the heart of the scientific enterprise. Scientists build models; they construct abstractions from observations (i.e., data) to generate explanations of phenomena. As currently practiced, modeling is very difficult for students because it requires a great deal of prior knowledge and mathematical ability. Models, especially computer-based models, are typically constructed from mathematical equations that represent phenomena. If high school or middle school students are expected to learn differential equations before they build models, they will be locked out of the central enterprise of science. By redefining the modeling task and providing appropriate support, however, modeling can be made accessible to these students.

The recent Project 2061 curriculum reforms suggest a high-level, qualitative approach to modeling:

> In modeling phenomena, students should encounter a variety of common kinds of relationships depicted in graphs (direct proportions, inverses, accelerating and saturating curves, and maximums

36

and minimums) and therefore develop the habit of entertaining these possibilities when considering how two quantities might be related. None of these terms need be used at first, however. 'It is biggest here and less on either side' or 'It keeps getting bigger, but not as quickly as before' are perfectly acceptable—especially when phenomena that behave like this can be described (American Association for the Advancement of Science 1993).

The challenge, then, in making modeling accessible to middle and high school students is to create a modeling environment that requires minimal prior knowledge from other domains, incorporates advanced interface design, enables rapid generation of simple models, and facilitates the learner's transition toward more expert modeling practices. Model-It supports learners first building qualitative models, and continues to provide assistance as they move toward more quantitative models with newly developed expertise.

A DESCRIPTION OF MODEL-IT

Model-It provides both a simulation environment *and* a modeling environment. Students can build and test models of their own, defining specific objects, factors, and relationships. The program is open-ended; students can work with many different types of simulations and can find more than a single answer to a given question. The distinction between modeling and simulating is critical: constructivist pedagogy strongly suggests that allowing learners to build and run their own models is cognitively more effective than allowing them to run someone else's model. Or, in the words of one 9th grade Model-It user, "[Model-It] makes you think more about a real-life situation, where there's no real answer. *You* set it up and everything."

The program uses Macintosh graphical user interface (GUI) components including windows, lists, pop-up menus, buttons, sliders, and editable text boxes. Sliders set initial values that can be changed while the model runs; new factors are automatically entered into lists and pop-up menus, and object pictures can be cut and pasted. Pop-up menu positions are carefully chosen. In the Relationship Maker window, the menus are used to define factors and qualitative relationships. With these menus, students do not have to remember and/or type factor names repeatedly.

In one of the program's two main screen views, World View, the background is an actual photo of Traver Creek, the stream behind Community High School in Ann Arbor, Michigan, where the 9th grade science class is exploring water quality. At the bottom of the screen, icons appear that can be inserted into the World View, representing factors such as weather and people (Humans may be fertilizing the park that borders the stream, for example. When it rains, the fertilizer is washed into the stream, changing its levels of nitrates, dissolved oxygen, and water quality, etc.).

To construct a model, students must create:

- objects—the pictured "things" in the model, such as houses, streams, and people;
- factors—the variables related to the created objects; and
- relationships between the objects and the factors.

With the Relationship Editor, students build a relationship from a string of phrases selected from drop-down menus. A relationship can be built, for example, between the nitrates (a factor) in the stream (an object) and the stream's water quality: "As Stream: Nitrates increase the Stream: Water Quality increases, by more and more." The graph at the right side of the screen is linked to this text expression; this graph changes as the text expression changes. The graph helps students transition to quantitative modeling. Differential equations are used to effect qualitative, textually-expressed relationships. In models such as these, the meters and graphs provide rich visualizations of model dynamics. While the program is running, an independent factor (in this case, the weather rainfall factor) can be changed to vary the simulation.

DESIGN PRINCIPLES UNDERLYING MODEL-IT

In designing software for education, we mindfully design for *learners.* In our group at the University of Michigan, we have developed a rationale for learner-centered design (Soloway, Guzdial, and Hay 1994; Jackson, Stratford, Krajcik, and Soloway 1996; Soloway, Jackson, Klein, Quintana, Reed, Spitulnik, Stratford, Studer, Jul, Eng, and Scala 1996). In this model, learners are also users and the principles of user-centered design always apply (Norman and Draper 1986). User-centered design guidelines are not sufficient to address certain unique needs of learners, however, such as intellectual growth, learning style diversity, and motivational needs. Learners should have software that represents information in a familiar way and also helps introduce more professional or symbolic representations.

The central claim of learner-centered design is that software can incorporate scaffolding, or learning supports, to address student needs.

Scaffolding enables the learner to achieve goals or accomplish processes normally out of reach (Vygotsky 1978; Wood, Bruner, and Ross 1975). The following examines some of the scaffolding provided by Model-It:

- *The photo-realistic representation* of the *particular* stream under study provides an authentic, concrete, and personalized grounding for the student. This picture reminds the student of specific actions (e.g., monitoring water quality) at the stream and provides an anchor for thinking. Students can paste their own picture(s) into the program (a stream, a meadow for a predator-prey model, or the atmosphere for a climate model, etc.) to represent a main theme or various objects.
- *The Relationship Editor* hides complexity from the student, who initially doesn't need to know that differential equations are needed to represent relationships. As students gain expertise, they can build a data table to develop specific relationships, in place of the scaffolding provided by the drop-down relationship-building text.
- *Multiple linked representations* help the student understand the complexities of running, dynamic models.
- *Model simulations* with meters and graphs provide immediate, visual feedback of the current simulation. Students can directly manipulate current factor values while the model is running and immediately gauge their effect. "What if?" questions are generated and answered nearly simultaneously; hypotheses can be tested and predictions verified within moments. This interactivity provides opportunities for students to refine and revise mental models by comparing the interactive feedback with the feedback they expected to receive.

Assessing the Effect of Model-It

Model-It has been used since 1993 at Community High School in Ann Arbor, Michigan, in its three-year Foundations of Science integrated curriculum. Approximately 400 students have used the program in one to two week sessions held one to three times during the school year. A range of systems have been explored, including stream ecosystems, predator-prey relationships, climate, air pollution, and weather. Student and teacher feedback from this project has been used to refine instructional goals and make technology changes. Studies indicate that a large majority of the Ann Arbor students are learning the science content underlying the studied systems, although there are still issues to be addressed such as helping students understand and use feedback relationships. Overall, however, the students are learning a key science process: how to build a dynamic model of complex phenomena.

In a detailed study, Stratford, Krajcik, and Soloway (1997) analyzed the final models of stream ecology developed by 50 pairs of students, as well as conversations and interviews with eight pairs of the students videotaped while they were building the models. Fully 75% of the analyzed models were scientifically meaningful, coherent, accurate, and reasonable. The models made sense and were non-trivial, indicating that the students knew what they were doing and were able to express what they knew about stream ecosystem phenomena in the form of a dynamic model. Six of the eight student groups videotaped while building models were engaged in thoughtful elements of scientific reasoning, including analysis, reasoning, synthesis, and explaining.

The results from Stratford's work have implications for both classrooms and software design. The creation of dynamic models provides students with a meaningful way to engage in important elements of scientific reasoning and to represent what they know in a dynamic manner.

Model-It has also been used at the 7th grade level in two Detroit, Michigan, schools. Here, initial observations indicate that 7th grade students can build worthwhile models. Although the content may not appear as rich as that at the 9th grade level, the sophistication is consistent with curricular objectives and what would be expected from students in the 7th grade.

SUPPORTING TEACHERS IN PROJECT PLANNING: PIViT, PROJECT INTEGRATION VISUALIZATION TOOL

The Project Integration Visualization Tool (PIViT) helps teachers visualize and plan complex integrated curricula such as those associated with project-based learning. Instructional planning is never an easy task, and truly innovative and project-based instruction is especially challenging. Creative teachers must do more than plan individual investigations, artifacts, and teacher activities; they must also make these instructional components relate to and complement each other, as well as build toward assessment goals. The various PIViT tools support these teacher planning needs.

This program enables teachers to create projects by adapting topic-based units and instructional materials, or using published project materials. With PIViT, teachers have adapted existing topic-based units and created original projects around questions such as, "Will it rain?" (weather), "Are there poisons in our lives?" (chemistry), "How do I stay on my skateboard?" (physics), "Is it alive?" (biology) and "What happens to all our lunch garbage?" (ecology).

A DESCRIPTION OF PIViT

The main feature of PIViT is the Project Design Window that supports teachers in creating a "project map," a graphic representation that highlights the connections among individual components including concepts, driving questions, curricular objectives, investigations, teacher activities, and artifacts. The creation of a project map for an investigation of acid rain, for example, is structured around the driving question: "Do we have acid rain in our community?" Linked to this question are five related sub-questions. Tied to each sub-question are key concepts, related state curricular objectives, student activities, and artifacts. In this example, the key concept "acid" is linked to the sub-question "What is the acidity of our rain water?" Also tied to this sub-question is the student investigation "Collecting, analyzing, and interpreting acid rain data." Each design component (e.g., driving question, teacher activity, student investigation) has its own shape.

PIViT also provides three additional design areas:

- *Concept maps* support teachers creating a plan of the content students will explore in a project. Nodes from the concept map can easily be placed in the project design by selecting a menu prompt. Teachers can anchor a project design around a few key concepts and the concept map can elaborate on the subject area.
- *The calendar function* supports teachers in sequencing and temporalizing non-linear project designs. Teacher activities, student investigations, and other project components can be inserted into the calendar from the design window. The program enables teachers to schedule activities and move upcoming activities as scheduling needs change. In addition, teachers can enter daily notes into the calendar.
- *Libraries, or mini-databases,* can be created to support teachers in collecting and reusing related components. Teachers can collect

a variety of information from commercial materials or other projects and store them in a student investigation library that they construct. These investigations can be retrieved and modified at any time. PIViT also contains a library of the Michigan state guidelines for science. This library can be used to guide and critique teacher designs. Teachers also can select specific state guidelines and easily copy them into the project design window.

Support Structures in PIViT

PIViT, like Model-It and the other ScienceWare tools, was developed with the principles of learner-centered design. The following examines some of the PIViT scaffolding that assists teachers in project planning.

Each design component (driving question, investigation, artifact, teacher activity, etc.) has its own shape. By clicking and dragging these components, teachers can create links that relate the elements. This visual modality makes it relatively easy to see the relationships among project elements. Visually-oriented operations (e.g., dragging components around, cutting and pasting components) afford a low-cost method for changing plans and exploring design in a "what-if" style. PIViT's graphic representations scaffold teachers by focusing their attention on the relationships among the activities, and how those activities are integrated into a coherent conceptual whole.

The various windows in PIViT—the project design window, the concept map window, the calendar, and the description fields—are linked to each other. These links streamline movement among the windows. For instance, the description field associated with specific project components can be accessed from either the project design window or the calendar. Moreover, a teacher can examine the project in a graphical view and, with a simple click, can view the project in a calendar form. Switching among the different representations, or views, supports teachers in seeing the design of the project as a whole and determining the best way to sequence the project.

Each project design component (e.g., student investigation) has an associated description template that prompts teachers developing a design. The templates do not need to be filled in; however, we encourage teachers new to project-based science to work through them. The template prompts require explicitness and reflection that is beneficial, particularly for less experienced teachers (Urdan, Blumenfeld, Soloway, and Brade 1992).

Assessing the Value of PIViT

PIViT was in development for five years, with repeated cycles of development and teacher testing. Although learning to use PIViT was found to be a straightforward process, nearly all of the program's features were revised as a result of user tests. In particular, the calendar design was strongly influenced by classroom teachers.

Overall, PIViT supports teachers developing an understanding of project-based science as they construct their own projects, modify existing projects, or adapt curriculum materials to fit a project framework. PIViT reflects the complex and dynamic nature of teacher planning. Linear planning, such as that supported by outlining programs, does not support linking among components or reflect the iterative nature of the way teachers actually plan (Clark and Yinger 1987). The "language" of PIViT plans can serve as a lingua franca as teachers collaborate and share project plans.

CONCLUSION

With ScienceWare programs like Model-It and PIViT, technology can scaffold challenging tasks for students and teachers and help promote sustained inquiry teaching and learning. This type of technology creates two opportunities. It gives students an entry to areas of science to which they literally had no previous access. In addition, it supports an inquiry-based pedagogy in critically important ways. With a class made up of one teacher and 30 students, each of whom may be working on a different investigation, it is imperative that technology provide supportive scaffolding. The teacher cannot work on 30 diverse projects at different levels simultaneously.

The prospects for meeting the high standards developed by the AAAS and the NRC have never been better; technologies such as Model-It are poised to play a key role in enhancing the all-important science education of today's youth—to better prepare them for tomorrow's world. Programs like PIViT provide teachers with a resource that helps them modify curriculum to meet the new constructivist instructional framework. The use of computational technologies as described in this chapter has the potential to enhance the process of teaching and learning.

We hope that the use of these technologies will promote sustained changes in science classrooms. Substantial questions must be addressed, however, to construct effective technology. We have only begun to explore the appropriate scaffolds for promoting learning. We also have much to learn about the way computational and communication technologies can support teacher collaboration and professional development. We are encouraged by our successes to date, but we recognize that we are still in the early stages of a substantial effort.

REFERENCES

American Association for the Advancement of Science. (1993). *Benchmarks for Science Literacy*. New York, NY: Oxford Press.

Blumenfeld, P. C., E. Soloway, R. Marx, J. Krajcik, M. Guzdial, and A. Palincsar. (1991). "Motivating Project-Based Learning." *Educational Psychologist* 26, 3: 369-398.

Brown, A. (1992). "Design Experiments: Theoretical and Methodological Challenges in Creating Complex Interventions in Classroom Settings." *Journal of the Learning Sciences* 2, pp. 141-178.

Brown, J., A. Collins, and P. Duguid. (1989). "Situated Cognition and the Culture of Learning." *Educational Researcher* 18, 1: 32-42.

Clark, C., and B. Yinger. (1987). "Teacher Planning." In *Exploring Teacher's Thinking*, edited by J. Calderhead. (pp. 84-103). London: Cassell.

The Cognition and Technology Group. (1990). "Anchored Instruction and Its Relationship to Situated Cognition." *Educational Researcher* 19, 6: 2-10.

Jackson, S., S. J. Stratford, J. S. Krajcik, and E. Soloway. (1996). "Making System Dynamics Modeling Accessible to Pre-College Science Students." *Interactive Learning Environments* 4, 3: 233-257.

Krajcik, J. S., P. C. Blumenfeld, R. W. Marx, and E. Soloway. (1994). "A Collaborative Model for Helping Middle Grade Science Teachers Learn Project-Based Instruction." *The Elementary School Journal* 94, 5: 483-498.

Linn, M. C. (1997). "Learning and Instruction in Science Education: Taking Advantage of Technology." In *International Handbook of Science Education*, edited by D. Tobin and B. J. Fraser. The Netherlands: Kluwer.

Lunetta, V. N. (1997). "The Role of Laboratory In School Science." In *International Handbook of Science Education*, edited by D. Tobin and B. J. Fraser. The Netherlands: Kluwer.

National Research Council. (1996). *National Science Education Standards*. Washington, D. C.: National Academy Press.

Newman, D., P. Griffin, and M. Cole. (1989). *The Construction Zone: Working for Cognitive Change in School.* Cambridge, England: Cambridge University Press.

Norman, D., and S. Draper, eds. (1986). *User Centered System Design.* Hillsdale, N. J.: L. Erlbaum & Assoc.

Resnick., L.B. (1987). "Learning in School and Out." *Educational Researcher* 16, 9:13-20.

Roth, W.-M. (1995). *Authentic School Science.* The Netherlands: Kluwer.

Salomon, G., D. N. Perkins, and T. Globerson, T. (1991). "Partners In Cognition: Extending Human Intelligence with Intelligent Technologies." *Educational Researcher* 20, 3: 2-9.

Soloway, E., M. Guzdial, and K. E. Hay. (1994). "Learner-Centered Design: The Challenge for HCI In the 21st Century." *ACM Interactions* 1, pp. 36-48.

Soloway, E., S. Jackson, J. Klein, C. Quintana, J. Reed, J. Spitulnik, S. Stratford, S. Studer, S. Jul, J. Eng, and N. Scala. (1996). "Learning Theory in Practice: Case Studies of Learner-Centered Design." *Association of Computing Machinery - Computer Human Interactive - 96 Conference*, Vancouver, B. C.

Stratford, S., J. S. Krajcik, and E. Soloway. (1997). "Secondary Students' Dynamic Modeling Processes: Analyzing Reasoning About, Synthesizing, and Testing Models of Stream Ecosystems." Paper presented at the annual meeting of the American Educational Research Association, Chicago.

Urdan, T., P. Blumenfeld, E. Soloway, and K. Brade. (1992). "IByD: Computer Support for Developing Unit Plans." In *Instructional Models In Computer-Based Learning Environments*, edited by S. Dijkstra. Secaucus, N. J.: Springer-Verlag.

Vygotsky, L. S. (1978). *Mind In Society: The Development of Higher Psychological Processes.* Cambridge, Ma.: Cambridge University Press.

Wood, D., J. S. Bruner, and G. Ross. (1975). "The Role of Tutoring In Problem-Solving." *Journal of Child Psychology and Psychiatry*, 17, pp. 89-100.

3

Technological Support for Project-Based Learning

MARK GUZDIAL

Projects play an important part in learning. In a project, students engage in a complex process of inquiry (e.g., "How does that work?") and design (e.g., "But I want it to do this!"). The result is an *artifact*—a product of student knowledge that can be shared and critiqued. Projects that have successfully been used with middle and high school students include designing a solar house, modeling the effect of water pollution on a stream, and simulating two-dimensional projectile motion.

Projects have many benefits over other forms of classroom structure, including lectures or discussions. A project typically involves more complex cognitive processing which can serve as a catalyst for

Acknowledgments: Thanks to collaborating researchers Janet Kolodner, John Stasko, Cindy Hmelo, Amnon Shabo, Roland Hübscher, Sadhana Puntembakar, Jennifer Turns, Noel Rappin, Matthew Realff, Pete Ludovice, Farrokh Mistree, Janet Allen, and David Rosen. Funding to support this work is from the National Science Foundation (RED-9550458, CDA-9414227, ESI-9553583), Defense Advanced Research Projects Agency (DARPA) CAETI Program, and the EduTech Institute through a grant from the Woodruff Foundation.

greater learning. The resulting artifact can be used as a focus for review and reflection, and its public display can motivate student involvement. Projects have a context associated with them and, properly chosen, the context can situate learning to improve transfer. And, projects founded in community situations and values can tie a school to its community.

Cognitive science has shown that learning improves when skills and knowledge are explicit (Brown, Bransford, Ferrara, and Campione 1983). Many skills and forms of knowledge are tacit or deeply embedded within a practice, however, and projects provide the best available method to help students learn these embedded or non-decomposable skills and knowledge.

It can be difficult to orchestrate learning situation projects in the classroom. A teacher has an enormous challenge in managing 30 students engaged in authentic project-based learning. The classroom management techniques designed to help structure classrooms working with project-based learning are not easy for teachers to learn and use. And, even when the orchestration works well, students still may not learn from a project. In some cases, students may not be able to recognize the learning goals of the project and may focus simply on completing tasks, rather than the process of learning.

Teachers and researchers are learning what makes projects work— what makes orchestration possible and what makes student learning more probable. Since 1993, research at the EduTech Institute at Georgia Institute of Technology (Georgia Tech) has focused on making design problems (a form of project-based learning) effective learning opportunities in both middle school and undergraduate classrooms. The lessons from EduTech and other researchers working in project-based learning point to several requiremens for success:

- Students need opportunities to reflect on their learning and the purpose of their project.
- For learning to occur, student goals must be focused on learning or knowledge building.
- Enough support must be provided so that students can succeed. Too much support, however, can be overwhelming and too little support can make the complexity of the task too great.

This chapter describes some of the educational technology research related to software use in support of project-based learning. Technology, while not absolutely necessary to the success of project-based learning, can reduce costs (e.g., as compared with the time and effort needed for a teacher to become a master in problem-based learning methods), improve learning benefits, and create practical project-based learning opportunities for large numbers of students.

A Model for Technological Support

When thinking about technological support for project-based learning, it is important to consider every stage of a project and the best way to support each with technology, support across project stages, and techniques to make the separate technology pieces coherent and usable.

I have developed a five stage model of project progression, based on a review of many expert project models. In my model, the five stages include: initial review, decomposition, composition, debugging, and final review. The following briefly explores each of these stages:

1. *Initial Review*. In this early stage, students work to understand the problem addressed by the project, design a solution process, and conduct research on the problem and potential solutions. In problem-based learning, students often invent a prototypical solution or potential solution to drive the investigation and design process.

2. *Decomposition*. Students begin to define the components of a solution. It is particularly useful to look at examples and cases here, to serve as reminders of potential or alternate solution components.

3. *Composition*. In this stage, students begin assembling the solution artifact. At this point, they must deal with meshing the pieces and making sure all of them are compatible with one another.

4. *Debugging*. Here students test the artifact, to learn if their current knowledge is complete, inappropriately structured, incomplete, or incorrect. Testing and changing the artifact to correct problems ("debugging" in programmer's parlance) provide the student a most important opportunity to fail and learn from that failure. Debugging differs in different domains. In the case of a public speech, for example, "debugging" occurs when the speech is changed after it has been delivered. With a model car, debugging might involve measuring its speed down a ramp and then modifying the car to increase the speed.

5. *Final Review*. A period of reflection at the end of a project offers an important opportunity for the development of metacognitive skills. Here the student can consider where a process may have failed, where it was successful, and what was finally accomplished.

The following hypothetical example of this model is drawn from the Learning by Design (LBD) project directed by Janet Kolodner at Georgia Tech's EduTech Institute. In this program, design projects are used to help middle school students in the Atlanta area learn math and science. To solve the "Tunnel Problem," LBD students design a high speed train tunnel to move people quickly from coastal Savannah, Georgia, to the city of Atlanta. The problem may be altered in a number of ways, but the following provides one example of the way it might fit the five stage model.

1. *Initial Review*. At the start, students talk about what goes into tunnels, what high speed trains need to run, and the challenges of tunnels. They might begin to define *criteria* for contrasting possible solutions such as cost, the amount of time needed to tunnel, and the amount of time needed to make the trip.

2. *Decomposition*. Here the students begin to define pieces of the problem. Tunneling through the swampland near Savannah is different from tunneling through the more hilly region near Atlanta. Consequently, different types of tunneling will be required and different types of tunnel supports are needed.

3. *Composition*. Students put together designs and make a plan for constructing the tunnel.

4. *Debugging*. Currently, students make presentations about their tunnels, answering questions from teachers and fellow students. Although there is no mechanism to directly test the tunnel designs and plans, we are exploring the use of simulations for this purpose.

5. *Final Review*. The students write reports on their designs, specifically developed for an audience of future students working on the same problem.

The five stages of project progression do not represent a linear sequence for experts or students. During the decomposition stage, for example, students may realize that they did not fully understand the problem. And, during the composition phase, students may need to return to the initial review stage. Learners clearly loop back to previous stages at several points in the program process. These distinct stages, however, also occur in many experts' problem-solving processes and are a reasonable place to begin thinking about the activities that need to be supported.

Some activities may appear in more than one stage. The most significant activity in our work is collaboration—working or discussing with others. This activity appears in several of the five stages, including:

1. *Initial Review*. Collaboration during initial review is particularly useful when students work to understand a complex problem. Different individuals have different perspectives, and each can become a local expert to support a *jigsaw* collaboration.

2. *Decomposition*. In collaboration during decomposition, individuals can help one another to find methods or components to create solutions. A shared library of useful solution pieces can be one form of collaboration during decomposition.

3. *Final Review*. Collaboration during final review is very useful in providing an audience for metacognitive reflection.

In the Learning by Design program, collaboration appears in several stages. During initial review, students discuss the problem, using whiteboards for noting known facts about the problem, ideas for solutions, and learning issues that will surface when developing ideas. During decomposition, students work in groups to report on their research and suggest ideas for their designs. The final report, reviewing the whole design, is handled as a group activity.

In terms of learning, collaboration is less useful in composition or debugging, but may be necessary in terms of task completion. Collaboration can allow students to tackle complex and potentially motivating problems which they might not be capable of solving alone. To support team completion of a complex task, collaborative composition of the artifact and collaborative testing and improvement of the artifact will be necessary. It is never easy, however. In the composition and debugging stages, collaboration may actually impede learning because of the high cost of synchronizing effort, a key component for task completion.

Finally, the organization of the supports themselves can be critical for success in project-based learning. Although it is easy to provide support for each of these stages with six different tools, the resulting task of learning to use each of the tools successfully becomes quite complicated. In addition, simply using an expert's existing tool or environment (an integrated suite of tools) is also prone to failure. Students do not have the characteristics of experts in terms of diversity, motivation, or prior knowledge. In addition, they are at the steepest part of the learning curve and their needs change dramatically in a short period. As a result, the design of multi-faceted software environments for project-based learners is a complicated issue.

51

ONE APPROACH

There are a variety of approaches to addressing the needs of each of the stages, cross-stage activities, and project organization. A MOO, or multi-user domain based on object oriented technology, (an online virtual community with a strong fantasy theme) provides a paradigm for supporting collaboration and a metaphor for organizing all of the tools and supports in a project-based learning environment.

I use "Cognitive Apprenticeship" as a description of the desired learning environment. In a cognitive apprenticeship, students learn cognitive skills in the situated, learning-by-doing, guided exploration style noted in apprenticeship learning. The role of the computer in a cognitive apprenticeship approach to project-based learning is to provide some of the supports that a master-teacher might provide. *Scaffolding* is the term for the support that a master-teacher provides, so *software-realized scaffolding* is a computer-based implementation of human scaffolding.

As an example of non-software scaffolding, consider the three different ways a master plumber might help an apprentice plumber:

Communicating Process: The master plumber might ask the apprentice to "Watch me while I do this. I'll explain what I'm doing as I go along."

Coaching: The master plumber may say, "Now you do it. I'll watch over your shoulder and help you if you need it."

Eliciting Articulation: The master plumber may ask the apprentice for an explanation of the task to be performed. "Now, before you do the next step, tell me how you're going to do it . . . Now, why are you going to do that? Good! Now, let's get started!"

In software-realized scaffolding, the computer plays the three roles:

Communicating Process: Human master-teachers typically convey a process by performing activities and explaining how and why they do what they're doing, that is, *modeling*. While there may be some value in watching a computer perform a task that a student will copy (although evidence has been decidedly mixed) (Palmiter and Elkerton 1991; Palmiter, Elkerton, and Baggett 1991), there are many other ways for the computer to communicate process, including checklists or carefully constraining the environment. By enabling only certain menu items at certain times, for example, the computer can constrain the environment as a way to communicate "these options are the ones available to you now."

Coaching: When a student is performing a task, the master-teacher or computer can monitor student progress and offer hints or suggestions as the student works. Computer coaching can provide the right information at the right time and help students to monitor their own progress.

Eliciting Articulation: An important role for the master-teacher is to talk with the student, encouraging the process of reflection and self-assessment. The computer can play a similar role by prompting the student for plans, predictions, journal entries, and other important opportunities for reflection. The Inquire software system developed by Bank Street College is an excellent example. This software is designed to help students with computer inquiry by providing extensive scaffolding.

In this this chapter, I present examples and experiences from three of the five stages of project progression, including collaboration as a stage-crossing activity. The significant stages chosen for this examination are Initial Review, Decomposition, and Debugging. This material draws primarily upon Georgia Tech research, but also refers to some research on these kinds of supports occurring around the country (Brunner, Hawkins, Mann, and Moeller 1990; Blumenfeld, Soloway, Marx, Krajcik, Guzdial, and Palincsar 1991; Krajcik, Blumenfeld, Soloway, and Marx 1992 and 1994; Krajcik and Layman 1990; Ladewski, Krajcik, and Harvey 1994).

INITIAL REVIEW

The key insight that we have learned in the initial review process is that it is not enough to simply elicit articulation. Recently, articulation— including writing and reflecting on process and knowledge—has played an important role in several learning theories (Bereiter and Scardamalia 1989; Collins, Brown, and Newman 1989; Scardamalia and Bereiter 1991; Scardamalia, Bereiter, and Lamon 1994; Scardamalia, Bereiter, McLean, Swallow, and Woodruff 1989; Scardamalia, Bereiter, and Steinbach 1984). While evidence suggests that articulation is very valuable, students need guidance in how to articulate, what to articulate, and what to reflect upon in the articulation. The process of talking about something doesn't necessarily lead to improved performance or learning. Drawing upon the software-realized scaffolding approach, we have learned that the communicating process and coaching must also be applied to the activity of eliciting articulation—the three software-realized scaffolding activities are not exclusive of one another.

To help students review a problem and plan a solution, we provide scaffolding for planning and a better integration of the planning activity with the rest of the problem-solving process. At the EduTech Institute, we have been developing a set of design problems for middle school science classes.

Most recently, we have been classroom testing WebSMILE (Web-Scaffolded Multi-user Integrated Learning Environment), a Web-based collaboration tool integrated with scaffolding to support student design actvities. Based on a design by Roland Hübscher, Web-SMILE provides students with a flowchart (developed by Sadhana Puntembakar) of the things they need to do in the problem-solving process (Figure 3.1). Clicking on a box such as "Figuring It Out!" (the initial review stage), leads the students to a page (Figure 3.2) that describes what needs to be done and how the collaboration tools can be used in this stage. The tools are directly accessible with a click from the stage description page. Web-SMILE communicates the process by describing how and when planning takes place, and links the scaffolding into tools for the design activity.

The GPCeditor (Goal-Plan-Code editor), a learning environment for high school students studying design through Pascal programming, also scaffolds the planning process and integrates it with the problem-solving process. Evidence suggests that integrated planning improves performance and that an improved, more reflective planning process results from using the GPCeditor. After working with the program, students demonstrate expert quality programming behavior, and retain that behavior even when programming in a more traditional environment. Comparisons of low-ability and high-ability students using the GPCeditor have shown that both groups of students develop programs with similar quality.

DECOMPOSITION

As students begin to define the components of a solution, a case library is an essential tool. An important form of communicating process, a case library describes what others have done and how they did it. "How To" books (How To Wire Your House, How to Fix Your Plumbing) are a good example of a case library. These books provide more

FIGURE 3.1

The Web-SMILE problem-solving process.

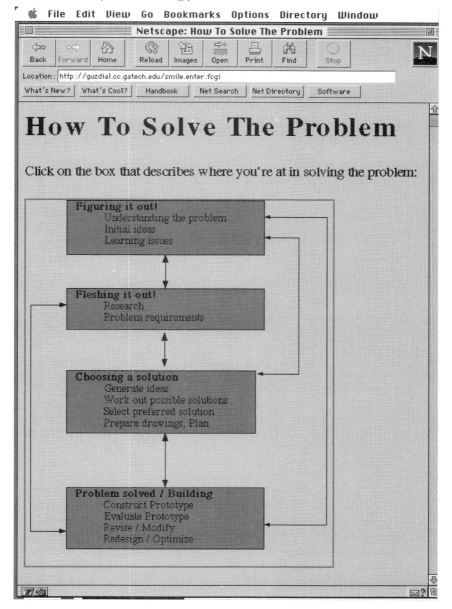

than lists of activities to be done in a specific order. They usually point out the right way (sometimes, multiple alternative right ways!) and the wrong way to do things, and offer pictures of people actually performing the tasks. How To books are often indexed by subject (type of repair, etc.) to help readers find needed information easily.

FIGURE 3.2

Web-SMILE: explaining the stage and linking to tools.

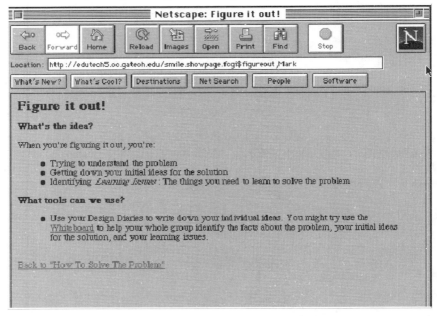

Imagine a "smart" How-To book that could identify a particular problem, identify the closest task it knew to fix that problem, provide information about that task, and perhaps even suggest how to fit that task to fixing your problem. That kind of "smart" book provides the same assistance as case-based reasoning.

Computer-based case libraries have taken the form of collections of components that can be re-used in new settings. The GPCeditor included a *plan* library where students could find pieces of program code and other things to re-use. Emile, a similar tool that supports high school students programming physics simulations, extended the re-use library to contain graphical user interface components such as buttons and fields, including a button that moved as if affected by gravity. Case libraries need not be constrained to highly technical components, however.

Case libraries also retain stories that help to convey important knowledge or skill. Case-based teaching with technological support has been used since 1991 with software that presents a story from a case library at an appropriate time or in an appropriate sequence (Bareiss and Beckwith 1993; Domeshek and Kolodner 1992; Ferguson, Bareiss, Birnbaum, and Osgood 1992; Hmelo, Narayanan, Hübscher, Newstetter, and Kolodner 1996; Kolodner 1995; Kolodner, Hmelo, and Narayanan 1996; Kolodner and Schwartz 199; Schank, Bareiss, Fano, Osgood, and Ferguson 1992).

In a newer use, case libraries facilitate student performance and enhance student learning. STABLE, the Small Talk Apprenticeship-Based Learning Environment, is an example of a case library used to facilitate performance and enhance undergraduate computer science student learning. A Web-based case library, STABLE includes more than a dozen projects exemplifying good object-oriented analysis, design, and programming practice. Each project is presented in a hierarchy of steps (Figure 3.3), to aid student progress. Each step is presented at a variety of levels of detail to allow students to fade the scaffolding to an appropriate level. In addition, each step is linked to several related resources, such as multiple representations of the project, related concepts, insight into the strategy behind a step, and a collaboration area where step and overall project discussions can take place.

Since 1996, STABLE has been used in a 75-student class. Each term, various formative evaluations are conducted and the information is used to continue to iterate on STABLE's design. Our research shows that students willingly use STABLE for a large number of hours, even though the interface is not nearly optimal. For these students, the benefit of the program is the valuable information provided for successful project completion. Our formative evaluation also suggests that we are getting the intended learning effects:

Students perform better with STABLE.

We developed STABLE by using winter quarter cases, offering STABLE for the first time in the spring quarter. The second assignment in the winter was to create a simple spreadsheet; three of those examples were in STABLE. The first assignment in the spring was to build a complex spreadsheet system. The first spring programming assignment was to extend the second programming assignment from the winter quarter. The spring quarter students also had access to three winter quarter cases. Using identical grading criteria, the spring students scored significantly higher than the winter class, suggesting that students are able to boost their performance with STABLE.

Students learn from STABLE.

On the final Spring quarter exam, the problems were designed to be isomorphic (very similar but not identical) to problems in the winter quarter final exam. Significant improvement was shown in program design. As case-based reasoning theory suggests, the design learning improved and better abstractions resulted as more cases were explored.

The biggest challenge with case libraries is easy access. A useful case library is large, but a large case library is difficult to browse. How do you find the information you need for a given problem? The key to case library usability is a good index, like the How To book index.

The indexing problem is particularly difficult with a user population (students) that changes dramatically as it learns during the course of the term. At the beginning of a course, an index phrase might not make sense, but the same phrase might be very clear later in the course. A student may not care about "How to replace a washer" until she or he learns that a "washer" is something in a faucet and that a faulty washer might lead to a leaky faucet. One of the major challenges facing case library designers is making indices work well for a wide variety of users.

DEBUGGING

The key to successful learning through debugging, the stage where students are working and getting feedback, is to ensure that student effort and potential failure are where learning should occur. In our work, careful design of the learning activity and environment proved to be more important than debugging support software. Cognitive science research says that students often learn from failure (Schank 1982, 1991; Schank, Fano, Bell, and Jona 1994). The challenge is to structure student activity so that recovering from a failure proides an opportunity to learn the objective, not a personal catastrophe.

In one of our research projects, we found that we could improve learning by getting students to debug more. DEVICE (Dynamic Environment for Visualization In Chemical Engineering) Version 1.0 is an

FIGURE 3.3

STABLE: example step page.

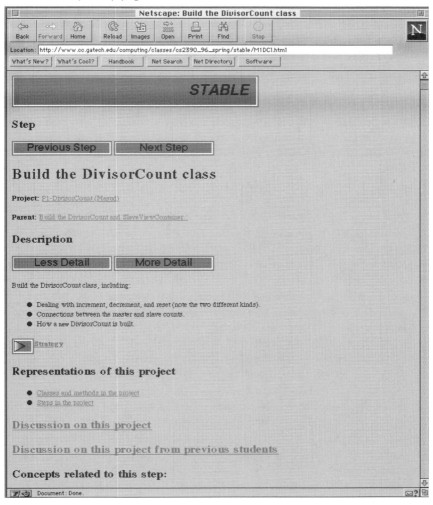

environment developed by Ph.D. student Noel Rappin to support undergraduate chemical engineering students modeling pumping problems. The program was designed to help students find a richer understanding of the way theoretical equations could be used to model real world problems. Students using DEVICE drew a diagram of a realistic pumping problem, set the parameters of various components, and checked the output of the system to see if it met the desired constraints. If the constraints were not met, the students would have to change the system by adjusting the diagram or the parameters. To strengthen the connection between the model and the equations, the system output was displayed in equation form, so that students could see the key values (e.g., the amount of work that a pump had to perform) in the context of other variables of the system.

While students were able to use DEVICE 1.0 successfully in a very short period of time, the learning results were not promising. In a post-test interview, one student questioned about the role of equations in the program replied, "What equations?" Analysis of the videotapes of students working with DEVICE led us to believe that students were not really connecting the problem to the equations—they simply used the equations to get their answers, not to note how the problem worked. We unfortunately had designed the problem to be simply set parameters until the right value popped up. The students were not connecting the equations with the problem to be solved.

In DEVICE 2.0, the problem was changed so that students had to explicitly construct equations and identify how each variable was connected to the real world problem. In Figure 3.6, a student must explicitly define ΔZ (the change in height) as the difference between the height of the feeder and holding tanks. By changing the environment, the student task had been changed into a task that required construction and, hopefully, an understanding of the equations. Working with a problem in DEVICE 2.0 involved more than just tweaking the system—the students also had to check the equations, and could fail at equation or system design. The new DEVICE 2.0 was much harder for students to use and took much longer for them to learn, but resulted in significantly better performance on post-test modeling problems with equations.

The lesson here is that the project task (debugging included) must be focused on the desired learning goal. If students can meet the project goal without meeting the learning goal, they probably will. This lesson fits non-computer contexts, too. When I was in high school, I took a

Latin class where we were asked to translate an ancient Latin text. To help us, the teacher provided an Olde English translation. That help completely changed the task from the goal of learning Latin. Instead, we learned a great deal about Olde English that semester as we focused on the (easier) Olde English translation. Beware the "help" that moves the task away from the learning goal.

CROSS-STAGE ACTIVITY: COLLABORATION

We have been working with collaboration in a variety of contexts (e.g., middle school, undergraduate, graduate classes) and domains (e.g., computer science, literature, chemical engineering, mechanical engineering). Our most significant lesson is simple in hindsight: Give the students something to talk about. We refer to this lesson as anchored collaboration.

Our first exploration of collaboration in support of project-based learning was in an undergraduate Mechanical Engineering class. Mechanical Engineering 3110 (ME 3110) at Georgia Tech is a required introduction to design for juniors. Students work in teams of four to six (seven to 10 teams per class), with all teams working on a common task. One class, for example, had to create a vehicle to climb a vertical length of pipe and then pop balloons attached to the top of the pipe. The tasks are too complex for an individual to solve in a single quarter (10 weeks), but simple enough for a team to complete.

The ME 3110 instructors approached us to help students in working together and integrating their activities. We designed a collaboration tool for ME 3110 called CaMILE (Collaborative and Multimedia Interactive Learning Environment). Our CaMILE design was heavily influenced by CSILE (Computer Supported Intentional Learning Environment by Marlene Scardamalia and Carl Bereiter at the Ontario Institute for Studies in Education, now published by Learning in Motion. Http://www.learn.motion.com/lim/kf/knowledgeforum.html/), a successful tool that has been widely used and carefully evaluated with positive results. The first version of CaMILE (used in Fall '95 in ME 3110) was a Macintosh-based program. With this program, students created notes in *threaded* discussions, where the chain of comments (one student commenting on another's note, which is a comment on another note) were displayed. When creating a note, students were asked to identify the *kind* of note they were creating (e.g., a rebuttal, an alternative idea, a new idea, a question), and were offered suggestions of phrases useful in a note of that type. This is an approach used in CSILE to support metacognition about the role of the student's note in the discussion. We believed that students would use CaMILE to communicate with one another outside of class, perhaps in lieu of meetings.

We used the Macintosh version of CaMILE for three quarters in ME 3110. Our recognition that something unexpected was happening came very early. Students only used CaMILE when required for assignments designed to encourage use of the program. The notes that they were posting often had little content, e.g., "I agree" as a complete note. And, students were not using CaMILE in lieu of meetings—in fact, they complained *in CaMILE* about the difficulty of scheduling meetings.

After interviewing and surveying the students, we decided that the most significant factor influencing the lack of CaMILE use was that students in the same group saw one another much more often than we had anticipated. As one student put it, "I'm in a group with my best friends. We take three or four classes together a quarter. Why do we need to talk over the computer?" The problem with scheduling meetings was caused simply because the students were too busy! The software was not offering an affordance, that is, it offered no new capability or benefit.

We redesigned CaMILE as a Web-based application where the emphasis was on providing opportunities for discussion which would *not* normally come up. In terms of prompting students for note types and phrase suggestions, Web-CaMILE worked much like the Macintosh-based CaMILE (Figures 3.4, 3.5). The new CaMILE was available cross-platform, so students could use it from their dorm rooms on their own computers. We added a new capability that was not available in the Macintosh-based CaMILE. Each note in Web-based CaMILE was accessible at a distinct address (URL) which could be referenced from another Web page as a link. We were now able to create *anchored collaboration*, where a discussion on a given topic (anchor) was accessible through a simple hypertext link.

We combined this new capability with a new emphasis in our description for students of the role for Web-CaMILE. Rather than using Web-CaMILE for within-group discussion (which was still acceptable and encouraged), our new focus for Web-CaMILE use was between-group and cross-class discussions.

Web-CaMILE was used as a forum allowing ME 3110 student groups to review and critique other groups' interim design reports partway through the quarter. Each report was placed on the Web, with a

FIGURE 3.4

Web-based CaMILE for college students: student prompt for note type.

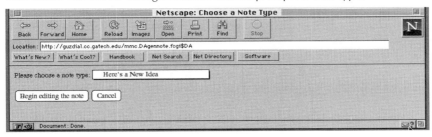

FIGURE 3.5

Web-based CaMILE for college students: composition page.

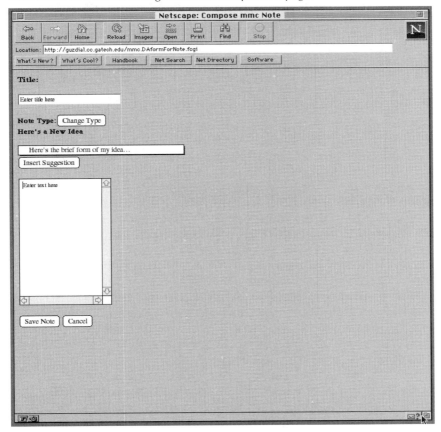

link to a note heading a *thread* (a continuous chain of notes commenting on one another) focused on discussing that particular report.

Similarly, in other classes, Web-CaMILE was used to create virtual study groups, where a set of exam review questions served as anchors. A click on a link from a review question took students to a collaboration space for discussing the problem and its solution.

The Web-CaMILE results were quite different. Students wrote notes with much more content. While not excited about using Web-CaMILE itself, the students were interested and excited in the activities that we were providing for them. Competing student design groups were eager to see one another's designs, as well as to critique and defend the designs. Web-CaMILE provided the opportunity for new kinds of collaborations.

In general, we found anchored collaborations to be useful in many classroom contexts. In most classrooms (especially project-based classrooms), there are artifacts to discuss or critique, from the latest open-ended design assignment to peer review of student work. Because Web-CaMILE facilitates anchored collaboration, it is now being used in several classes around Georgia Tech's campus. More than 800 Tech students have used the program in the last two years.

Web-CaMILE inspired the creation of a tool for middle school science classes, Web-SMILE (Figure 3.6), mentioned earlier in this chapter. The middle school science classes that we work with use problem-based learning approaches to structure problem understanding in the group. Here, students use whiteboards to define problem components before doing research and developing a solution—the whiteboards list facts, ideas, and learning issues.

In Web-SMILE, the whiteboards have been attached to a CaMILE-like discussion space, so that students can report back on their work in the discussion space, while linking to the problem components defined in the whiteboard space (Figure 3.7). When working on the "Tunnel Problem," students might identify "hardness of rocks and how difficult it is to tunnel through" as a learning issue on the Web-SMILE whiteboard. As the group investigates rock hardness and tunneling techniques, the members can attach their findings in the Web-SMILE discussion area and connect them (using the notion of anchored collaboration) to the original learning issue note.

We interviewed the students after their use of Web-SMILE to ask them about the tool and its use. In the excerpt below, we see that the students report that Web-SMILE served the role of organizing their work and facilitating collaboration.

FIGURE 3.6

Web-SMILE for middle school students: the discussion area can be linked to whiteboard entries.

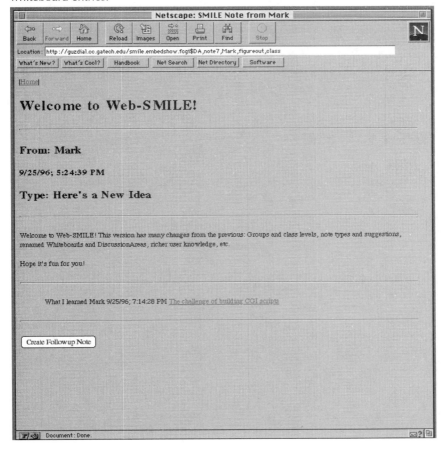

FIGURE 3.7

Web-SMILE for middle school students: the whiteboard area.

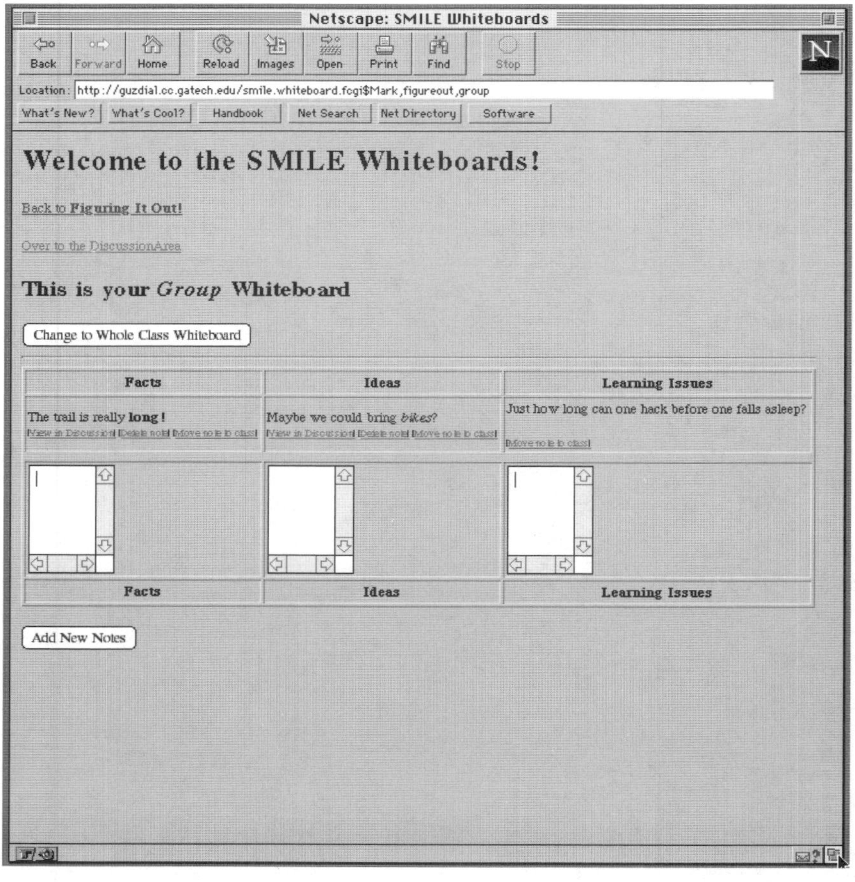

Interviewer (I):	How would you compare the computer version of the whiteboards with the paper version of the whiteboards?
FS:	It's more organized.
I:	What's more organized?
FS:	The computer is.
MS:	You don't have to write anything.
FS:	I hate writing. I type faster and also, like, you have a better...your notes can be saved on the computer, and you have a better chance of keeping notes instead of losing the notes that you wrote down on paper.
I:	OK, what about the whiteboards? Was that helpful in sharing information?
MS:	Yeah, because you could find out what other kids in your class like knew.
MS:	I think it helped us, because you get organized better.
FS:	Tell why.
FS:	If you didn't know everything yourself, you got an idea from other people.

In summary, we are finding that giving students something to talk about encourages collaboration. In Web-CaMILE, the anchored collaboration created collaboration opportunities that were not available previously. In Web-SMILE, the connection between the whiteboards and the discussion area served as an organizing metaphor and encouraged collaboration.

CONCLUSION

In our research at Georgia Tech, we have been exploring how to support project-based learning in a variety of study areas, with a wide range of students—from middle school students studying science to undergraduates studying chemical engineering and computer science. Placed in the context of what research teams are learning about project-based learning, we can begin to specify guidelines and critical issues for the use of technology to support this type of learning. While our experiences point the way toward effective supports for project-based learning, it is clear that significant research is yet to be performed.

INTEGRATION INTO THE CLASSROOM ENVIRONMENT

There is much more to the classroom experience, or any learning experience, than the tools and resources available to the student. The teacher's role with respect to the technology, the teacher's comfort with the technology and the way the curriculum or task (e.g., in a workplace setting) mesh with the technology are all critical factors. Teachers must be taught to work with technology at this level; their role as the gate-keeper and shepherd of innovation is critical for student success.

INTEGRATION INTO RESEARCH ON PROCESS

A significant amount of research today explores our under-standing of tasks and process, such as Jean Lave's work among tailors and housewives (Lave 1977, 1988; Lave and Wenger 1991). This re-search is changing the way we think about effective student process and about tasks and processes that individuals actually use in their daily lives. As this research influences work on technological support for project-based learning, we may see a better integration of learning supports into daily living, supporting the concept of life long learning. We will also probably see different kinds of technology that fit better with student work styles, e.g., handheld computational devices that can coach students as they work at Lego or clay, units more flexible than a desktop computer.

The research in technological support for project-based learning is promising. The field has learned a great deal about how to support students working on projects in real classrooms. In the near future, we hope that this kind of support will lead to more and better project-based learning opportunities for all students.

For more information on the EduTech Institute and the Learning By Design project, please visit the World Wide Web page:
http://www.cc.gatech.edu/edutech/

From that page, you can get information on CaMILE, DEVICE, STABLE, and Web-SMILE. CaMILE is freely available for educational use and can be found at:
http://www.cc.gatech.edu/gvu/edtech/CaMILE.html

REFERENCES

Bareiss, R., and R. Beckwith. (1993). "Advise the President: A Hypermedia System for Teaching Contemporary American History." Paper presented at the annual meeting of the American Educational Research Association.

Bereiter, C., and M. Scardamalia. (1989). "Intentional Learning As a Goal of Instruction." In *Knowing, Learning, and Instruction: Essays in Honor of Robert Glaser*, edited by L.B. Resnick. (pp. 361-392). Hillsdale, N.J.: Larence Erlbaum Associates.

Blumenfeld, P.C., E. Soloway, R.W. Marx, J.S. Krajcik, M. Guzdial, and A. Palincsar. (1991). "Motivating Project-based learning: Sustaining the Doing, Supporting the Learning." *Educational Psychologist* 26, 3: 369-398.

Brown, A.L., J.D. Bransford, R.A. Ferrara, and J.C. Campione. (1983). "Learning, Remembering, and Understanding." In *Handbook of Child Psychology: Cognitive Development*, Vol. 3, edited by W. Kessen. (pp. 77-166). New York: Wiley.

Brunner, C., J. Hawkins, F. Mann, and B. Moeller. (1990). "Designing Inquire." In *Design for Learning*, edited by B. Bowen. (pp. 27-35). Cupertino, Ca.: Apple Computer.

Collins, A., J.S. Brown, and S.E. Newman. (1989). "Cognitive Apprenticeship: Teaching the Craft of Reading, Writing, and Mathematics." In *Knowing, Learning, and Instruction: Essays in Honor of Robert Glaser*, edited by L.B. Resnick. (pp. 453-494). Hillsdale, N.J.: Lawrence Erlbaum and Associates.

Domeshek, E.A., and J.L.Kolodner. (1992). "A Case-based Design Aid for Architecture." In *Proceedings of the Second International Conference on Artificial Intelligence and Design*, edited by J. Gero.

Ferguson, W., R. Bareiss, L. Birnbaum, and R. Osgood. (1992). "ASK Systems: An Approach to the Realization of Story-based Teachers." *The Journal of the Learning Sciences* 2, 1: 95-134.

Hmelo, C., H. Narayanan, R. Hübscher, C.W. Newstetter, and J.L. Kolodner. (1996). "A Multiple Case-based Approach to Generative Environments for Learning." *VIVEK: A Quarterly in Artificial Intelligence* 9, 2-18.

Kolodner, J. (1995). "Design Education Across the Disciplines." Paper presented at the Second Congress on Computing in Civil Engineering. Atlanta, Ga.

Kolodner, J.L., C.E. Hmelo, and N.H. Narayanan. (1996). "Problem-based Learning Meets Case-based Reasoning." Paper presented at the International Conference on the Learning Sciences. Northwestern University.

Kolodner, J.L., and B. Schwartz. (1997). "Roles of a Case Library as a Collaborative Tool for Fostering Augmentation." Paper presented at the Computer-Supported Collaborative Learning (CSCL) 1997 Conference. Toronto, Ontario, Canada.

Krajcik, J.S., P. Blumenfeld, E. Soloway, and R. Marx. (1992). "Enhancing the Teaching of Project-based Science." Proposal to the National Science Foundation program in Teacher Preparation and Enhancement.

Krajcik, J.S., P.C. Blumenfeld, R. W. Marx, and E. Soloway. (1994). "A Collaborative Model for Helping Teachers Learn Project-based Instruction." *Elementary School Journal* 94, 5: 483-497.

Krajcik, J.S., and J.W. Layman. (1990). "Middle School Teachers' Conceptions of Heat and Temperature: Personal and Teaching Knowledge." Paper presented at the meeting of the National Association for Research in Science Teaching. San Francisco, Ca.

Ladewski, B.G., J.S. Krajcik, and C.L. Harvey. (1994). "A Middle Grade Science Teacher's Emerging Understanding of Project-based Instruction." *The Elementary School Journal* 94, 5: 499-516.

Lave, J. (1977). "Tailer-made Experiences in Evaluating the Intellectual Consequences of Apprenticeship Training." *Quarterly Newsletter of the Institute for Comparative Human Development* 1, 1-3.

Lave, J. (1988). *Cognition in Practice*. New York: Cambridge University Press.

Lave, J., and E. Wenger. (1991). *Situated Learning: Legitimate Peripheral Participation*. Cambridge, U.K.: Cambridge University Press.

Palmiter, S., and J. Elkerton. (1991). "An Evaluation of Animated Demonstrations for Learning Computer-based Tasks." Paper presented at the CHI'91: ACM Conference on Human Factors in Computing Systems, New Orleans, La.

Palmiter, S.L., J. Elkerton, and P. Baggett. (1991). "Animated Demonstrations Versus Written Instructions for Learning Procedural Tasks: A Preliminary Investigation." *International Journal of Man-Machine Studies* 34, 5: 687-701.

Scardamalia, M., and C. Bereiter. (1991). "Higher Levels of Agency for Children in Knowledge Building: A Challenge for the Design of New Knowledge Media." *Journal of the Learning Sciences* 1, 1: 37-68.

Scardamalia, M., C. Bereiter, and M. Lamon. (1994). The CSILE Project: Trying to Bring the Classroom into World 3." In *Classroom Lessons: Integrating Cognitive Theory and Classroom Practice*, edited by K. McGilly. (pp. 201-228). Cambridge, Mass.: MIT Press.

Scardamalia, M., C. Bereiter, R. McLean, J. Swallow, and E. Woodruff. (1989). "Computer-supported Intentional Learning Environments." *Journal of Educational Computing Research* 5, 1: 51-68.

Scardamalia, M., C. Bereiter, and R. Steinbach. (1984). "Teachability of Reflective Processes in Written Composition." *Cognitive Science* 8, 173-190.

Schank, R.C. (1982). *Dynamic Memory*. Cambridge, London, New York: Cambridge University Press.

Schank, R.C. (1991). "Case-based Teaching: Four Experiences in Educational Software Design." Technical Report 7. The Institute for Learning Sciences, Northwestern University.

Schank, R.C., R. Bareiss, A. Fano, R. Osgood, and W. Ferguson. (1992). "Agents in the Story Archive." Draft from the Institute for Learning Sciences.

Schank, R.C., A. Fano, B. Bell, and M. Jona. (1994)." The Design of Goal-based Scenarios." *Journal of the Learning Sciences* 3, 4: 305-346.

Assistive Technology for Young Children in Special Education

Michael M. Behrmann

Introduction

As we approach the millennium, it seems that nearly every segment of society is predicting a dramatic change in the education of the future. Much of this shift is expected to result from new technology and its effect on living and learning. Even now, computer and computer-based advances are leading to classroom reorganization. Technology has opened many educational doors to children, particularly children with disabilities. Alternative solutions from the world of technology are accommodating physical, sensory, or cognitive impairments in many ways.

Much of the technology we see daily was developed initially to assist persons with disabilities. Curb cuts at street corners and curb slopes, originally designed to accomodate people with orthopedic disabilities, are used more frequently by families with strollers or individuals with grocery carts than by persons with wheelchairs or walkers. The optical character reader, developed to assist individuals unable to read written text, has been adapted in the workplace to scan printed documents into computer-based editable material, saving enormous amounts of data entry labor. Closed captioning television technology, developed to enable persons with hearing impairments to watch television, is now used extensively in noisy sports bars.

Technology can be a great equalizer for individuals with disabilities that might prevent full participation in school, work, and the community. This is most evident in the case of individuals with mobility, hearing, or vision impairments, but is also true for individuals with limitations in cognition and perception. With technology, an individual physically unable to speak can communicate with spoken language. Using a portable voice synthesizer, a student can ask and respond to questions in the "regular" classroom, overcoming a physical obstacle that may have forced placement in a special segregated classroom or required a full-time instructional aide or interpreter to provide "a voice."

Improvements in sensor controls enable subtle motor movements to control mobility devices such as electric wheelchairs, providing independent movement through the school and community. Text and graphics enhancement software can enlarge sections of a monitor enough to be seen by persons with vision impairment. Text can be read electronically by a digitized voice synthesizer for a person who is blind. For persons with hearing impairments, amplification devices can filter extraneous noise from the background or pick up an FM signal from a microphone on a teacher's lapel. Word processing, editing, spell checking, and grammatical tools commonly found in high-end software facilitate the inclusion of students with learning disabilities in regular classrooms by allowing them to keep up with much of the work. Not inconsequentially, the children often feel better about themselves as active learners.

Technology is providing more powerful and efficient tools to teachers who work with children with disabilities. These tools enable teachers to offer new and more effective means of learning while individualizing instruction to the broad range of student learning needs. Educators are using computers as tools to deliver and facilitate learning beyond drill and practice, to provide environments that accommodate learning, and to ensure enhanced and equitable learning environments to all students.

Access to the World Wide Web, e-mail, listservs, and other electronic learning environments is common in many classrooms. In these environments, students around the world can interact in real time via onscreen messaging or video and audio transmissions. In most of these learning situations, a disability makes no difference at all.

This chapter is a personal reflection on the effect of assistive technology in the lives of children with disabilities, spanning nearly two decades. It examines legislative reforms related to assistive technology, the reason this technology is important to young children with disabilities, and the way technology is removing barriers to learning, living, working, and playing in our society for persons with disabilities. In addition, it includes speculation on what we might see after the turn of the millennium.

ASSISTIVE TECHNOLOGY

The Technology Related Assistance Act of 1988 provided funds to each of the 50 states to supply assistive technology to all citizens. One of the first national laws for persons with disabilities that addressed individuals of all ages, this bill did not distinguish between adults or children. Assistive technology (AT) was defined in the legislation as "any item, piece of equipment, or product, whether acquired commercially, off the shelf, modified, or customized, that is used to increase, maintain, or improve the functional capabilities of individuals with disabilities" (P.L. 100-407 1988). The definition has been used in subsequent legislation, including the Individuals with Disabilities in Education Act of 1990 (P.L. 101-476) and 1997 (P.L. 105-15) which reauthorized and renamed P.L. 94-142, the Education for All Handicapped Children's Act, and the Americans with Disabilities Act (P.L. 101-336).

The definition of assistive technology applied to education is extremely broad, encompassing "any item, piece of equipment, or product system whether acquired commercially off the shelf, modified, or customized, that is used to increase, maintain, or improve functional capabilities of individuals with disabilities." As a result, the potential range of AT devices is incredibly large, and both "high-tech" and "low-tech" devices are included. High-tech devices may be computers, electronic equipment, or software. Although electronically operated, high-tech devices need not be expensive. A simple low cost switch that controls a battery-operated toy can be considered a high-tech device, as can a tape recorder. Low-tech devices are manually, not electronically, operated. This group includes devices such as pencil grips, mouth sticks, and mechanical hoists.

Under this definition, AT devices can be home-made, customized, or purchased commercially. Nearly any device is considered potentially assistive. Blocks of wood used to raise a table to fit a wheelchair would be considered a type of home-made assistive technology. A joystick could be used as purchased off the shelf or customized by adding a special grip.

This definition also expands the consideration of potential educational applications with its focus on devices "used to increase, maintain, or improve the functional capabilities of persons with disabilities." As educators, we try to *increase* or add new academic, social, and daily living skills and knowledge to the functional capability of all children. This is a basic goal as we prepare children to take their place in society. In the case of children with degenerative impairments such as muscular dystrophy, educators may be working to keep children functioning at their current level. They may be striving to help students *maintain* their capability to function in the world. And, teachers work with students to *improve* skills and knowledge, making existing skills and knowledge even more functional, and improving fluency so that functional capabilities may be generalized into many different settings.

It is critical to understand the implications of this definition to comprehend its effect on children with disabilities in our schools. It is fairly easy to understand the how the definition is applied with regard to children with physical or sensory disabilities. To see a young child who had been unable to speak for her first five years say her first sentence with a speaking computer device presents an exciting and clear picture of assistive technology. The benefit of AT is also easy to comprehend when a child who cannot hear can understand his teacher's directions because real-time captioning converts the teacher's speech to text projected onto his laptop computer. Similarly, a child with a visual impairment can use a computer that speaks the names of computer icons, making it easy for the child to operate software applications.

The definition of assistive technology devices also applies to the more difficult to gauge tools that teachers use to deliver and facilitate learning, including instructional applications of technology. These applications range from drill and practice tutorials (from the direct instruction behavioral model) to facilitated learner-based environments provided through the Internet or interactive hypermedia and multimedia-based instruction (from constructivist models).

Both models have their place in providing appropriate assistive technology instructional interventions for children with disabilities. Mathematics drill and practice programs can be used to *maintain* or *im-*

prove skills that a child with mild retardation needs in functional math and money skills. Improvement is associated with the concept of fluency building in academic skills, where failure to attain fluency is one of the most prevalent reasons children are referred to special education. The child may understand the concepts, sometimes slowly, while falling farther and farther behind because he or she may not have developed the fluency needed to learn new skills.

Multimedia-based learning environments, however, such as those featured in anchored instruction (Hasslebring and Goin 1994), are based upon constructivist learning in which children can explore relationships and use various visual, auditory, and kinesthetic learning experiences to develop new skills and knowledge and build upon previous learning to *increase* their knowledge and skills. These models often co-exist in both technology-based and nontechnology-based instruction, and their successes are often the result of teachers who understand that teaching is both an art and a science.

It is important to understand that virtually all applications of technology—tools for children to learn, as well as tools for teachers to provide learning opportunities—can be defined as assistive technology. This is true for individual children with disabilities whose disability has primary impact on academic performance (e.g., learning disabilities) or functional performance (e.g., multiple physical and visual disabilities).

LEGAL AND MORAL REQUIREMENTS

The mandate to provide assistive technology to children with special needs is grounded in the moral concerns protected by the U.S. Constitution and its amendments. The Education for All Handicapped Children Act (P.L. 94-142) was based upon the Supreme Court's 1954 Brown v. Board of Education decision that separate education was not equal education under the 14th Amendment to the Constitution. At the time the law was passed by Congress in 1975, nearly two million children were excluded from schools in the United States. With the legislation, the President and Congress established a legal requirement for a "free appropriate public education in the least restrictive environment" for children with disabilities. That law turned education around for children with disabilities and, as a result, the field of special education began to flourish for the first time in nearly 75 years.

Many controversies surfaced, however, about the extent of the required educational services and the cost to society for those services. The major debates have focused on the need for a clear definition of an "appropriate" education in the least restrictive environment and the requirement to provide assistive technology devices and services to all individuals with disabilities.

"APPROPRIATE" EDUCATION

The requirement for an "appropriate" education in the least restrictive environment has led to the development of a separate educational system designed to meet the needs of children with disabilities. Some educators contend that this is the same type of separate system that the Supreme Court found unconstitutional in 1954. These individuals suggest that all children, regardless of ability, should be educated with their neighborhood peers in their local school.

Others in favor of the special education system argue that it is necessary to meet the educational needs of all children with disabilities, particularly the "continuum of services" mandated by the Individuals with Disabilities in Education Act (IDEA). In their view, children must have specific intervention designed to "mainstream" them back into regular education. Without the intervention, these individuals believe that students will be doomed to continued and more significant failure. They also note that, while the goal of "mainstreaming" is reasonable, some children may not benefit appropriately from a full inclusion program.

Although there are many arguments on both sides of the issue, it is apparent that new technologies can provide the tools to bring more children with disabilities into "regular" educational settings. In my opinion, assistive technology will certainly mainstream more and more children in wheelchairs, children who cannot physically speak, see, or hear, and children who need computers to write, organize, think, and function educationally.

THE AT REQUIREMENT

The second debate centers on the requirement to provide assistive technology to all students. The initial legislation, the Education for All Handicapped Children Act, did not require schools to provide assistive technology devices and services to individuals with disabilities. The current assistive technology mandate was created by later legislation[1] and prompted by the technological revolution resulting from the development of the microcomputer.

The subsequent legislation passed by Congress[2] encouraged states to develop services designed to provide assistive technology to all persons with disabilities and required the provision of AT as a special education service (trained special education teachers in special classes), related service (occupational, physical, speech therapies, and other services needed to access education), or supplemental service (services necessary to maintain a child in regular education classes).

Many states have not yet addressed the AT issue, since assistive technology devices and services were identified as requirements only fairly recently.[3] This may be due to a fear of "breaking" instructional budgets by purchasing high cost equipment in already cash-short school systems. Concern also exists that the rapid evolution of technology creates the potential of costly investment in devices that may have a relatively short life span.

A close look at the situation will show that these concerns are not well grounded, however. Schools already use extensive amounts of AT, and need only to identify it as such. Nearly any use of computers falls into this category, as do tape recorded instructions or homework, copies of notes from a classmate or teacher, switch-operated toys, drawing paper taped to table tops, as well as large pencils and crayons. All of these could be noted, as required, in Individual Education Plans (IEPs) and Individual Family Service Plans (IFSPs).

TOOLS FOR YOUNG CHILDREN

Assistive technology tools for young children fall into the functional categories of vision, hearing, communication, motor movement, and cognition and perception. The following describes some of the major tools in each of these domains.

---

[1] As defined in P.L. 100-407, The Technology Related Assistance Act of 1988, and applied to the recent reauthorizations of P.L. 94-142, most recently the 1997 Individuals with Disabilities Education Act (IDEA, P.L. 105-15).

[2] P.L. 100-407, The Technology Related Assistance Act of 1988, and P.L. 101-176, the Individuals with Disabilities Education Act (IDEA) of 1990.

[3] The Individuals with Disabilities in Education Act (IDEA) was reauthorized in 1990 (P.L. 101-476) and in 1997 (P.L. 105-15).

VISION TOOLS

AT tools for persons with visual disabilities address the needs of individuals who are blind or have severe visual impairments. These tools generally fall into three basic categories: computer screen enhancement, speech output, and hard copy output.

Enhancement. Computer screen enhancement can be as simple as obtaining a monitor with a large screen (today's screens measure up to 35 inches). Generally, a 20 inch monitor can provide sufficient screen enlargement for persons with visual impairments of many types. Software can enlarge portions of the computer screen from two to 20 times, showing enlarged portions in detail. A closed circuit television with a camera and zoom lens can be used to enlarge non-computerized text and three-dimensional objects. As video technologies improve and become more compact, these systems will become less expensive and intrusive, and will easily integrate with computers for videoconferencing on the Internet and other multimedia applications.

Speech Output. Speech output is critical to persons who are blind. For many years, these technologies have been limited to tape recorded "talking books" and instructions and other communication recorded on portable tape recorders. Now, text to speech software translates computer-based text to spoken language. When combined with other technology, such as a scanner and optical character recognition, the software can be used to translate hard copy text to speech. Computer-based text readers can use a camera to "read" text from a book or other hard copy.

These AT devices may be particularly useful to young children with limited reading ability. Since receptive language generally precedes reading, the ability to use such devices can be of great assistance to young children. Multimedia "talking books" can easily be adapted for young children with visual impairments. In addition, software can be used to provide pictures and translate the pictures to words to be spoken or written as text.

For older children, portable note-taking devices can use either a keyboard or braille entry to input text which can be translated to speech. Braille can also be translated to and from text, making communication between braille users and non-braille using teachers possible.

Combining these technologies can be a challenge. As with most software and peripheral devices, conflicts in hardware requirements and configurations are common and it takes persistence and knowledge to make the different technologies work together. Not all speech output devices can identify graphic images, for example. Even changing from one computer operating system to another may require the purchase of new equipment.

Hard Copy Output. Hard copy can be categorized into tactile or large print output. Braille is the primary tactile output. It can be produced in hard copy or with technology that uses small needle-like projections to make lines of refreshable, or "erasable," braille. Additional devices can produce tactile displays of graphic images, allowing a child with a vision impairment to touch and feel these images. Large print output has become increasingly simple, a result of word processors that can easily enlarge fonts and graphic images, and format text for easy reading.

HEARING TOOLS

Devices have been available to assist persons with hearing impairments since Alexander Graham Bell invented the telephone in 1876 to assist his hearing impaired wife. These devices fall into four basic categories: devices for telecommunication, translation, and amplification, and environmental sensors and indicators.

Telecommunication and Translation Devices. Telecommunication devices allow hearing and non-hearing persons to communicate over the telephone. Telecommunications Devices for the Deaf (TDDs) and Teletypewriters (TTYs) act much like electronic mail: a message is typed on a keyboard at the sending end and auditory modem-type signals are translated to printed text at the receiving end. Devices such as IBM's Phone Communicator or Auditory Display's TE98 Communicator use a touch tone phone to type in a message that is translated into text on a computer monitor or a small portable liquid crystal display (LCD) device carried by a person with a hearing impairment. Other devices allow a non-speaking person with a hearing impairment to type a message that will be spoken by a voice sythesizer to a hearing recipient.

Translation. AT services include sign language interpretation, which is quite expensive because of the labor cost. Some multimedia instructional software has been designed to accommodate sign language users. Close captioning is a translation system that has been integrated into all of the televisions produced in the United States. Recently, court stenographers have used video projectors or links to laptop computers to provide real-time translation services to readers. This technology can also assist persons with vision impairments; the text can be saved as class notes and used with voice output. As voice recognition systems are perfected, individuals will merely speak into a microphone and the speech will be immediately translated to text. Young children with good expressive language could use this system as a writing tool. Commercial products claiming a high reliability for real-time voice recognition are already on the market.

Amplification Devices. Tools to amplify or modify auditory input are another means of providing assistive technology. FM radio loops can be installed in classrooms, allowing microphone speech input to be picked up by special hearing aid receivers. Other common devices include telephone volume controls and high tech hearing aids that filter out background noise or customize frequencies to be audible to a person with a hearing impairment.

New technology in development will slow speech down for better understanding. This device will digitally delay auditory input, emphasizing each sound or phoneme. This technology may be particularly useful for young children with auditory processing difficulties.

Other technologies include the cochlear implant, a prosthesis in the inner ear that replicates the cochlear hairs that translate the auditory vibration into nerve impulses. This assistive technology enables function that may not have been available from birth. It is exciting to think that it could enable a child who has never heard a sound to hear his mother speak his name for the first time.

Environmental Indicators. Visual and tactile indicators are another source of AT for children with hearing impairments. Lights are commonly used as substitutes for telephone rings, fire alarms, and doorbells. Other useful technologies include vibrating pagers and motion detectors that alert an individual when someone has entered a room. Hearing ear dogs are also being used to alert users to environmental hazards and noises. As sensory technology improves, it is likely that many low-cost sensor devices will be used by hearing and non-hearing persons in many segments of our society.

COMMUNICATION TOOLS

Augmentative communication supplements or replaces spoken language with other means of communication. Included in this field are sign language, lip reading, and total communication (combined signing and lip reading), as well as specific devices that use pictures, objects, icons, symbols, and words in graphic or spoken form to facilitate communication.

AT devices range from low-tech to high-tech and from simple to quite complex. A simple yes/no communication board is an example of a low-tech communication device. Complexity is developed as the number and type of choices increase for both low- and high-tech devices. The primary difference between the two devices is the manner in which choices are made and the nature of interactive communication (immediate one to one interaction, or delayed or "across the room" interaction). Selection (or input) to the device may be made by pointing (e.g., with a finger or a cursor), eye gaze (looking at a selection), or by scanning rows and columns of selections with a moving cursor or pointer until the correct selection is highlighted.

Varying language level and complexity is possible with high- or low-tech devices, but may be easier to provide with high-tech equipment. The high-tech device may offer more or easier choices and may perform additional non-communication functions. Higher levels of communication can also be achieved by layering "pages" of choices in a notebook binder or a computer program. Different "pages" may contain language for different environments (e.g., home, library, classroom) or may be organized by grammatical structure (nouns, verbs, etc.).

High-tech devices may be as simple as a battery-operated device that provides digitally recorded voice output when one of two switches is pressed. Pictures or words can be placed on the switches to depict the message to be conveyed: a single word, a phrase, or even a short speech (e.g., Yes./I need help./Please take me to the bathroom and wait outside until I am finished). Young children often start with simple high-tech or low-tech communication boards and progress to complex systems, using multiple layers or pages of symbols that have their own syntax and meaning within different contexts—a shorthand language requiring high cognitive functioning. The icon for "apple" could mean fruit, school, or the color red, depending on the context. The user can define the meaning of a symbol and the computer will intelligently determine the output based on context. Output may be in the form of a printed tape, LCD or computer monitor display, or voice output. Such devices often have other computer functions such as word processing with spell and grammar checking, environmental control (turning on the television or lights), and e-mail. These devices can be software-based and loaded on a portable or desktop computer, or can be portable stand-alone devices costing as much as $10,000 or more.

ORTHOPEDIC TOOLS

AT orthopedic devices fall into three categories: mobility, environmental adaptation, and computer access.

Mobility Devices. The universal disability icon representing a person in a wheelchair is what most people think of when asked about a disability. Today, however, the standard hospital wheelchair has often been replaced by a lightweight "racing" wheelchair with titanium frames and canted wheels to enhance speed, maneuverability, and decrease physical fatigue. Electric wheelchairs have been greatly improved by the addition of lightweight batteries, better control systems, infrared or radio interfaces to computers, cellular phones, and new driving technology. Advances in battery and motor technology make these devices more robust and less likely to fail—and an individual less likely to be stranded. Four wheel drive chairs have even been designed to handle rough terrain.

Cost is a significant factor, however. Specialized wheelchairs can cost upwards of $25,000. And mobility comes at a high price when a special chair is combined with an adapted van with hydraulic suspension, automatic ramps, wheelchair locks, and electronic driver controls that may cost an additional $40,000 or more.

Young children who cannot drive automobiles can operate other less expensive means of assisted and independent mobility. Strollers have been adapted to be lighter and easier to use. Adapted chairs can take children safely along on family outings with parents who are runners or bikers. Electric toy cars can provide independent mobility for preschoolers for hundreds, rather than thousands, of dollars. These "cars" are a big success in school hallways, as the student motors from room to room, leaving every kid in the hall envious.

Environmental Control Devices. These devices can be low-tech ramps or grab bars, or high-tech voice operated environmental controls. Many are finding their way into commercial markets. Young and old use remote controls for televisions, stereos, and VCRs. Larger buttons on these devices or computerized controls can make a child significantly more independent because fine motor control is not required for operation.

Architectural spaces in schools, homes, and communities are being re-designed with wider halls and doors, adapted restrooms, and ramps to provide access to persons with disabilities. "Smart homes" provide computer control for home security, lighting, cooking, enter-

tainment, and opening drapes, all at the touch of a button. If a child who is blind enters a room at night, the lights automatically turn on (lights may not be necessary for the child, but the smart environment provides a more "natural" situation for non-disabled persons who might be surprised to find someone in a dark room). Smart environments can be incorporated into schools or other environments, responding to any movement or timed to provide stimulation and interactive learning opportunities.

Smart environments for learning, working, and living should be commonplace in a few years. We will be controlling our environment with voice commands or systems smart enough to anticipate our requests, learning about them over time, so that we do not have to think about many of the activities of daily living. These interactive environments, designed to meet the needs of everyone, will be particularly useful to persons with disabilities.

Computer Access Devices. Hardware or software adaptations have been called the "electronic curb cuts" of the information age. While these high-tech assistive technologies currently can be classified as either hardware or software, they appear to be slowly merging into one entity. Voice recognition is a good example of one such merger. Once hardware-based, voice recognition is now software-driven. Microcomputers and multimedia features enable computer navigation by voice alone. The software still requires a mostly noise-free environment, but it is possible to dictate directly to a word processing program. For a high level quadriplegic, this technology will enable complete control of computer software.

New systems reaching the market put speech into context for a high rate of dictation reliability with a more natural language. Other intelligent systems may soon be able to ask questions to young children with high receptive language, enabling them to have improved control of their computer based learning.

Hardware adaptations include devices such as switches, alternative and adapted keyboards, touch screen monitors, and pointing devices. The switches can be mechanical or sensor-based, used alone or in combination to enable a child to interact with a computer or battery-operated toy. As a result, a child who may only have voluntary control of a toe, finger, eye blink, or gaze can interact with the computer. A mechanical switch, such as a joystick or a small or large button, can activate the computer and move the cursor. Adapted trackballs and mice are also available. Some toy companies are even marketing large trackballs for young children that help them use less developed motor control to activate the computer.

Eye gaze technology, originally developed for military purposes, enables a child to simply hold eye gaze on a single point on a monitor to activate a command or make a selection. A camera notes the position of the eye and the computer reads that the child is saying yes, selecting a letter or word, or moving the cursor.

Keyboard adaptations may be as simple as a piece of plexiglass with holes over the keys where a hand can rest on the keyboard and a finger or touch stick can be placed in the hole to activate a key. Extended keyboards (essentially an array of single switches, each programmed for a different function) can be as large as a serving tray or as small as a hand, made of touch-sensitive plastic to resist spills and moisture. These keyboards can be programmed to respond to different keyboard overlays or activate only when pressure is applied for a predetermined length of time to enable the child to slide a hand across the keyboard without making undesired keystrokes.

The number of keys on the keyboard can be as few as one or two, or as complex as a standard keyboard and designed in different layouts—perhaps in alphabetical order, the way young children learn their ABCs. Some extended keyboards also have a paint tray graphic with colors, an eraser, and a number pad that might be more understandable for a young child. Small keyboards can be designed so that all of the keys are accessible with a single hand. Touch screen monitors are also available, enabling the child to directly interact by touching the monitor to activate and navigate the software. This interface accommodates varying cognitive levels and facilitates a more concrete interaction.

Software adaptations are also available to help a person with a disability control the computer. Most operating systems such as Mac OS and Windows have special features that enhance access by persons with disabilities. Sticky keys allow a user to press the shift key and a single key in two movements, rather than one, to make a capital letter and select upper case keystroke commands. Screen enlargement is another accommodation, and an effort is underway to develop Internet access for persons with disabilities.

The concept of "Universal Design" in operating systems, Internet access, and application software is being accepted by developers, partly due to federal access requirements, as well as the fact that design accessibility provides many useful features that make a product more marketable to many different segments of society. These features, like other hardware, cost a small amount if they are incorporated during initial production, but require a large investment if added to the system later.

EARLY INTERVENTION AND ACCESS

As computers became prevalent in schools in the early 1980s, it seemed appropriate to focus research on young children identified as having disabilities. In part, this strategy was developed to avoid intervening research variables, such as the effects of a lifetime of unintentional learning by a 17-year-old living in an institution.

The earlier we intervene with a child who has a disability, the less impact the disability will have on that child's ability to learn and function. Research supports that early intervention leads to better ultimate functional levels of persons with disabilities and lower long term costs to the individual and society as the child grows to adulthood (Schnorr and Schnorr 1989).

In the early 1980s, many professionals in the field did not see the potential of technology to improve the lives of children with disabilities. One grant reviewer for a field-initiated research proposal responded that, "you cannot teach babies or preschoolers to use computers," and that was that. Yet, 10 years later, a federal Request For Proposals was issued that focused on the way software could enhance learning in young children.

Early findings on cause and effect and early learning (Behrmann and Lahm 1984) and later findings on the effects of various features of software designed for young children (Lahm, Behrmann, and Thorp 1993), supported common sense about children and the literature on general child development and developmental stages. Early research found that babies could understand cause and effect at a couple of months of age. That is, they could activate or control a device in their environment, such as a mobile or a music box, with a simple switch. Today, toys are available nearly everwhere with microswitches that play music and activate movement.

More recent research findings are less clear, but do appear to show that children respond best to multimedia features such as animation, music, and, particularly, voice. They also tend to prefer open-ended exploratory activities, but respond to opportunities to practice skills. Times have changed radically since the early 1980s; a trip to the software aisle confirms that computers are for young children. At this point in time, there is probably more educational software available for this population than any other age group in the commercial market.

Technology can provide a mechanism for young children to interact with their learning environment in a developmentally appropriate manner. For example, assistive technology enables children who cannot speak to use technology to interact with speech or singing. A young child can participate in "Circle Time," using a switch to activate a computer software program to sing her part of a song. The child can even lead the group, using the computer to start the song. Often, this child is envied by the other children because of the special technology, and this technology may help to break down social barriers within the peer group. Independent play and work can also be enhanced as part of the learning environment. Children who cannot physically push a toy car around may be able to activate a battery-operated or remote-controlled car with the use of single switches. Children who cannot hold a crayon to draw and paint can use a computer-based drawing program and "paint by numbers," or they can construct their own drawing with stamps and drawing elements available in specific software programs. These drawings can be printed out in full color and taken home to be displayed on the refrigerator or a classroom bulletin board with other children's work. Using technology to provide full access to the learning environment in school, there are fewer reasons to place children with disabilities in separate classes.

TOOLS FOR TEACHERS

As technology has become pervasive in our society it is clear that young children have no fear of it. By the age of four, children can use various devices, with or without adaptations. They can dial a telephone, operate a television and stereo, guide computerized toys, and play video games. Young children today are growing up with technology infused into every aspect of their lives.

Since the 1950s, most technologies have been passive, providing information to the learner in a linear format. Technology became more interactive when it could be controlled by a remote interface that allowed individuals to pause, rewind, and start the instruction. To be interactive, the instructional design of linear programs such as Sesame Street encouraged active response in children, yet did not enable them to directly engage with the technology. Computer technology has moved us to a new model of interactivity. Video and multimedia on CD and LaserDiscs (now an "old" technology) have enabled children to access the power of multimedia in an interactive learning environment.

Web TV is also emerging as an interactive learning tool. The challenge now is to develop instructional designs that take advantage of these technologies and develop effective learning environments.

It is incumbent on teachers to make good instructional decisions regarding how and when to incorporate technology into teaching environments. This responsibility is unlikely to change, even as the technologies become more powerful and user friendly. Technology-based instruction can be used to enhance thematic-based instruction, as well as for specific academic and daily living skill development and maintenance.

In teaching specific skills such as reading and writing, teachers can use multimedia books that highlight and "speak" words and phrases. Talking dictionaries may also be embedded in the book. As children get more facile with the technology, they can access information resources such as electronic multimedia encyclopedias and dictionaries through the Internet. Computers and keyboarding skills are already replacing penmanship in the curriculum and may be particularly important to children with physical and perceptual-motor disabilities. Technology enhancements such as extended keyboards, software that matches pictures to words (enabling a child to understand the idea without worrying about the "words"), word prediction software that assists with word recall, and macros that shorten the number of keystrokes can be used. Talking wordprocessors for auditory feedback, story illustration with graphic images, built-in prompting, and spelling and grammar checks are features that can enhance learning to write by using technology.

Currently, teachers are able to engineer technology-based learning environments to enhance both teacher and self-directed learning, but it takes a knowledge of technology, curriculum integration, and instructional design associated with planning, as well as persistence to make all of these components work together. Teachers must first determine what a child needs to learn and then provide the tools for the child to achieve that objective. We must not underestimate the importance of directed instruction to develop specific skills in children and assist them to develop fluency in using those skills. The lure of a multimedia-based constructivist-based learning environment is powerful, but we will still have children who do not flourish in such an environment until they are provided with the skills and knowledge to do so.

A behavioral model of instruction may provide the best technology-based approach, using tutorial software for acquisition of skills or knowledge where new skills can be attained independently. Drill and practice software may also be used for developing fluency and maintenance of skills and knowledge. We must keep in mind that, whether using direct instruction (behavioral) or facilitated instruction (constructivist), young children learn by practice combined with multiple opportunities to repeat and apply newly acquired skills. It is also feasible to introduce simulations (microworlds) that encourage independent problem solving as skill building toward independent facilitated learning. Microworlds often incorporate tutorial, drill and practice, and interactive and exploratory learning in an extended learning environment.

Other tools are available to the creative and energetic teacher willing to put time into developing computer-based instruction. Authoring software enables teachers to customize instruction and develop instructional software with multimedia features. Computer hardware is getting increasingly powerful, smaller, and more portable, and peripheral devices such as scanners, cameras, and voice input and output are making computers easier to use and are providing more capacity for each dollar spent. More powerful computers, combined with new development tools not requiring "programmer" skills, rather good content and instructional design capability, are enabling the development of multimedia and hypermedia based instruction that can be individualized to learner needs.

It is apparent that teacher-facilitated learning is increasingly important in the education of all children, with and without disabilities. Access and use of information will be a critical skill for children working and living in tomorrow's world. The constructivist approach to teaching where independent, interactive, and exploratory learning opportunities are provided, is appropriate and desirable for young children who learn by playing, even on a computer. This approach has the added benefit, for young children with disabilities, of being able to present and receive information in various auditory, visual, and tactile modes.

Multiple modality learning is supported and enhanced by technology. Using more than one modality strengthens the learning process and enables teachers to use computer-based assistive technology to teach to the child's learning strengths (e.g., auditory, visual, and tactile/kinesthetic) and remediate the child's learning weakness (through practice). Self-directed instruction is enhanced and learning is made meaningful for children. Children make decisions on what is important to learn, and learn at their own pace. Children learn to work independently, but also can engage in peer collaborative learning. Thus, both independent interactive and exploratory learning opportunities are provided. It is important to remember that young children learn by playing, using the skills of watching (watching a cartoon animation), doing (making a character speak with a click of the mouse), using (moving the animated character through the town), constructing (making a face by positioning the cursor and selecting various images of eyes, ears, mouth, etc.), and creating (drawing a picture with "paint" software tools) (Behrmann and Lahm 1994).

FUTURE TECHNOLOGIES

As technology improves, we will probably see the development of specific technologies followed by "smart" technologies that can integrate various instructional and assistive access technologies with minimal or no installation or configuration by teachers and children. Control systems will use multimedia features to simplify and extend the child's ability to interact with the technology. Instructional and tool software applications will have training and remediation embedded within the system to support and accommodate memory, perceptual, and physical needs of the individual user.

As the applications and tools get more complex, smart navigation systems will enable the user to keep oriented within the software. Teachers will have access to performance data on every aspect of the learning environment and will be able to instantly display the progress of individual students in a graphic format. "Smart" learning environments will progress through instructional software integrated into performance charts. Software will also determine the level of performance and challenge necessary for each child. The physical environment will also be "smart," providing options for the child and teacher through voice commands or other input. If the child is unresponsive, the environment will provide different types of stimuli and learning activities that motivate that child.

Virtual reality environments will be developed that enable children to explore ideas and concepts, even though confined to a high-tech wheelchair. Such technology will enable these children to practice real world tasks such as moving about their community before they actually go out on their own. New input technologies will anticipate the user, (although the user will have the option to over-ride the system). As the Web develops, children will be able to explore environments in their community and the global village, using video, audio, text, and graphics in real-time. They will be able to have experiences that may have been previously unavailable due to a disability. New video conferencing technologies will assist teachers in assistive technology evaluation by providing access to AT experts around the world.

We may also see changes in our most basic curriculum. Literacy may no longer be as focused on the skills of reading and writing. Just as Gutenberg's printing press technology made reading and writing important curricular skills for society, intelligent computer systems may change our curricula to focus on communication, thinking, and problem solving using information technology that does not require reading or writing. We will be able to speak to the computer and it will speak back to us or provide us with multimedia output. Video and audio, including spoken language, will be the interface for learning and may remove the education barriers that now label many of our children as having a learning disability—not because they cannot learn, but because they have difficulty with reading and writing skills.

With computer technology, the proven efficacy of early intervention will continue to be enhanced, leading children to function at a higher potential in a world that will continue to change rapidly. The only caveat to working with children with disabilities in this and the next millennium is: Do not underestimate the capability of the child! When the appropriate technology is available and used in a way that supports the individual strengths and needs of the child, a young child can achieve success, fulfill her or his full potential, and experience life through active engagement with his or her surroundings, becoming a more productive and independent member of society.

REFERENCES

Behrmann, M., and E. Lahm. (1984). "Using Computers with Young and Low Functioning Children. In *Handbook of Microcomputers in Special Education*, edited by M. Behrmann. (pp. 139-157). San Diego, CA.: College Hill Press.

Behrmann, M., and E. Lahm. (1994). "Computer Applications in Early Childhood Special Education." In *Young Children: Active Learners in a Technological Age*, edited by J.L. Wright and D.D. Shade. (pp. 105-120). Washington, DC.: National Association for the Education of Young Children.

Hasselbring, T., and L. Goin. (June 1994). *Advanced Institute: Anchored Instruction Multimedia for Enhancing Teacher Education.* Presentation at Vanderbilt University, Nashville, TN.

Lahm, E., M. Behrmann, and E. Thorp. (1993). *Features that Work for Teachers: Software Features in Early Childhood Special Education.* Technical report. Center for Human disAbilities, George Mason University, Fairfax, VA.

Public Law (P.L.) 100-407. The Technology Related Assistance Act of 1988.
P.L. 101-476. The Individuals with Disabilities in Education Act of 1990.
P.L. 105-15. The Individuals with Disabilities in Education Act of 1997.
P.L. 94-142. The Education for All Handicapped Children's Act of 1975.
P.L. 101-336. The Americans with Disabilities Act of 1990.
Schnorr, L.B., and D. Schnorr. (1989). *Within our Reach: Breaking the Cycle of Disadvantage.* New York: Anchor Books.

WEB SITES TO EXPLORE

For information on special education and links to other organizations, the Council for Exceptional Children:
  http://www.cec.sped.org/ericec/links.htm

For information on technology access in early childhood special education, the National Center for the Improvement of Practice (NCIP):
  http://www.edc.org/FSC/NCIP/

For information on barriers to accessing the World Wide Web, the Alliance for Technology Access:
  http://www.ataccess.org/access.html

For information on the integration of software into the curriculum, Clara Clutterbuck's (an Australian Special Ed teacher) home page:
  http://www.ataccess.org/access.html

For books on assistive technology, the University of Kansas:
  http://www.sped.ukans.edu/~dlance/book.html

For information on assistive technology in the schools, the University of Kentucky:
  http://serc.gws.uky.edu/www/ukat/ukatmenu.html

For more general information on resources for assistive technology and computer access, the Trace Center home page:
  http://www.trace.wisc.edu/

To contact Dr. Behrmann and see the activities that he is involved in, visit the Center for Human disAbilities at George Mason University:
  http://chd.gse.gmu.edu/

Part III

Extending Learning Communities

Technology and Learning in Schools for Thought Classrooms

SUSAN M. WILLIAMS, KATHERINE L. BURGESS,
MELINDA H. BRAY, JOHN D. BRANSFORD, SUSAN R. GOLDMAN,
AND THE COGNITION AND TECHNOLOGY GROUP AT VANDERBILT
(CTGV)

INTRODUCTION

In this chapter, we explore ways teachers and students can use modern and time-honored technologies to support learning. We do so by focusing on an education project currently being conducted in a number of schools throughout the United States called the Schools for Thought (SFT) Project (Lamon, Secules, Petrosino, Hackett, Bransford, Goldman 1996; Secules, Cottom, Bray, Miller, and the SFT Collaborative, 1997). The goal of this project is to restructure curriculum, instruction, assessment, professional development, and community participation in ways that help students develop the competencies and confidence necessary for success in the 21st century.

Schools for Thought evolved from three programs developed by independent groups of university researchers working in collaboration with classroom teachers:

- Fostering Communities of Learners (Brown and Campione 1996);
- Computer-Supported Intentional Learning Environments (Scardamalia, Bereiter, and Lamon 1994); and
- Anchored Instruction (The Cognition and Technology Group at Vanderbilt [CTGV] 1990, March 1993, 1994, 1997).

The Schools for Thought project is part of an exciting consortium, "Reinventing Communities of Learners," which is analyzing this project and similar reforms from different disciplinary perspectives in an attempt to understand the processes needed to take programs "to scale."[1] In this chapter, we focus on Schools for Thought in Nashville, Tennessee.

There are currently 30 SFT classrooms in the Metropolitan Nashville Public Schools: eight 1st grades, six 5th grades, eight 6th grades, six 7th grades, and two 8th grades. In addition, special education teachers collaborate with the 5th and 6th grade classroom teachers. Thanks to a Technology Challenge Grant awarded to the Nashville school system by the U. S. Department of Education's Office of Educational Research and Improvement, these numbers will increase substantially over the next four years. The ultimate goal is to create Schools for Thought classrooms throughout the school system from kindergarten through 8th grade. Researchers and educators are also working to develop SFT in high schools.

Schools for Thought classrooms are both child-centered and knowledge-centered. They are child-centered in using insights from research on cognition and development in the design of curriculum, teaching practices, and assessments. They are knowledge-centered in their belief that thinking and "learning to learn" require a solid grounding in traditional disciplines such as mathematics, science, literature, history, and social studies. The Schools for Thought project emphasizes the articulation of "big ideas" or "deep principles" in each of these areas (Brown and Campione 1994), rather than the memorization of sets of facts. The project also emphasizes the importance of establishing a

---

[1]Our collaborators on the Reinventing Communities of Learners project include Ann Brown, Joe Campione, Ed Haertel, Milbrey McLaughlin, Lee Shulman, Judy Shulman, and Joan Talbert.

"community of learners" in which teachers and students share the responsibility for defining and achieving the learning goals of the group.

STUDENT RESEARCH

To develop deep understanding, SFT students conduct sustained research and inquiry on important problems such as, "Why have many animal species become endangered or extinct?" or "What are the important legacies of early Greek, Roman, and Egyptian civilizations?" Once a teacher introduces a problem, students generate a list of questions that they must answer to address the problem. Students then classify these questions into topics for research, working in small research teams to examine different topics connected to the overall research problem.

Students reassemble into "jigsaw" groups composed of at least one "expert" in each topic. These experts share what they have learned during their research so that everyone has an understanding of the big picture. Along the way, the students receive multiple opportunities to "test their mettle" and revise and improve their work.

The students do their work with an eye toward completing "consequential tasks" that represent a synthesis of all topics. In one endangered species unit, for example, students constructed models of ecosystems and explained the features of these models as part of a poster fair held at a nearby university.

TECHNOLOGY AS A TOOL

The Schools for Thought project is based on the assumption that teacher and principal leadership is essential for enhancing school achievement. Technology alone can never make up for the power of effective teachers and administrators, but technology can make it easier for them to do their work.

Most SFT classrooms use a wide range of modern technologies to help students conduct research, collaborate, revise their work, and communicate their findings. These technologies include computers, videodiscs, CD-ROMs, the Internet, and (in some cases) desktop videoconferencing. In addition, there is also a strong reliance on time-honored technologies such as writing paper, pencils, and books.

In this chapter, our discussion is organized around four ways that Schools for Thought students and teachers use technology:

- to bring important problems into the classroom;
- to provide resources and scaffolds that enhance student learning;
- to provide opportunities for feedback, reflection, and revision; and
- to overcome the isolation of individual classrooms by connecting students and teachers to homes, communities, and the world.

We end this chapter with a discussion of teacher learning and the ways technologies help teachers become lifelong learners who are able to learn from one another.

Bringing Important Problems into the Classroom

Schools for Thought teachers use technology to encourage problem finding and problem solving by bringing real-world problems into the classroom and illustrating them realistically. Students attempt to solve problems such as "How can we save this wounded eagle?" "How can we design a playground that fits the constraints of this neighborhood?" and "How can we determine if this river is polluted?" The complexity of real-world problems like these can create difficulties for learners who have limited experience, knowledge, and reading skills. Many students may have trouble understanding complex problem situations presented as text. By providing a dynamic representation of events that includes visual and spatial information, video technologies allow students to form more accurate mental models of the problem situation that can act as a support for comprehension (Sharp, Bransford, Goldman, Risko, Kinzer, and Vye 1995). Video environments also can include numerous scenes designed to scaffold students' learning. (The issue of scaffolding is discussed later in this chapter.)

The interactive technology environment in Schools for Thought classrooms is very important in helping students manage the complexity of a problem and achieve in-depth understanding of content. Interactive video allows students to scan rapidly forward and backward to locate important information about a problem. Although it is possible to use videotape for this purpose, videodiscs and CD-ROMs controlled by barcode readers or computers offer more flexibility and greater opportunities for collaborative re-examination and exploration. With the random access capabilities of this technology, teachers can instantly access important scenes to use as illustrations for class discussion, and students can show data from the video as evidence to support their solutions to problems.

COLLABORATIVE PROBLEM SOLVING

Solving complex problems is an important part of the program's goal to promote understanding of deep principles or big ideas. Complex problems also help students appreciate the value of working collaboratively, because it is unlikely that any one student can solve the problems alone (CTGV May 1991, April 1993, 1997). The organization of instruction around the collaborative solution of realistic problems is quite different from classroom organizations where individual students spend most of their time learning facts from a lecture or text and answering questions at the end of a chapter. The following describes some of the ways technology is used to introduce problems in Schools for Thought classrooms.

Jasper Adventures. The Jasper Woodbury Problem Solving Series consists of 12 interactive video environments that invite students to solve authentic challenges requiring the understanding and use of important mathematical concepts (for data on Jasper, see CTGV 1992, 1993, 1994; 1997; Vye, Goldman, Voss, Hmelo, Williams, and CTGV in press; Vye, Schwartz, Bransford, Barron, Zech, and CTGV in press).

In the adventure "Rescue at Boone's Meadow," a character named Larry teaches a woman named Emily to fly an ultralight airplane. During the lessons, Larry helps Emily learn about the basic principles of flight and the specific details of the ultralight she is flying, such as its speed, fuel consumption, fuel capacity, and the amount of weight it can carry. Not long after Emily's first solo flight, her friend Jasper goes fishing in a remote area called Boone's Meadow. Hearing a gunshot, he discovers a wounded bald eagle and radios Emily for help in getting the eagle to a veterinarian. Emily consults a map to determine the closest roads to Boone's Meadow, then calls Larry to ask about weather conditions and if his ultralight is available. Students are challenged to use all of the information in the video to determine the fastest way to rescue the eagle.

After watching the video, students review the story and discuss the setting, characters, and any unfamiliar concepts and vocabulary. After they have a clear understanding of the problem, small groups of students work together to break the problem into subgoals, scan the video for information, and set up the calculations necessary to solve each part of the problem. When all of the groups have a solution, they compare their work and try to choose the best plan for rescuing the eagle. Like most real-world problems, Jasper problems have many correct solutions. Determining the optimum solution involves weighing factors such as safety and reliability, as well as making the necessary calculations.

Larry teaches Emily about the ultralight airplane in the Jasper Adventure, "Rescue at Boone's Meadow."

The Jasper series focuses on providing opportunities for problem solving and problem finding. It is not intended to replace the entire mathematics curriculum. Frequently, while attempting to solve these complex problems, students discover that they do not have the necessary basic skills. Teachers use these occasions as opportunities to conduct benchmark lessons that review the necessary concepts and procedures. (In a later section on scaffolds for student learning, we discuss the many opportunities that technology provides for presenting and practicing basic skills in the context of the original problem situation.)

Scientists in Action. In the Scientists in Action series, students are invited to solve video-based challenges that require them to learn about important science concepts such as ecosystems and interdependence (CTGV Fall 1992, 1997; Goldman, Petrosino, Sherwood, Garrison, Hickey, Bransford, and Pellegrino 1996; Sherwood, Petrosino, Lin, Lamon, and CTGV 1995). In the "Stones River Mystery" episode, students explore a polluted river to find the source of the pollution and clean it up. They engage in research cycles that require an understanding of water quality indicators (e.g., pH, macroinvertebrate, and dissolved oxygen testing) and their interrelationships (Vye, Schwartz et al. in press).

Young Children's Literacy. This series introduces kindergarten, 1st, and 2nd grade students to problems in the form of literacy challenges that encourage them to research and write books to solve the challenges (CTGV 1997). In "Ribbit and the Magic Hats," for example, children write stories to warn animals on the Little Planet about the mean tricks of a character named Wongo.

The Internet. World Wide Web sites, such as the American Schools Directory's Challenge Zone (http://www.asd.com/), also can introduce students to important problems. One Challenge Zone problem involves an exploration of ways to engineer the environment to help increase the eagle population. Students and their teachers are encouraged to conduct research about specific sub-topics related to this problem. The Challenge Zone suggests other resources, including Internet sites, books, and videos. Students can work together as a class to consult these resources, write short essays about important sub-topics, and publish their work on the Web site, where they can see their own publications and those developed by other students.

Each challenge is designed to last approximately one month. During that time, students are encouraged to increase their knowledge by reviewing the accumulated publications, revising their work, and continuing to publish. The Challenge Zone is designed so that students will have developed a solid understanding of several concepts and their interdependence by the end of a particular challenge. In working to save the eagle population, for example, students can develop a deep understanding of interdependence, habitats, and eagle recovery.

Computer-Supported Intentional Learning Environments (CSILE). CSILE, a communal database used in Schools for Thought classrooms, provides students with opportunities to initiate and discuss new problems electronically. In the following example, a 6th grade student brings her classmates a problem inspired by her research.

> [New Information] Dear Group, I was reading and I found out that if Spanish conquerors wouldn't have burned the Mayan library in Yucat'an we would know a lot more about Mayan Civilization. Only three books were salvaged. Then I started thinking about it and I discovered something. What would happen if all the books ever written were destroyed? What if only three remained? What three, if you had a choice, would you choose to save? This is a really interesting concept to me. I am going to ask Mrs. Jones if I can start a discussion note on it. Would you guys want to join? [CS]

FIGURE 5.1

Internet sites such as "The Challenge Zone" introduce students to important problems and the resources for solving them.

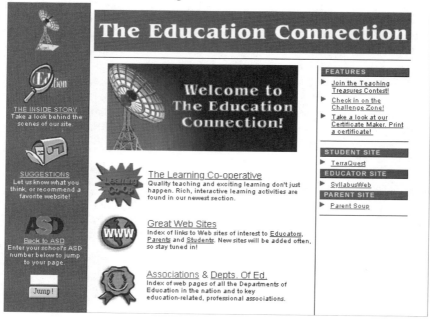

In all CSILE communications, each entry is preceded by a category identifier indicating information type, and is followed by the initials of the person posting the entry.

Time-Honored Technologies. Schools for Thought classrooms also use time-honored technologies such as books to create problem contexts. In these classrooms, books are not simply read and summarized by students; they are used to encourage learners to define issues, conduct research, and create a product that reflects their learning. For example, teachers use *Hatchet* (Paulsen 1987), a novel about a boy who survives a plane crash in the wilderness, to help students explore issues of personal survival in potentially hostile environments. SFT classrooms in Oakland, California (Brown and Campione 1996), use the book *The Day They Parachuted Cats on Borneo* (Pomerantz 1969/1993) as a context for exploring issues of endangered species. Students working with this book research endangered species and interdependence to understand how the disruption of the food chain on Borneo led to an outbreak of bubonic plague.

PROVIDING RESOURCES AND SCAFFOLDS FOR LEARNING

In addition to introducing interesting problems, technology in Schools for Thought classrooms also provides resources and scaffolds for learning. SFT classrooms often follow a model that begins with problem-based learning, such as the use of Jasper, Scientists in Action, or the Young Children's Literacy series, and then proceeds to project-based learning during which students engage in actual local community activities. The use of problem-based activities has been shown to scaffold student learning, allowing the development of higher quality projects (e.g., Barron, Schwartz, Barnsford, Goldman, Pellegrino, Morris, Garrison, and Kantor under review; CTGV 1997).

The problem-based adventures used in the Schools for Thought project also contain resources and scaffolds. The Jasper and Scientists in Action adventures include "embedded data" and "embedded teaching" scenes that help students understand issues related to the overall challenges. In a scene in the Jasper geometry adventure, "Blueprint for Success," an architect demonstrates the use of graph paper and a protractor in determining the length of the legs needed to make a ladder of a certain height.

The Young Children's Literacy series includes software that helps students use hints about picture order to sequence the pictures related to a story. The software also allows children to write a summary of the story, receive spelling help when needed, record their voices reading the story, and add music to their stories. These activities encourage in-depth understanding of the affective and narrative elements of stories. Eventually, the students print their stories as books to take home and share with their parents.

FIGURE 5.2

With the Young Children's Literacy series, children use multimedia software to write books.

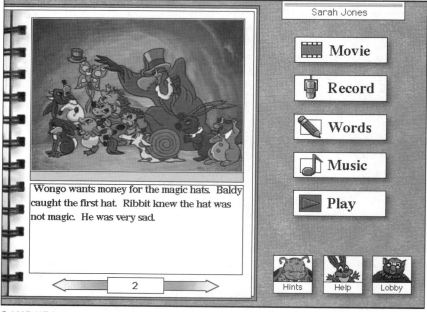

© 1997 ALT, Inc.

Other software supports the development of expository compre-hension and writing skills. The program, Notetaker, assists children do-ing research by helping them understand how to identify relevant information, structure notes about specific research topics, and organ-ize information to write reports (Weise, Scharnhorst, and Bransford 1997). It also helps children understand the distinction between narra-tive elements of a story and factual information embedded in a story or other type of text.

CSILE also serves as a scaffold in Schools for Thought classrooms. By logging onto CSILE, students can receive information from their peers that can help to solve the problems that interest them. Experts in various content areas can log onto CSILE servers from their homes or offices and help students explore important topics by providing tips and suggesting relevant articles and books. The following interchange illustrates the kind of asynchronous discussions students engage in over CSILE.

[I need to understand] Why does the fish stay around the coral? [ET]

[My Theory] I think that the fish stay around the coral because the fish need a place to hide. [ET]

[New Learning] Yesterday, we watched a film on the Great Barrier Reef. I found out a lot. The reef provides food, shelter, and hunting grounds. Fish called Remoras help out big manta rays by cleaning them. There are also small fish called Cleaner fish. They clean fish of small particles.[BW]

[Comment] BW, I agree that the fish stay by the reef for protection and food. I guess I really didn't think about that. When you were talking about the fish that eat parasites and how they help clean them I was very interested. Could you give me some information on where I can find some more things about that? [ET]

Internet sites also serve as information resources in SFT classrooms. The project's Mission to Mars curriculum (Petrosino 1995) has a Web site that includes pictures and content material relevant to space travel (http://relax.ltc.vanderbilt.edu/mars/short.html). An Internet site on eagles helps students understand how to change the environment to promote the survival of a species (http://peabody.vanderbilt.edu/projects/funded/sft/eagle/eaglewb1.htm). The Challenge Zone in the American Schools Directory site (http://www.asd.com/) also provides resources relevant to the various challenges presented there.

PROVIDING OPPORTUNITIES FOR FEEDBACK, REFLECTION, AND REVISION

Technology in Schools for Thought classrooms is designed to allow students to receive frequent feedback about their thinking and the opportunity to revise their understanding as necessary. When teachers working with the Jasper adventure "Blueprint for Success" had difficulty finding time to give feedback to students on playground designs, researchers developed a simple computer interface that cut teachers' time in providing feedback by more than half (CTGV 1997). Similarly, researchers developed an interactive Jasper Adventureplayer software program that allows students to suggest solutions to Jasper problems and see a simulation of the effects of these suggestions. This program clearly improved the quality of the solutions students generated (Crews, Biswas, Goldman, and Bransford in press; Williams 1994). Opportunities to connect to real scientists over the Internet also provide rich resources for feedback and revision.

SCIENTIFIC AND MATHEMATICAL ARENAS FOR REFINING THINKING (SMART)

The SMART Challenge series uses technology to provide multiple resources for feedback and revision. Students working to create a business plan as part of the Jasper adventure "The Big Splash" can visit the SMART Lab Web site where they can examine data submitted by other students. The data show a number of different estimates of revenue and expenses relevant to the adventure—only some of which are accurate. Students locate their own points in these data, see alternatives generated by others, and can use this information to revise their business plans. Students can also visit the SMART Toolbox, where they receive just-in-time tools to help them test their thinking, (e.g., a timeline tool to help assess the feasibility of their plans for "The Big Splash").

SMART has been tested in a number of contexts, including Jasper and Scientists in Action. Data indicate that adding the SMART formative assessment resources increases achievement over use of the same curriculum without these assessments (CTGV 1997; Vye, Schwartz et al. in press).

CSILE AS A SOURCE OF FEEDBACK

With CSILE in Schools for Thought classrooms, students can get a great deal more feedback on their ideas than would be possible if the teacher were the only feedback source. Peers can generate questions and provide feedback, often leading students to revise their thinking. On other occasions, teachers or outside experts can participate in the discussion to stimulate students thinking (Scardamalia, Bereiter, and Lamon 1994). One SFT teacher (designated "RB") began a critical dialog in CSILE by asking students to compare the experiences of Miyax and Brian, two protagonists from different books, and decide who had been in the most treacherous survival predicament. Miyax, in *Julie of the Wolves* (George 1972), was trained by her father in wilderness survival skills and runs away from home when he is presumed dead after failing to return from a hunting trip. Brian, a self-proclaimed "city boy" in *Hatchet* (Paulsen 1987), gets stranded in the Canadian woods after a plane crash. After students generated their initial responses on these characters, RB inserted the following note to foster deeper discussion on the issue.

> [Comment:] To Everyone: We have a definite "split" in our opinion on whose situation is worse. Read everyone's theories and see if you can bring someone of a different opinion around to agreement with you by asking specific questions or clarifying, perhaps, a misconception. [RB]

This prompt stimulated students to provide the following comments and feedback to their peers:

> [Comment]: To Brett: Didn't Miyax have grass and stuff that she could eat? [WD]

> [Comment]: CF, what do you mean that the girl is going to die in the cold? [DP]

> [Comment]: DP, I am saying that she is in more danger than Brian. [CF]

> [I Need To Understand]: Jamie: Don't you think that Brian's condition is worse than Miyax's because he has no food or anything and Miyax does?

CURRICULUM-BASED MEASUREMENT (CBM)

Curriculum-based measurement is an assessment system that enables teachers and students to follow the path of student learning over the course of the school year (Fuchs, Fuchs, Hamlett, and Stecker 1991). These assessments are sampled from the range of competencies expected by the end of the school year at a particular grade level. Students complete short assessments several times per month, which are scored by the computer. Each score becomes a data point on an individual child's graph. By looking at the shape of the graph over time, students and teachers can quickly see whether or not performance is improving. A more detailed analysis of a student's correct and incorrect answers helps teachers determine which curriculum areas to concentrate on with the student. Teachers have found the results of CBM assessments to be powerful ways of providing parents with information about their children's learning and development.

BUILDING COMMUNITIES

A major goal of the Schools for Thought project is to create a community of learners (Brown and Campione 1994) who work together within the classroom and are connected to others outside the classroom (e.g., CTGV 1994). Technology plays an important role in developing both of these types of communities.

BUILDING COMMUNITY WITHIN CLASSROOMS

Schools for Thought classrooms use a variety of methods to develop a sense of community within the classroom, including dividing the class into interdependent research groups that rely on one another for needed content information. The use of CSILE technology also supports community building by allowing students to see their peers' thoughts in the form of comments and questions. The asynchronous, permanent nature of the database has advantages over the fleeting oral conversation of a traditional in-class discussion. As one student said, "If I'm absent I can find out what was talked about by looking at the database."

Technology helps to connect students with communities both inside and outside of the classroom.

Connecting Classrooms to the Broader Community

Common anchors for problem solving, such as the Jasper and Scientists in Action adventures, also foster community building outside the classroom, within and across groups of students, teachers, parents, and community members. Parents, administrators, college students, business representatives, and other community members have participated in the adventures and attempted to solve the challenges. Because the tasks are challenging and take time, even for adults, the students who have solved these adventures can act as mentors to groups of adults, keeping them on track without giving them the answers. The result has been an exciting experience for the students and the adults (CTGV 1997).

These programs and projects also allow adults to share their expertise with students. Adults in various communities have taught students about ultralights after seeing the Jasper adventure "Rescue at Boone's Meadow." Similarly, business representatives from a local bank have shared their expertise with students creating business plans around the Jasper adventure "The Big Splash." One bank executive provided a visual representation of his group's solution and presentation. The 6th graders who were meeting with them said, "That looks just like the solution from Jenny's group." Indeed, the student group's visual representation of their solution and presentation was almost identical to the adults'.

In a study conducted by Burgess (in preparation), inner-city 5th grade students who had solved "Rescue at Boone's Meadow" helped a college class solve the adventure. The 5th graders kept the college students from getting off track, but did not tell them the answers. They also helped the college students learn to use the interactive technologies necessary to search the video. Both groups learned a great deal from working with each other.

In a focus group session after the college class, the 5th graders were asked what they had learned by watching the college students. The students' answers were extremely perceptive. A number mentioned their surprise that the college students were not afraid to ask questions. All were impressed that the college students "knew their math facts," and they agreed that they should learn them, too. The 5th graders also remarked that the college students did not need to return to the video as much as their class had needed to; the college students tended to remember the relevant information needed to solve the challenge. When asked to explain why the older students remembered so much, the 5th graders remarked, "Because they all paid attention." They pointed out that disruptions in their 5th grade classroom often got in the way of learning.

Interviews with the teacher of the 5th grade students indicated that the youngsters had returned to the school with great enthusiasm about helping the college class, and a realization that their classroom could be better if they acted more like the older students. Feedback from parents confirmed that the 5th graders talked a great deal about their "college" experiences when they returned home. It is doubtful that the 5th graders' experiences would have been as positive if they had simply visited a college class with no preparation. By coming "armed" with knowledge about how to solve a complex problem, the 5th graders were able to teach as well as learn.

TWO-WAY VIDEOCONFERENCING

Realistic problems also provide an excellent context for the use of technologies such as two-way videoconferencing to connect with other community members. In a class at Vanderbilt University, college students first solved the Jasper adventure "The Big Splash," then mentored inner-city 6th graders as they worked with it and developed their business plans. The groups of college students and 6th graders met once in person. After that, all interactions occurred over inexpensive desktop videoconferencing. The college students and the 6th graders indicated that the experience was highly valuable. The use of videoconferencing made it possible for the college students to connect to the 6th grade classroom on an ongoing basis.

Two-way videoconferencing also makes it possible for students in Schools for Thought classrooms to connect with students in distant locations. One group of SFT students was preparing for a debate on Hawaiian sovereignty, which required that they understand the state and its relationship with the continental United States. A search for information led to a Web site created by a class in Hawaii which, in turn, led to a videoconference organized by the students' teachers. The SFT students were able to share what they had learned and get feedback from other students living in Hawaii.

GREAT BEGINNINGS CHALLENGE

Nashville's Great Beginnings Challenge illustrates another way to use problem-solving adventures to create community connections. The Challenge is organized around adventures from the Young Children's Literacy Series developed for students in grades K-3. Working with the series, students write a book to save the creatures on the Little Planet from falling prey to the wiles of an evil character named Wongo. The animated adventures contain information relevant to literacy, science, and mathematics.

Students share the adventures with interested community members who attempt to create stories, music, videos, and other new products related to the series. Some 5th grade students, for example, are writing stories related to Little Planet themes for 1st grade readers. In addition, Nashville musicians, writers, and storytellers are creating music videos related to various series themes. High school video production classes are working with video industry professionals to showcase teachers and students using these products, as well as the community members who helped create them. The overall goal is to create a community of learners that contributes to "great beginnings" for each child.

PROFESSIONAL DEVELOPMENT

Teachers engaged in the Schools for Thought approach are the agents and orchestrators of the technology used in these classrooms. They employ technology to bring discussion, debate, and research into the classroom. They rely on technology for teaching resources, use it to obtain information about student learning, and to provide feedback. In addition, teachers use technology to form professional development communities important to their own learning and reflection on teaching practice. Clearly, technology helps Schools for Thought teachers to be lifelong learners in many ways.

By design, the uses of technology for professional development parallel those for student learning. One assumption in this professional development model is that teachers need to experience the activities in which they will engage their students, including the uses of technology (CTGV 1997). Teachers prepare to teach a Jasper adventure such as "The Big Splash" or "Blueprint for Success" by working in teams to find a solution, in much the same way their students will. Professional development facilitators model the kinds of activities and guidance that teachers will later use in their own classrooms and an interactive video provides additional teaching support for the Jasper series (CTGV 1997). In addition, teachers work with the same technology-based problem anchors, resources, and scaffolds that will be available to their students.

Teachers also use technology to support the reflection that occurs in a variety of forms and is sometimes anchored around specific examples of student work. CSILE notes generated by students on the "Blueprint" adventure can become the focus of a teacher discussion on student learning and understanding. Teachers also can look at CSILE notes to gauge what students understand and to determine the type of student assistance needed. Analyzing student learning in this way enables teachers to reflect on the kinds of questions, prompts, comments, and ideas that could be used to "seed" database discussions.

Reflective discussion of student learning and teaching practice also can be anchored around video of specific classroom situations, such as a group of students working together. In a particularly interesting research project, one teacher watched a group of students comment on their own work (Cohen, Friedlander, Baecker, and Rosenthal 1996). She was amazed at how the students were learning "behind her back." Teachers have also used simpler technologies such as audio tape recorders to tape student discussions. These are helpful in augmenting written group products because the oral discussions are often much richer than the written material.

TEACHER COMMUNITIES

Teachers often voice dissatisfaction about a sense of isolation from professional peers. Creating teacher networks is a powerful way to develop a sense of professionalism, a professional identity, and increased understanding of learning, assessment, and educational reform (Lieberman 1995). This appears to be as true for electronic communities as it is for face-to-face communities. The important dimension appears to be the existence of common causes or activities as community anchors. During professional development sessions, Schools for Thought teachers use CSILE for their own reflections, even as they are learning how the program works. E-mail and the Internet also serve as powerful tools for sustaining conversations among professionals at remote locations. This is particularly important when there are only one or two teachers at the same site working on the Schools for Thought project.

SUMMARY

Our goal in this chapter has been to discuss the ways that technology supports learning and enhances teaching in Schools for Thought classrooms. First, video, computer, and Internet technology bring information about important problems into the classroom. These technologies communicate complex problem situations in ways that support student understanding and allow the review, study, and collaboration necessary to find solutions to real-world problems.

Second, technology provides resources and scaffolds that enhance learning. In SFT classrooms, students attempt to solve complex problems that require sustained effort. Video and interactive computer-based tools encourage in-depth exploration and help students achieve deeper understanding.

Third, tools such as computer-based simulations provide opportunities for feedback, reflection, and revision. SFT teachers also provide frequent feedback to students by using computer-based tools to administer and score assessments and communicate results.

Finally, technology supports collaboration among students, teachers, and the community. Computer-mediated communication provides opportunities for students to discuss their work with each other, with their teachers, and with members of the community outside their classrooms. In addition, technology allows teachers to enhance their own learning by participating in discussions on practice with other teachers and university colleagues, both near and far.

REFERENCES

Barron, B.J., D.L. Schwartz, N.J. Vye, A. Moore, A. Petrosino, L. Zech, J.D. Bransford, and CTGV. (under review). "Doing with Understanding: Lessons from Research on Problem- and Project-Based Learning."

Barron, B.J., N. Vye, L. Zech, D. Schwartz, J. Bransford, S.R. Goldman, J. Pellegrino, J. Morris, S. Garrison, and R. Kantor. (1995). "Creating Contexts for Community-Based Problem Solving. The Jasper Challenge Series." In *Thinking and Literacy: The Mind at Work*, edited by C.N. Hedley, P. Antonacci, and M. Rabinowitz. Hillsdale, N.J.: Lawrence Erlbaum Associates.

Brown, A.L., and J.C. Campione. (1994). "Guided Discovery in a Community of Learners." In *Classroom Lessons: Integrating Cognitive Theory and Classroom Practice*, edited by K. McGilly. Cambridge, Mass.: MIT Press.

Brown, A.L., and J.C. Campione. (1996). "Psychological Theory and the Design of Innovative Learning Environments: On Procedures, Principles, and Systems." In *Innovations in Learning: New Environments for Education*, edited by L. Schauble and R. Glaser. Mahwah, N.J.: Erlbaum.

Burgess, K.L. (in preparation). "University-Public School Collaboration in Schools for Thought."

Cognition and Technology Group at Vanderbilt. (1990). "Anchored Instruction and Its Relationship to Situated Cognition. *Educational Researcher* 19, 6: 2-10.

Cognition and Technology Group at Vanderbilt. (May 1991). "Technology and the Design of Generative Learning Environments. *Educational Technology* 31, 5: 34-40.

Cognition and Technology Group at Vanderbilt. (1992). "Anchored Instruction in Science and Mathematics: Theoretical Basis, Developmental Projects, and Initial Research Findings." In *Philosophy of Science, Cognitive Psychology, and Educational Theory and Practice*, edited by R. A. Duschl and R. J. Hamilton. New York: State University of New York Press.

Cognition and Technology Group at Vanderbilt (Fall 1992). "The Jasper Series as an Example of Anchored Instruction: Theory, Program Description, and Assessment Data." *Educational Psychologist* 27, 4: 291-315.

Cognition and Technology Group at Vanderbilt. (1993). "The Jasper Series: Theoretical Foundations and Data on Problem Solving and Transfer." In *The Challenges in Mathematics and Science Education: Psychology's Response*, edited by L.A. Penner, G.M. Batsche, H.M. Knoff, and D.L. Nelson. Washington, D.C.: American Psychological Association.

Cognition and Technology Group at Vanderbilt. (March 1993). "Anchored Instruction and Situated Cognition Revisited." *Educational Technology* 33, 3: 52-70.

Cognition and Technology Group at Vanderbilt. (April 1993). "The Jasper Experiment: Using Video to Furnish Real-World Problem-Solving Contexts." *Arithmetic Teacher* 40, 8: 474-478.

Cognition and Technology Group at Vanderbilt. (1994). "From Visual Word Problems to Learning Communities: Changing Conceptions of Cognitive Research." In *Classroom Lessons: Integrating Cognitive Theory and Classroom Practice*, edited by K. McGilly. Cambridge, Mass.: MIT Press.

Cognition and Technology Group at Vanderbilt. (1997). *THE JASPER PROJECT: Lessons in Curriculum, Instruction, Assessment, and Professional Development.* Mahwah, N.J.: Erlbaum.

Cohen, A., N. Friedlander, R. Baecker, and A. Rosenthal. (July 1996). "MAD: A Movie Authoring and Design System: Making Classroom Process Visible." *Proceedings of the International Conference on the Learning Sciences* (ICLS). Charlottesville, Va.: Association for the Advancment of Computing in Education.

Crews, T.R., G. Biswas, S.R. Goldman, and J.D.Bransford. (in press). "Macrocontexts Plus Microworlds: An Anchored Instruction Approach to Intelligent Learning Environments." *Journal of AI in Education.*

Fuchs, L.S., D. Fuchs, C.L. Hamlett, and P.M. Stecker. (Fall 1991). "Effects of Curriculum Based Measurement on Teacher Planning and Student Achievement in Mathematics Operations." *American Educational Research Journal* 28, 3: 617-641.

George, J.C. (1972). *Julie of the Wolves.* New York: Harper and Row.

Goldman, S.R., A. Petrosino, R.D. Sherwood, S. Garrison, D. Hickey, J.D. Bransford, and J. Pellegrino. (1996). "Anchoring Science Instruction in Multimedia Learning Environments." In *International Perspectives on the Design of Technology-Supported Learning Environments*, edited by S. Vosniadou, E. De Corte, R. Glaser, and H. Mandl. (pp. 257-284). Hillsdale, N.J.: Lawrence Erlbaum Associates.

Lamon, M., T.J. Secules, T. Petrosino, R. Hackett, J.D. Bransford, and S.R. Goldman. (1996). "Schools for Thought: Overview of the Project and Lessons Learned from One of the Sites." In *Innovations in Learning: New Environments for Education*, edited by L. Schauble and R. Glaser. (pp. 243-288). Mahwah, NJ: Erlbaum.

Lieberman, A. (April 1995). "Practices that Support Teacher Development." *Phi Delta Kappan* 76, 8: 591-596.

Paulsen, G. (1987). *Hatchet.* New York: Bradbury Press.

Petrosino, A.J. (1995). *Mission to Mars: An Integrated Curriculum.* Technical Report SFT-1. Nashville, Tenn.: Learning Technology Center, Vanderbilt University.

Pomerantz, C. (1969/1993). *The Day They Parachuted Cats on Borneo*. LaSalle, Ill.: Open Court Publishing Co.

Scardamalia, M., C. Bereiter, and M. Lamon. (1994). "The CSILE Project: Trying to Bring the Classroom into World 3." In *Classroom Lessons: Integrating Cognitive Theory and Classroom Practice*, edited by K. McGilly. (pp. 201-228). Cambridge, Mass.: MIT Press.

Secules, T., C. Cottom, M. Bray, L. Miller, and The Schools for Thought Collaborative. (1997). "Creating Schools for Thought." *Educational Leadership* 54, 6: 56-60.

Sharp, D.L.M., J.D. Bransford, S.R. Goldman, V.J. Risko, C.K. Kinzer, and N.J. Vye. (1995). "Dynamic Visual Support for Story Comprehension and Mental Model Building by Young, At-Risk Children." *Educational Technology Research and Development* 43, 4: 25-42.

Sherwood, R.D., A.J. Petrosino, X. Lin, M. Lamon, and the Cognition and Technology Group at Vanderbilt. (1995). "Problem-Based Macro Contexts in Science Instruction: Theoretical Basis, Design Issues, and the Development of Applications." In *Towards a Cognitive-Science Perspective for Scientific Problem Solving*, edited by D. Lavoie. (pp. 191-214). Manhattan, Kan.: National Association for Research in Science Teaching.

Vye, N.J., S.R. Goldman, J.F. Voss, C.E. Hmelo, S.M. Williams, and the Cognition and Technology Group at Vanderbilt. (in press). "Complex Mathematical Problem Solving by Individuals and Dyads. Cognition and Instruction.

Vye, N.J., D.L. Schwartz, J.D. Bransford, B.J. Barron, L. Zech, and the Cognition and Technology Group at Vanderbilt. (in press). "Smart Environments that Support Monitoring, Reflection, and Revision." In *Metacognition in Educational Theory and Practice*, edited by D.J. Hacker, J. Dunlosky, and A.C. Graesser. Mahwah, N.J.: Erlbaum

Weise, R., U. Scharnhorst, and J. Bransford. (1997). "Tools for Enhancing Learning Across Disciplines." Paper presented at the annual meeting of the American Educational Research Association in Chicago, Illinois.

Williams, S.M. (1994). "Anchored Simulations: Merging the Strengths of Formal and Informal Reasoning in a Computer-Based Learning Environment." Unpublished doctoral dissertation, Vanderbilt University, Nashville, Tenn.

The Cognition and Technology Group at Vanderbilt (CTGV)
http://peabody.vanderbilt.edu/ltc/general/
CTGV is a collaborative, multidisciplinary group of approximately
70 researchers, designers, and educators. CTGV members are currently working on a variety of projects in the areas of mathematics,
science, social studies, and literacy. Project Web sites include:

Schools for Thought:
http://peabody.vanderbilt.edu/projects/funded/sft/
general/sfthome.html
Scientists in Action:
http://peabody.vanderbilt.edu/projects/funded/sia/sia.html
Mission to Mars:
http://relax.ltc.vanderbilt.edu/mars/short.html
Little Planet Times:
http://www.Littleplanet.com
American Schools Directory:
http://www.asd.com/
The Education Connection:
http://www.asd.com/asd/edconn/page5nf.htm
Challenge Zone:
http://www.asd.com/asd/edconn/chzone/zone2.htm

Publishers of programs mentioned in this chapter:

The Jasper Series is published and distributed by LEARNING, Inc., a
divison of Lawrence Erlbaum Associates, 10 Industrial Avenue,
Mahwah, NJ 07430-2262; 1-800-9-BOOKS-9 (http://www.erlbaum.
com/). Jasper is currently being used in classrooms in every state in
the United States and in other countries. http://peabody.vander-
bilt.edu/projects/funded/jasper/Jasperhome.html

Ribbit and the Magic Hats is published by Little Planet Publishing,
5045 Hillsboro Road, Nashville TN 37215. The Ribbit Collection was
awarded the Software Publishers' Association 1997 "Codie Award"
for "Best Curriculum Software for Early Education."

Computer-Supported Intentional Learning Environments (CSILE)
http://csile.oise.utoronto.ca/
CSILE is distributed by Learning in Motion, 500 Seabright Ave.,
Suite 105, Santa Cruz, CA 95062-3481; 1-800-560-5670.

Union City Online:

An Architecture for
Networking and Reform

MARGARET HONEY, FRED CARRIGG, AND JAN HAWKINS

"This school system is undergoing a remarkable transformation
I want the rest of the country to know about it, and I want every-
body in the country to be able to emulate it."
> President Clinton
> Address to Union City (NJ) Schools
> February 15, 1996

I n February 1996, President Clinton and Vice President Gore selected
Union City, New Jersey, as the site for the announcement of a new
multi-billion dollar initiative known as *America's Education Technology Challenge*. The White House recognized that the Union City
School District's comprehensive educational reform program had resulted in remarkable improvements in student learning and achieve-

ment. Closely tied to this reform program was Project Explore, an innovative school-business partnership with the Bell Atlantic Corporation. This partnership pioneered the use of home/school networking technologies to provide students and teachers with in-depth access to communications and information resources.

OBJECTIVES

Building on the work of Project Explore, Union City Online: An Architecture for Networking and Reform was designed to investigate the potential of Internet technologies in a context where systemic educational reforms have taken root. The program, which officially began November 15, 1995, was funded by the National Science Foundation (NSF) for three years. In partnership with the Union City Board of Education and Bell Atlantic, the Education Development Center's (EDC) Center for Children and Technology (CCT) has helped to develop a technical infrastructure that delivers high speed Internet connectivity to the 11 schools in the district. This effort links more than 2,000 personal computers (PCs) in classrooms, library media centers, computer labs, and teacher and student homes to the network. In addition to this technical infrastructure, the program was charged with the development of an effective and sustainable *human infrastructure.*

Union City Online began with seven core goals:

1. Produce information about effective architectures for high speed school networking and the transfer of technical and design expertise from corporate and nonprofit collaborators to the local community.
2. Establish effective teacher training practices to support teachers in *integrating* Internet resources into the curriculum and introduce them to *authoring* techniques and design principles for building original World Wide Web resources.
3. Develop Web-based curricula that support research-driven, interdisciplinary learning and make extensive use of Internet resources.
4. Create a model for community authoring initiatives that brings together teachers, students, and community agencies to create World Wide Web resources.
5. Integrate the network into the district's Parent University initiative to facilitate parental involvement.

6. Draw upon other National Science Foundation-funded projects as key contributors to the district's math and science reform efforts.
7. Provide opportunities for the extensive dissemination of project outcomes by the school community and by project collaborators at state and national levels.

The overarching mandate of the Union City Online project is to document, synthesize, and evaluate information that can help multiple audiences (including teachers, school and district administrators, educational leaders, and policy makers) develop a broader understanding of the power of networked technologies as tools for teaching, learning, and community involvement. Union City's extensive networking infrastructure makes this school system one of the most comprehensively wired urban districts in the country. In addition, the district's reform efforts have fundamentally altered the nature of teaching and learning taking place in the schools. As a result, the project offers a rich opportunity to learn more about the dynamics of technology integration and educational reform. This chapter examines the project's goals and strategies, and the lessons learned as Union City built an architecture for networking and reform.

SYSTEMIC REFORM AT THE DISTRICT LEVEL

Union City, located in northern New Jersey's Hudson County, sits perched on top of the Lincoln Tunnel directly across the Hudson River from Manhattan. It is the most densely populated city in the United States (42,000 residents per square mile), with a student population that is 92% Spanish speaking. In the 1960s, the ethnic composition of the city changed dramatically from Italian to Cuban as the city became home to refugees fleeing Castro's rise to power. Today, Union City continues to have the largest concentration of Cuban-Americans outside of Miami. A bus, known locally as "La Cubana," leaves daily for the long journey to Miami. In recent years, however, the city's Latino population has diversified as Union City has become home to many former residents of the Caribbean, Central, and South America.

Families who make the long journey to Union City come with the intention of giving their children a better way of life. Many adults arrive with limited formal education. According to the 1990 census, about half of the officially reported adult population had completed high school. For this community, schooling is important because it represents an opportunity for a better life.

The Union City Board of Education serves approximately 9,000 students in 11 schools (three elementary, five K-8, one middle, and two high schools). The school district is one of 30 special needs districts in the state, as defined by the New Jersey Quality in Education Act. A special needs district is an area with a poor economic base recognized by the state of New Jersey. In a 1976 court case, these districts alleged that the inadequate funding of urban schools denies poor and minority students the equal educational opportunity mandated by the New Jersey Thorough and Efficient Education law. The New Jersey Supreme Court subsequently upheld this claim.

Like many urban school systems, Union City has confronted serious educational challenges and, in 1989, was among a handful of New Jersey districts facing state takeover. In response, the district implemented a five year plan to bring about substantive and systemic changes in the educational system. Under the umbrella of a whole language approach to learning, the district created a curriculum to support the development of thinking, reasoning, and collaboration skills throughout the disciplines, de-emphasizing rote learning and whole-group lecture modes of education.

In addition to changes in the curriculum, the district implemented a number of additional reforms. Schools no longer only bought textbooks for individual students; instead, class and free voluntary reading libraries were established. Teacher inservice time was increased from less than eight hours a year to up to 40 hours yearly, with increased opportunities for voluntary staff development. To encourage student research, major scheduling changes were implemented. At the elementary level, English, reading, and writing were combined into a single 111 minute communications period. Math was extended to a 74 minute period and, whenever possible, combined with a 37 minute period of science to create a 111 minute math/science block. Block scheduling was initiated at the two high schools in September 1996, creating 80 minute blocks of time in most subject areas. School buildings have been significantly refurbished. Windows have been replaced, classrooms and hallways painted, and individual student desks replaced by cooperative learning tables.

With additional funding from New Jersey's Quality in Education Act, the district made a significant investment in technology resources to support the curriculum reform goals. During the last seven years, approximately 2,200 instructional computers have been installed in the district, establishing a four to one ratio of students to computers.

Union City Online, a hardware base connected by a state-of-the-art networking infrastructure, offers a good opportunity to examine the effect that networking technologies can have on teaching, learning, and community involvement in the context of a well-established systemic reform initiative.

THE GOALS

The remainder of this chapter examines in detail each of the seven goals of the Union City Online project, as well as the specific strategies used to meet these goals.

Goal 1. Produce information about effective architectures for high speed school networking and the transfer of technical and design expertise from corporate and nonprofit collaborators to the local community.

When the Union City Online project was first conceptualized, the project team planned to build on the networking infrastructure that Bell Atlantic had begun to deploy through Project Explore at two district schools, the Christopher Columbus Middle School and the Emerson High School. This infrastructure was owned and operated by Bell Atlantic and, in theory, it made sense for the school's corporate partner to continue in its role as district personnel gradually assumed responsibility for network ownership and maintenance.

During the first two months of the project, however, it became clear that the school district would have to assume the responsibility for running and managing the network much sooner than anticipated. This was essential for several reasons:

- to promote ownership of the networking technology at the district level and ensure that the networking infrastructure was genuinely responsive to district needs,
- to begin to build technical expertise at the district level as soon as possible, and
- to ensure the efficient growth and maintenance of the networked environment.

As soon as the decision was made to place the responsibility for network management within the Union City Board of Education, board staff moved quickly to design the networking infrastructure. Under the direction of the district's Supervisor for Computer Operations, the board evaluated the effectiveness of ISDN versus T1 telecommunications line options, wrote detailed technical specifications for vendor bids, and established a mixed architecture of school board owned and maintained UNIX, Windows NT, and Macintosh servers at the central office. The district also moved away from the proprietary Lotus Notes platform used in Bell Atlantic's Project Explore to an open standard-based TCP/IP architecture.

As part of the district's 1996-1997 budget, the Union City Board of Education approved an additional $1.2 million to build the technical infrastructure. This allocation represented the district's first significant investment in building its wide area network capacity. Currently, the district allocates approximately 3% of its $110 million operating budget to technology expenditures.

During the 1996-1997 year, the district built fiber backbones in each of its 11 school buildings and created a wide area network to connect 11 schools, two public libraries, the city hall, and day care center through T1 lines to the central office server. Approximately 25% of the district's 2,200 instructional computers are connected to the network.

By investing and building expertise locally, the district was able to make dramatic progress in ensuring equitable access to technology for all students and families in its service area. Specific initiatives, designed by the district to support the equity of access agenda, included the following:

- *Computer training for the public at the public library.* The district hired several full time trainers to work with the 1,000 community members who signed up for computer courses.
- *Extended hours for schools*, during which students and parents can access technology resources (7:00 a.m. - 9:00 p.m.).
- *An innovative technology rebate program.* The schools receive a rebate when Union City families sign up for Internet access with Bell Atlantic. The rebate income is invested in the district's technology programs.
- *A computer purchase program for parents.* Thomas A. Edison Elementary School, the state's largest elementary school, ran a computer purchase program for parents. Approximately 60 families joined.
- *Laptop computers for the classroom.* Using Title I resources, the district purchased 150 Toshiba laptops through the Microsoft/Toshiba SchoolNet project. As a result, as many as 90 6th and 7th grade students can use laptops all day in class.

- *Alpha Smart laptop keyboards are used extensively for student writing projects.* The keyboards are Macintosh compatible word processing devices that enable students to write at home and download and edit at school.
- *The purchase of additional Internet technology* is being explored, including Web TV and other low-cost Internet devices.

To document the growth of the Union City Online network infrastructure, the Center for Children and Technology created a hypermedia document that describes and explains the evolution of the district's network model. Available on the Union City web site (http://www.union-city.k12.nj.us), the documentation includes everything from network diagrams to specific bid requests and security solutions. This information, focusing on the lessons learned in Union City, is intended particularly for school districts implementing or expanding an information infrastructure.

Goal 2. **Establish effective teacher training practices to support teachers in *integrating* Internet resources into the curriculum and introduce them to *authoring* techniques and design principles for building original World Wide Web resources.**

In Union City public schools, staff development is a process, not an event. The district learned a great deal in the early years of its restructuring, especially during the massive staff retraining in the whole language philosophy of literacy acquisition (1989-1993). For this project, the district used a five stage model to support the teachers as they worked toward proficiency in the new educational paradigms. The model currently is being used to integrate technology into the daily curriculum with the support of the National Science Foundation, the State Systemic Initiative (SSI), and a host of local and state funding sources.

The five stages of this teacher support model include: awareness, practice, sharing, peer coaching, and mentoring.

Stage 1: Awareness.

At this stage, work is done in large groups during which broad and (or) new elementary concepts are introduced to the faculty. Examples include the first inservice of each new year, during which revised curriculum guides are presented and discussed with grade level or department level faculty. Whole language and cooperative learning technique orientations also are presented through awareness workshops. In addition, hundreds of faculty members are funded for single and multiday training sponsored by professional groups out-of-district and at state and national conferences.

Stage 2: Practice.

The second stage, and the most commonly used approach to staff development, is *practice*. This is particularly effective for computer orientation. Basic computer skills, such as Beginner Macintosh (locally funded) and Internet Explore (funded by NSF and SSI), are introduced and practiced over a series of several days. The district also offers intermediate and advanced Macintosh camps. During the winter of 1997, the district introduced a two day beginner HTML faculty workshop funded by NSF and run by staff from the Center for Children and Technology.

Stage 3: Sharing.

In a workshop, practitioners of new approaches discuss their experiences, both successful and not so successful, and share their adaptations with peers. At least two of these half-day sessions are held each year. They are run by local School Improvement Teams (SITs) and lend themselves well to a site-based approach. At times, the district will gather team members from several schools to participate in more advanced workshops. In the summer of 1996, for example, three teams (one middle school and two high school) of four members participated in a two day interdisciplinary cross-curricular thematic unit. Their goal was to find common ground across the disciplines for collaborative support and team building.

Stage 4: Peer Coaching.

In this model, teachers with experience and confidence in a new approach open their classrooms to coach and team teach with teachers working with new ideas. The model was used successfully in the early '90s with the district's conversion to whole language philosophy, a student-centered educational approach using authentic reading materials. In the 1997/98 school year, coaches experienced in integrating the Web-based, student-centered curriculum into daily practice will spend two days to a full week working with protégés, team teaching, and providing suggestions and ideas on successful practices.

Stage 5: Mentoring.

An extension of the peer coaching concept, this program partners a mentor with no more than three protégés for an extended period of time, such as a marking period or a full school year. The Union City school district has implemented several successful teacher-to-student and teacher-to-teacher mentoring programs. Teacher-to-teacher mentors most often are seasoned faculty paired with new non-tenured teachers. Teacher-to-student mentoring activities include the highly successful Computer Applications Mentoring Program (CAMP) at Emerson High School. During the 1996-1997 school year, this program involved more than 20 faculty and 30 students. For the 1997-1998 school year, an honors camp program has been started. For this program, nine students and a district Web master will develop and maintain the Union City Online Web site (http://www.union-city.k12.nj.us/ .

As staff development and inservice activities are planned and implemented, the district recognizes that change occurs over time and at various personal and professional levels. Workshops, activities, and professional experiences are planned to be responsive to the evolving needs of the Union City staff. Since the start of the Union City Online project, more than 400 teachers have received training in the use of new technologies and more than 20 faculty members have mentored other faculty and students working on technology-based projects.

Goal 3.   Develop Web-based curricula that support research-driven, interdisciplinary learning and make extensive use of Internet resources.

As part of a five-year plan for reforming the school system in Union City, the Board of Education organized a group of teachers in the summers of 1996 and 1997 to develop online curricula to be used in the 1997/98 school year in grades 7-12. In these Web-based curricula, the tremendous educational resources available on the Web have a role in the classroom equal to traditional print material. The proficiencies and syllabi for Marine Science 530, for example, include a list of URLs, or Internet "addresses," related to marine science, a traditional textbook in marine science, and multimedia material such as *Oceanography* from Optical Data Corp. (1990). The online course material is located at http://www.union-city.k12.nj.us/science/ .

In its curricular reforms, the district's primary consideration was to provide an information-rich environment to foster research through multiple sources of information. As students are allowed a more active role in designing their assignments, decision-making skills are reinforced across the curriculum. And, critical-thinking skills are developed by encouraging students to self-reflect and seriously evaluate their own efforts.

In this Web-based redesign of the curriculum, the teacher, while still the primary guide of the learning process, becomes more of a "facilitator," encouraging students to collaboratively discover alternative methods of problem solving and creative expression. In addition, cooperative learning strategies promote social skills, self-confidence, and meaningful communication.

The Web-based curricula are an extension of Union City's curricular reform efforts. The district's whole language approach, immersing students in a print-rich environment of authentic literature, has been expanded to the Web. The social studies curriculum can be found online at http://www.union-city.k12.nj.us/uc_curriculum/socstu_hs/ . The science curriculum, currently being converted to HTML by one of the Union City teachers, will soon be online. Block interdisciplinary scheduling (the 111 minute math/science block, for example) also facilitates cooperative and project-based learning, allowing students to take advantage of the district's online connectivity.

Goal 4. Create a model for community authoring initiatives that bring together teachers, students, and community agencies to create World Wide Web resources.

In the spring of 1996, the Center for Children and Technology worked with district administrators to design a summer course to train high school students to develop Web sites for local community-based agencies. The course, titled Business, Community, and Educational Applications of Technology, was approved by the Board of Education for the summer of 1996. The program ran for six weeks in the summer of 1996, five days a week, from 8:30 a.m. to 12:30 p.m. Students who successfully completed the course received five high school credits. The program was continued in the summer of 1997.

The district's curricular emphasis on collaborative learning through project work, independent research, and the communication of findings through reports and publications provided an ideal framework for this Web-authoring course. Well designed Web sites would support and enrich the district's student learning agenda. The project would involve levels of complexity not often demanded in student work. Students would have an opportunity to develop many types of skill and understanding, including:

- Mastery of content knowledge
- Information gathering, interpretation, and synthesis
- Knowledge of design principles (what counts as good design)
- Awareness of an audience (Who are we making this for? What interests them?)
- Technical complexity

- The ability to collaborate (identify and distribute tasks, trust, the ability to reassemble)
- Critique and revision

The success of the Business, Community, and Educational Applications of Technology course has been widely recognized by district educators and community members. A number of tangible outcomes have resulted from this effort, including:

- Summer course students initiated a weekly HTML training course for their fellow classmates. The students plan to teach elementary students in the spring.
- Several students created Web pages for local businesses as after-school jobs.
- The Board of Education adapted this model as part of the regular curriculum. Teachers are working with teams of students to create multimedia presentations, students are helping teachers to develop their technical skills, and teachers are helping students to develop research skills through the synthesis of information and content.
- Students presented their work to several prominent audiences, including the New Jersey Education Summit and Governor Christine Todd Whitman, the New Jersey State Board of Education, the U.S. Department of Education Office of Bilingual Education and Minority Language Affairs, and the National Science Foundation.
- The course Business, Community, and Educational Applications of Technology will be offered again in the summer of 1997. The class will be run officially by Union City teachers and administrators, with some assistance from the Center for Children and Technology.

A detailed report on this program can be found on the Well Connected Educator page at the Global Schoolhouse Web site (http://www.gsh.org/wce).

Goal 5. Integrate the network into the district's Parent University initiative to facilitate parental involvement.

Due largely to the success of the Project Explore collaboration with Bell Atlantic, school administrators believe that providing access to technology resources for families without home computers is critical to furthering the education of Union City's students. In the fall of 1996, the Union City Online program built on Project Explore by linking the city's two public libraries with a computer network. The libraries offered free classes on computer use and the Internet as part of the district's Parent University initiative. To be eligible for enrollment, an individual had to be a Union City Resident, show a library card, and register in person by filling out a form at one of the two libraries during designated hours. The offered classes included: Introduction to Computers, Introduction to Microsoft Word, Introduction to Excel, Introduction to Microsoft PowerPoint, Computer Class for Seniors, Internet Basics; Career Planning/Job Search on the Internet, and Colleges and Scholarships on the Internet.

In October 1996, with absolutely no advertising, 100 people signed up. In December 1996, a single flyer was distributed throughout the community and in a matter of weeks more than 800 people had signed up. That number had risen to 1,000 by the end of February 1997.

To learn why people were attending these classes, a database was created to gather information on demographics and motivation, as well as course evaluation. A preliminary examination of this data suggests attendees are motivated by the need for a job and other work related reasons, a desire to upgrade job skills, and an interest in helping children with school work.

While interest in the classes no doubt is generated by the general national interest in the Internet, local events also play an important role. The citizens of Union City are motivated to understand more about computers and the Internet as a result of pride in their community's accomplishments, the success of their schools, and the national recognition the schools have received. In addition, parents want to be able to help their children and want to be able to see what their children are learning.

Goal 6. Draw upon other National Science Foundation-funded projects as key contributors to the district's math and science reform efforts.

Union City Online developed collaborations with several National Science Foundation-funded technology initiatives. These include: the Stevens Institute of Technology's Networking Infrastructure for Education project, the New Jersey State Systemic Initiative, Swarthmore College's Math Forum, and Stanford Research Institute (SRI) International's *Tapped In* Project. Collaborations with other organizations outside the district have proved to be enormously valuable. These groups bring resources and expertise to the district and the collaborations often result in new and creative ways of looking at issues and solving problems.

Stevens Institute of Technology's Networking Infrastructure for Education Project
(http://k12science.ati.stevens-tech.edu/)

The Stevens Institute of Technology is working with a team of four Union City high school teachers to develop an interdisciplinary Internet-based curriculum that builds on fourth marking period themes. The topics under consideration center around the novel *Great Expectations* and include DNA data analysis, environmental issues, and the industrial revolution. The Stevens Institute also offers Internet classes to schools involved in the New Jersey Statewide Systemic Initiative and those in special needs districts. Union City teachers are able to take these courses at no cost.

In addition, district teachers have taken advantage of the EBSCO online database resource also offered at no cost to special needs districts and schools that are part of the New Jersey State Systemic Initiative. This database is currently available through the district's two high school library media centers.

New Jersey State Systemic Initiative
(http://k12science.ati.stevens-tech.edu/)

Union City is a key Thrust II site for New Jersey's State Systemic Initiative (SSI). Thrust II districts are intended to be models of reform in math, science, and technology. The SSI grant has been used for a broad range of professional development activities. Currently, the district is participating in the following programs sponsored by the New Jersey State Systemic Initiative:

RST2-Remote Sensing Technology. This project incorporates the use of primary real time data from remote sensing satellites to create an experientially driven classroom environment.

The Watershed Project. This National Science Foundation-funded project focuses on the Passaic/Hackensack watershed. Students obtain data from ongoing monitoring programs via the Internet and communicate with research scientists.

Goals 2000. This three-year, U. S. Department of Education Grant/ State of New Jersey project to introduce teachers to new core curriculum standards has a preschool through 2nd grade focus. Partner sites for professional development are the New Jersey Institute of Technology, Fairleigh Dickinson University, and Jersey City State College.

Rutgers Consortium for Educational Equity. The Union City school district participates in various programs in professional development that focus on equity issues, including science teams, family science and math, and family tools and technology.

Woodrow Wilson Scholars-Lego-Robotics Program. This project incorporates cooperative learning, mathematics, science, and technology.

Hackensack Meadowlands Development Commission (HMDC) "Adopt-A-Class Program." This initiative partners Union City teachers with educational specialists at the HMDC's environmental center.

NASA/Goddard - Online mentoring program with NASA scientists at Goddard Space Flight Research Center. A partnership with the Stevens Institute of Technology, teachers and students receive scientific mentoring from Hispanic engineers at Goddard.

Swarthmore College's Math Forum
(http://forum.swarthmore.edu/)

A group of approximately 25 Union City middle and high school teachers have been collaborating with the Math Forum project at Swarthmore College in a project designed to increase the use of the Internet in the district's math classrooms. A series of Math Forum workshops introduced Union City teachers to Math Forum resources and provided Math Forum staff with information on the teachers' areas of concern in teaching mathematics.

As part of this effort, a Web site, *Linking Math Proficiencies to Internet Resources*, has been developed (http://forum.swarthmore.edu/teachers/union_city/). Union City teachers use this site to post requests for help on specific mathematics topics relevant to the Union City curriculum and receive feedback from other Math Forum teachers.

In September 1997, the Math Forum hosted a group of 30 Union City high school sophomores and juniors. This event was part of the district's Road to College program designed to expose students to a range of higher education opportunities. In addition to arranging a tour of Swarthmore College, Math Forum staff members ran several Internet-based math workshops for the high school students.

Stanford Research Institute (SRI) International's *Tapped In* Project
(http://tappedin.sri.com)

Union City teachers have begun to experiment with SRI International's *Tapped In* project, a Web-based professional development community for teachers. Using *Tapped In*, teachers can hold virtual meetings, conduct planning sessions, and exchange information about mathematical challenges their students are facing. Several teachers have *Tapped In* running on their home PCs and are working with the Math Forum project to explore *Tapped In* as a virtual mathematics learning environment.

Goal 7. Provide opportunities for the extensive dissemination of project outcomes by the school community and by project collaborators at state and national levels.

State testing data collected on 8th graders since 1992 clearly demonstrates that Union City students have shown consistent improvement in learning in a short period of time. Reading scores between 1992-1995 improved by 53.6%, writing scores by 42.9%, and math scores by 29%. Students in Union City consistently outperform other special needs districts by an average of 27% in each of these three core subject areas.

Evidence that technology can make a real difference in student outcomes can be found in the performance of the cohort of Project Explore students with consistent access to networked technologies from both home and school since 1993. As 7th graders, this cohort of students had the highest overall scores among district peers. As 8th graders, this group had the highest pass rate in the district for reading and writing, and the second highest pass rate for math. In addition to significant accomplishments on standardized measures of achievement, more of these students qualified for the 9th grade honors program than any other district class. As a result, an additional honors class was added to the high school program at Emerson for the first time in many years. As 9th graders, this trend continued. The cohort was outperforming their peers by 20% in writing; 15% in math, and 7% in reading.

Union City Online staff and students have presented this information at conferences, workshops, and meetings around the country, including:

Consortium for School Networking
The International Conference on Telecommunications and
     Multimedia in Education (Tel*Ed 1995 & 1996) sponsored by
     the International Society for Technology in Education (ISTE)
Latino Summit
The National Educational Computing Conference (NECC)
     1996 & 1997
The National Governor's Association National Education Summit
National Information Infrastructure: Kick Start Initiative
New Jersey Association of Supervisors and Administrators

New Jersey Association of Supervisors of Curriculum
  Development
New Jersey Business/Education Summit
New Jersey State Board of Education
New Jersey Teachers of English Speakers of Other Languages/
  Bi-Lingual Educators
Software Publishers Association

FIVE FACTORS FOR SUCCESS

The story of Union City is a remarkably compelling one, offering evidence that the American dream is still a possibility. Here, public education does work and schools can be re-crafted to meet the diverse needs of children's cultural and learning experiences.

The tale of Union City is as complex as it is successful, however. It would be nice if this project offered a formula for success—a kind of one-size-fits-all model of education reform. Unfortunately, a uniform model for change is an impossibility in an education system that prides itself on plurality.

Some important aspects of Union City's success can be identified and distilled for others to review, interpret, and implement in their own school communities. While changes in educational philosophy, design, and the implementation of the curriculum have been at the center of the district's success, a number of other comprehensive changes have occurred during the past seven years. These additional reforms have helped to establish both a climate and an infrastructure that support and embrace innovation. These five factors include:

1. Key parties working together.

Support from district leadership, including the superintendent, Board of Education, and the teachers union was crucial to the success of Union City's efforts. This support, combined with the strong vision and leadership of the Executive Director of Academic Programs, was invaluable in the reform process.

To enlist the support of the superintendent and Board members, the Executive Director headed a research and planning program during the 1989-1990 academic year. A committee of teachers and curriculum supervisors was formed to review the extensive literature on successful teaching and learning. Evidence gathered by this committee supported the move from a fact-based curriculum to one grounded in whole language, cooperative learning, and inquiry.

2. A strong base of teacher support.

Another piece critical to the district's success was the ability and strong commitment to involve teachers at every level of the curriculum reform and restructuring process. When the process began in the 1990/91 school year, the Executive Director of Academic Programs had a strong base of teacher support. As the former head of the district's Bilingual/English as a Second Language (ESL) program, he had worked closely with more than a third of the district's 800 teachers.

Many of the district's Bilingual/ESL teachers were involved in the early process of rewriting the curriculum and restructuring the classroom. They supported the changes that were being instituted; many of their classrooms became demonstration sites where teachers could observe first-hand the effect the reforms were having on student learning. For skeptical teachers, this opportunity to look "before leaping" was key to building interest and momentum in the district's schools. Equally important was the fact that the effort was voluntary; no one was required to participate until they were ready.

3. Teachers at the center of curricular revision and school decision making.

For six summers, teams of teachers created and revised curriculum, worked on the identification and integration of technology resources, and participated in substantial professional development. This process developed teacher ownership in the reforms and often put at the building level a knowledgeable teacher able to aid colleagues in implementing the new curricular ideas and practices.

Teacher ownership in decision making also was aided by the establishment of building level school improvement teams. Prior to the reforms, each school budget was tightly controlled by the central office. Teachers had little knowledge of how money was spent, and no input into budgetary decision making. The establishment of school improvement teams dramatically shifted the locus of control. Each school team is made up of teachers, students, and parent representatives, and is allocated funds—$200 per student—to spend as it sees fit. In addition, school budget and central office expenditures are reviewed with team members, and there is an opportunity for teachers to provide administrators with feedback on the most effective use of monetary resources.

4. Sufficient funding from a variety of sources.

In 1990, the New Jersey legislature passed the Quality of Education Act (QEA), a public law that redirected education funding from more affluent suburban communities to big city urban districts. Union

City has used this funding to invest in technology and teacher professional development. The funds from the Union City Online project and the New Jersey State Systemic Initiative also are used by the school district for similar purposes.

5. A close connection between curriculum and technology.

In Union City and many other districts, curriculum and technology are administered in distinct and separate areas. In Union City, however, district administrators have built a successful working relationship between the offices of Academic Programs and Computer Operations. The two departments plan collaboratively on the purchasing, design, and deployment of new technologies. As a result, curriculum representatives from each of the district's 11 schools are involved from the outset in the district's technology planning process. This collaborative environment has created a technical infrastructure genuinely responsive to the goals and objectives of the curriculum, to the requirements of the teachers, and to the needs of students and their families.

A LESSON IN PUBLIC RELATIONS

The partnership with Bell Atlantic taught the Union City school district a great deal about the potential and importance of public relations. In addition to expanded technology resources, this business partnership provided a strong public relations program that helped the local community and the nation see, understand, and reflect on the significant achievements of Project Explore and Union City schools. And, while the spotlight was shining on Union City, the community and the nation had an opportunity to learn about the importance of school reform and restructuring.

For the Project Explore technology trial, Bell Atlantic launched the enormous public relations effort before program results in the form of student success stories were available. At this early stage, the communications effort focused on the real story of Union City—the magic in the systematic program of educational reform taking place in the district. Technology was shown to be an extremely valuable learning tool, but restructuring was emphasized as an essential component of successful technology integration efforts.

With its large corporate resources, Bell Atlantic was able to get this message out to a very big audience in a relatively short time. As a result, the Union City school district, the Center for Children and Technology, and Bell Atlantic receive daily requests for site visits and program information. Educators from nearly every corner of the globe want to duplicate Union City's success in their own communities. To date, district staff has hosted visits for groups from the United States Department of Education, the Education Ministry of the People's Republic of China, educators from Brazil and the Netherlands, as well as individuals from local and state boards of education.

To accommodate the growing tide of information requests, Union City again turned to technology. With funding from Bell Atlantic, the Center for Children and Technology developed a Web-based virtual tour of the district. This Web site (http://www.union-city.k12.nj.us/virtual_tour/) uses new multimedia technologies to construct a true story of education reform from a variety of linked vantage points, telling the stories of administrators, teachers, parents, students, and key collaborators. In the true spirit of the program, the Center continued to build technology skills in the Union City community by including district administrators, teachers, and students as collaborators and designers of the site.

REFERENCES

Living Textbook Laserdisks and Optical Data Corp. (1990). *Oceanography*. Englewood Cliffs, N.J.: Prentice Hall.

7

Integrating Internet Services into School Communities

Eileen M. Lento, D. Kevin O'Neill, and Louis M. Gomez

In his history of educational technology, *Teachers and Machines*, Larry Cuban (1986) reminds us that schools have a long-standing and largely uninspiring relationship with technological trends. Since the 1920s, a number of new technologies have been paraded before school teachers and administrators with the promise of "breaking down the classroom walls." These have included film, radio, television, and, most recently, computers. Today, a new generation of computing and network technology is making its way into schools, again with the assurance of abating the historical isolation of classrooms and teachers. If computer networking is to become more than a marginal enterprise in the classroom, schools must take an informed approach to its adoption. This chapter will offer advice for successful school networking, based on the results of a five year effort in the development and use of Internet resources for science teaching, the Learning Through Collaborative Visualization (CoVis) Project[1] (Pea 1993).

[1]The research reported here was generously supported by the National Science Foundation's Programs in Advanced Applications of Technology and Networking Infrastructures in Education under

MATCHING TECHNOLOGIES TO PEDAGOGY

Before examining the CoVis project, it is important to understand the thinking behind the project. The CoVis development team believes that an underlying philosophy is reflected in all school technology use. This philosophy may be explicit in technology plans and other documents, or it may be implicit in the general approach to teaching and learning in the school community. Whatever form the philosophy takes, school technology use is most successful if the technology "fits" the schools' vision of pedagogy and its articulation into classroom practice. No one philosophy is correct for every situation, and countless schools of thought exist. Even within the reasonably tight sphere of modern constructivist thinking, there are several philosophies of teaching and learning, from learning through exploration to learning through apprenticeship (Schank & Jona 1991).

This philosophy directly affects the ease or difficulty of integrating technology into a school community. If learning through guided exploration is the core philosophy of a school, technology applications that are highly scripted in the way that students see and use material most likely will be integrated only with great difficulty.

The CoVis work has been guided by the idea that learning is facilitated by participation in communities of practice (Lave & Wegner 1991), groups of people who share common purpose through language, work practices, tools, and intellectual values. Scientists form communities of practice in their subdisciplines, as do teachers and others. When communities of practice work well, they organize themselves to encourage what Lave and Wegner (1991) call legitimate peripheral participation. In the CoVis project, we theorized that communications technology can be used to create distributed learning communities where teachers and students can participate in and learn about multiple communities of practice (Edelson, Pea and Gomez 1996; Pea and Gomez 1992). This perspective has shaped our efforts in technology development and the design of instructional materials.

This perspective, when matched with the philosophies of the schools using CoVis materials, shapes their view of its utility (Shrader, Gomez, Lento and Pea 1997). We have seen, for example, that school

grants no. RED-94547429 and MDR-9253462. Additional funding was provided by the Illinois State Board of Education through the Eisenhower Program.

communities that have engaged in community-wide conversations about teaching and learning find it easier to use CoVis curriculum and technologies. This sort of "reflective conversation," as Schön (1983) calls it, is essential because new standards-based reform curricula (American Association for the Advancement of Science 1990, 1993; National Council of Teachers of Mathematics 1989, 1991; National Research Council 1996) depend critically on each community's unique insights into the way the curriculum could and should be realized in the local situation. In this way, today's curriculum standards are even more dependent upon local "capacity" than previous reforms (Elmore and Furman 1994).

The new curricular reforms lack elaborate images of the instruction they are designed to promote because they are still being worked out by scholars (Ball and Wilson 1997). In addition, the new reform pedagogy is likely to be weakly defined because reformers argue that educators teach in ways that cannot be precisely specified by external agents. Some reformers (Meier 1995) argue that it is only through ownership of the reform that powerful ideas about use emerge. This is entirely consistent with the constructivist approach to learning that underlies most of the previously mentioned instructional reforms. Constructivist curriculum developers frequently develop less well-defined materials that leave teachers and others room to construct their own understanding.

THE CoVIS PROJECT

The CoVis Project is a testbed (Hunter 1993) for teaching and learning with technology composed of teachers, scientists, museum staff, industry personnel, and researchers working in concert to reform science education in middle and high school classrooms. During the 1995-96 school year, the CoVis Project involved more than 100 teachers and 3,000 students using telecommunications as a critical leveraging technology to develop a wide array of new resources for classroom learning. This testbed is now creating multiple opportunities for learners to engage in open-ended inquiry and new kinds of learning relationships. In essence, the CoVis Project has established a community of invention that has spent the past five years constructing, experiencing, and evolving new kinds of science learning environments.

The CoVis Project is founded on the premise that classroom science learning should more closely resemble the open-ended, inquiry-based approach of science practice. As stated in our January 1992 National Science Foundation proposal:

We believe that science learning environments should look and act more like the collaborative, connected work environments of scientists. To this end, teachers and students need ways to *reduce the complexity of getting access to resources* that are inaccessible locally. These resources include human expertise in the form of other teachers, scientists, and graduate students in business, industry, and research settings, and other learners. They also include tools, instrumentation, hands-on materials and labs, museum exhibits, and computing and telecommunications infrastructures...

[We] aim: To examine how geographically dispersed teachers, students, and collaborators can *integrally and readily use* advanced information technologies to facilitate the types of collaboration and communication demanded by project-enhanced science learning.

The CoVis Project set out to create "distributed multimedia learning environments" to serve the emerging needs of pre-college science education, highlighting learning through guided inquiry and affiliated new roles for teachers (National Research Council 1996). With advanced computing and communications technology, pre-college science education can foster science learning with Internet-based science "doing." In our research, we have been investigating the requirements and challenges related to placing distributed multimedia learning environments into classrooms.

The implementation and sustained use of such technologies on a large scale basis in K–12 school communities presents a challenging design problem. The Learning through Collaborative Visualization Project has provided a wide-band high-speed computer network, a desktop video conferencing network, structured groupware for collaboratively developing and conducting scientific inquiries, and scientific visualization tools that provide access to wide-ranging data sets on climate, weather, and other global parameters. The development of the CoVis learning environment and its components was guided by a question-centered and collaboration-focused pedagogy that recognizes that students and teachers will continue the design process by innovating uses and suggesting revisions to their functionality.

In designing CoVis classroom activities, we quickly realized that there were vast distances, both cultural and physical, separating classrooms from scientists. In the community of science practice, the tools used and the data collected or re-used for investigations are critical to the scientists' abilities to formulate, think about, and work on their problems. In designing CoVis classrooms, we sought to take advantage of this practice by providing students with the ability to access the same data and the same tools used by scientists. Providing access to these tools, scientists, and other professionals is one of the key design techniques we used to attempt to create a sense of legitimate peripheral participation. This attempt to bring access to tools and people together in a common activity framework is a key aspect of CoViS design.

By now, most of us are at least peripherally aware of the great volume of information available to schools through the World Wide Web. It is already clear that access to the Internet significantly changes classroom operations. Teachers in classrooms with Internet access can direct students to Web sites instead of libraries. Curriculum developers can create Web pages that anyone with a computer with Internet access and appropriate modem speed can use, instead of making and distributing hundreds of paper copies at great expense.

These changes, in themselves, are superficial. As impressive as ease of information access may be, the challenges of classroom teaching are not related to scarcity of information, they are related to the difficulty of orchestrating the right kinds of *activity*. As more teachers and students use and contribute to the growth of the Web, it will be important to maintain a focus on crafting activities that make effective use of Web resources to leverage school goals for improving curriculum and outcomes. In other words, allowing students to surf the Net cannot be the sole reason to get a school online, just as channel surfing was not the point of instructional television.

Over the lifetime of the CoVis Project, participants at 40 schools, two universities (Northwestern University and the University of Illinois Urbana-Champaign), and a hands-on science museum (the Exploratorium in San Francisco) have developed and experimented with network-supported curricular activities that provide both students and teachers with unique learning experiences. One of our primary objectives has been to help realize the potential of networking to bridge K-12 science classrooms with the world of professional science. Our experiences have led us to believe that teachers must be able to exercise an uncommon range of skills and freedoms to make the most of networking in their curricular repertoires.

In this chapter, we will use our experiences from the CoVis Project to explore the conditions for success with educational networking. These include a reliable hardware and software setup, compelling and progressive activities for students and teachers on the network, participatory virtual communities, and audiences for teacher work outside of the school. Each of these needs has implications for the work lives of teachers and administrators, as well as the schoolwide policies they enact.

Reliable software and hardware is essential to this process. Too often, a reliable infrastructure is treated as an afterthought in the consideration of the benefits that technology will bring to a school. We believe that these benefits are often not realized because school communities underestimate the challenge of creating and maintaining a robust technical infrastructure. With some attention, however, it is possible and well within the reach of most schools to create such an infrastructure.

NETWORKS

The first set of important needs associated with school networking stems from the nature of present-day computer networking technologies. These technologies are quite different from other kinds of school equipment and infrastructure (sports equipment, plumbing, electrical wiring, etc.) and must be considered differently when schools and communities decide to commit financial resources to them.

A large part of the difference between network infrastructure and other types of school infrastructures lies in maintenance. Despite enormous progress in the usability and reliability of network software and services over the past five years, the technology remains a considerable distance from the "plug and play" ideal. The set-up of this technology is technically difficult and the daily "torture testing" from students in school environments is far from the office use it was designed to experience. Modern microcomputers have gained their tremendous multimedia and networking capabilities at the cost of additional complexity, and this complexity requires troubleshooting and maintenance.

In a relatively common scenario, a science teacher designs a classroom activity that involves six groups of students, sitting at six different computers, all pulling up the same Web page at the same time. Unfortunately, when the teams attempt this task, all of them receive a mysterious error message on their screens that reads "no DNS entry." What has gone wrong? The problem may be result from the individual computers in the room (where an incorrect or out of date bookmark is stored), the network wiring inside the room (which has been accidentally kicked out of place by a student), a server down the hall in the school building (which is malfunctioning due to a brief, early morning power failure), the offices of an Internet service provider across town (overloaded during peak hours), or the physical location of the Web site itself. It is also possible that there is no malfunction; the Web site the students are attempting to access may simply be too busy to respond to them. Determining which of these problems is occurring is something that all Web-using teachers learn, largely through classroom experience.

The Internet is a changing and dynamic place, and the networked classroom requires a new set of expectations on the part of teachers and students. K-12 school communities will need to develop strategies to accommodate the characteristics of a networked environment, just as the business community and higher education have. Scenarios like the one above are important to consider in developing these strategies, since technical problems can add measurably to a teacher's lesson-planning burden if they cannot be diagnosed and fixed within five or 10 minutes. Knowing that technical problems may derail a lesson plan, teachers burdened with an unreliable network must begin each day equipped with a contingency plan. This is certainly one way of accommodating the characteristics of network technology, but a far better accommodation would take place at the school staffing level.

STAFFING AND STAFF DEVELOPMENT

We believe that parents and administrators should not make an investment in network hardware and services without committing to a simultaneous investment in the human infrastructure that sustains them, school-based technical staff. In our experience, schools that do not have dedicated technical support staff *housed in the building* generally experience "network and computer rot," a gradual decline in the reliability of the network that leads to declining network use.

Schools must do two things to ensure that their investment in network hardware and services is not wasted:

- Hire dedicated technical staff for the district.
- Invest in ongoing training for teachers and provide incentives for them to take it.

TEACHER TRAINING ISSUES

Since technical difficulties are inevitable with networking, teachers must have a working knowledge of technology that will allow them to effectively communicate any problems to the resident "tech." This knowledge takes time to develop, but eventually every successful teacher learns a basic set of technical terms and tactics.

Lessons in network troubleshooting and use can be learned in a variety of professional development forums such as the CoVis workshops held each summer at CoVis schools. To be most effective, these events should be framed to make the school district's commitment to network-supported learning explicit. To do this, school officials must attend to difficult questions such as:

- Who pays for Internet training for teachers?
- If held during the summer, will the teachers be paid by the district?
- How many teachers will have the opportunity to attend Internet training?
- Should teachers be required to attend?
- Given the importance of meaningful classroom activity, how in-depth should the technology component of the training be?

Once a school has a reliable network in place and is prepared to maintain it, teachers can use it regularly in ways that will further the pedagogical commitments of the school and district. In this effort, the focus should be on creating or adapting curriculum-based activities that will keep network use from becoming marginal and sporadic, in the way that television and film are used in classrooms.

CoVis Interschool Activities

To model curriculum-centered network use for our participating schools, CoVis staff have designed a number of scheduled project events that make extensive use of Internet tools. We refer to these as CoVis Interschool Activities, or "CIAs" (Lento 1996). These activities are intended to help teachers begin long-term science projects with their students and facilitate network-based collaboration either between classrooms or between students and volunteer mentors. Our hope is that, in time, participation in these interschool activities will lead teachers to design similar projects on their own and distribute them throughout our virtual community.

To date, CoVis curriculum development efforts have focused on the geosciences. Each CIA addresses a specific topic in that domain and is based on a core idea that is called the *project seed*. Often, the seed idea can be accomplished in a variety of ways, using a variety of resources. Each CIA affords teachers both the ability to tailor a project to fit their own goals for student learning, and the means to do so.

As an example, the seed for our Land Use Management Planning CIA appears below:

> Students will develop a land use management plan for a specific area. First, they must define the existing environmental problems of their area. Then, they must propose a plan to solve them. Students should be creative and logical in developing their strategy. Plans must be workable for the designated area. Students must provide evidence that demonstrates the feasibility of their proposal.
>
> At a minimum, the following interests and needs must be included in each plan:
>
> - Industries: lumber, mining, agriculture, service, etc.,
> - Tourism: hotels, restaurants, rentals, environmental facilities, etc.,
> - Private residences,
> - Energy source(s),
> - Solid waste disposal,
> - Water treatment facilities,
> - Educational facilities,
> - Infrastructure: transportation systems, roads, railways, water, sewer systems, etc.,
> - Places of worship, and
> - Governmental type and structure.

In our CoVis Teacher Resource Guide, we supply guidance materials for implementing each project seed in a way that capitalizes on unique CoVis software and other network resources. Our Weather CIA, for example, calls for the use of our unique data visualization environment, the CoVis Weather Visualizer. The Land Use Management Planning CIA invites the use of our shared laboratory notebook, the Collaboratory Notebook. (See the CoVis web site, http://www.covis.nwu.edu, for in-depth descriptions of this software.)

Teachers are free to use the published resources to conduct a project at any time. In addition, a period of time is scheduled each school year to enable a number of volunteer teachers to conduct each CIA together. At this scheduled time, CoVis staff provide participating teachers and their students with supplemental support and resources. These may include the facilitation of cross-classroom collaboration between teachers and students, mentoring by scientific professionals, and virtual field trips (via Internet-based teleconferencing) to science museums, universities, and research labs. During the scheduled time for the Land Use Management Planning CIA, the CoVis team arranges for students to correspond via e-mail with environmental engineers or knowledgeable local residents from each of seven locations under study: Kalispell, Montana; Harrisburg, Pennsylvania; Portland, Oregon; Sao Paulo, Brazil; Calcutta, India; Tokyo, Japan; and Mexico City, Mexico.

Through a regular newsletter and an annual summer conference, CoVis teachers are encouraged to craft alternative implementations of the project seeds and share these with the CoVis community. In this way, we hope to build a rich library of projects for a range of science topics appropriate to various state and local standards. By providing a forum for these development efforts, CoVis aims to support teachers in migrating from their customary role of curriculum consumers to a more involved role as curriculum tailors or designers.

To date, five CoVis Interschool Activities have been enacted:

Land Use Management Planning (LUMP)—the study of land use management
It's Weather, Man!—the study of weather systems
A Global Warming Summit—the study of global warming
Native Soil—the study of soil science
WaterFall—the study of water quality

The *Global Warming Summit*, also a flexible CIA, approaches project work and cross-classroom collaboration from a specific angle. As earth science and environmental science teachers are aware, the controversy over global warming has been growing over the past few decades. There is an enormous amount of ongoing scientific research and policy development in this area, and the interdisciplinary nature of this work affords teachers the flexibility of approaching the project from a perspective which best meets the needs of their unique student cohorts. The seed idea for the Global Warming Summit, as it appears in our Teacher Resource Guide, is as follows:

Students will study global warming by participating in a conference where they represent countries and study global changes. Global warming provides an opportunity for students to see how studying science can be relevant to their lives and to the whole world. Hearing scientists disagree helps students see that science is not cut and dried, but is still being figured out. Important issues for students to consider include:

- The problem of making policy decisions on the basis of incomplete scientific evidence and varying risk estimates.
- "Time bomb" environmental problems that require significant

sacrifice to fix now, but whose effects will not show up for decades.

- The interrelationships of global ecology where changes in one part can have systemic impact (e.g., increasing global temperatures could melt glaciers, causing higher oceans, causing increased atmospheric carbon levels, and so on).
- The regional impacts of global changes (e.g., global warming might cause deserts in some areas and help agriculture in others).

The technology-intensive implementation of this CIA requires students to research the various dimensions of global warming (as determined appropriate for each class by the teacher) so that they can ultimately critique an existing government policy. A series of scaffolding activities (for instance, experiments and labs that explore the scientific factors underlying global warming) are provided for teachers to choose from so that their students can intelligently speak to the impact of a given policy. Along the way, student research is guided by online mentors. After personal introductions are made via e-mail, students across classrooms challenge one another with questions surrounding the global warming debate. Teachers and mentors must facilitate this process to ensure that student groups raise and respond to issues pertinent to effectively rewriting an existing policy.

What do we believe makes these activities a compelling use of school networking? Primarily, they allow students and teachers to pursue research in a way that wouldn't otherwise be possible. Depending upon the project, students may be accessing the latest available data on a phenomenon (as with the CoVis Weather Visualizer), pursuing work with distant collaborators (mentors or fellow students), or addressing an audience with whom they don't normally have contact. In addition to these immediate, curriculum-related benefits, we continue to revise the CIAs to better achieve long-term outcomes of teacher professional development, including:

- the scaffolding of teacher development around project-based pedagogy,
- the use of next generation technologies (e.g., scientific visualizations) by students and teachers for day-to-day classroom work, and
- the use of collaboration tools by diverse users in various settings (e.g., urban students collaborating with suburban students or university scientists).

VIRTUAL COMMUNITIES

School networking also can transform classroom activity through the support and development of innovative activities and ideas by like-minded people. A variety of online computer networks enable groups of people to communicate about common interests and share ideas, despite very different working schedules and vast geographical distances. We refer to these kinds of ongoing communications among many participants as "virtual communities." The CoVis community encompasses a number of these communities.

VIRTUAL COMMUNITIES FOR STUDENTS

The media projects a picture of school networking as students talking in real time with one another across the continent or the world while seeing each other on computer screens. This activity is done increasingly often, but it is almost universally a hit-and-run affair in terms of curricular goals. That is, student-to-student videoconferencing is most often a brief demonstration made to reinforce a point, rather than teach something new. The videoconference is over in a few minutes and may not be repeated for several weeks or months.

As many teachers and researchers have been finding in recent years, establishing and maintaining ongoing, curriculum-based virtual communities among students can be quite difficult (Gomez, Fishman, and Pea in press). Often this difficulty stems from the compartmentalization of the school day into short periods (which make real-time communication across schools difficult), the lack of regular convenient access to the network, curricula that do not allow teachers and students to focus on a single topic for very long, and student reticence to rely on remote collaborators for grades. Despite these barriers, carefully-crafted projects that capitalize on linguistic, cultural, or geographic differences among students can effectively motivate distant collaboration. During a soil science CIA called Native Soil, for example, two classrooms decided to share data derived from local samples via e-mail.

Two notes of caution should be sounded when designing activities for remote collaboration among students. First, if the student collaboration is not a natural part of the activities' goals, teacher management tasks tend to grow more complex and time consuming. When students don't see the point of working with distant partners, they must be coerced into the activity with increasingly complex and intrusive assessment routines that demand more time from their teachers. Under these circumstances, it is unlikely cross-classroom or cross-school collaboration will ever be a useful component of planned curricular activities.

Second, when teachers and students in distant classrooms do collaborate on learning activities, differences in classroom customs need to be negotiated between the cooperating teachers. In particular, if students in different classrooms work together on a project, it could be considered unfair for them to be assessed on different criteria. Therefore, the teachers need to work together to craft rubrics for student assessment. Here, mutual adherence to national science standards may help significantly.

VIRTUAL COMMUNITIES FOR TEACHERS

One of the more promising opportunities that networking can provide is linking teachers to communities of fellow teachers and other knowledgeable adults to support work on innovative curricula. Organized properly, this kind of virtual community can foster new partnerships among teachers and other adults that tap pockets of expertise to make curricular experiments, such as those associated with networking, more successful and less risky.

A virtual gathering of colleagues may initially encourage discussion, but when the demands of daily teaching are mounting, the knowledge provided by the online community must directly support classroom activity. To successfully support online professional development, online discussions should have a facilitator or moderator who ensures that concrete contributions are sparingly supplemented with theoretical underpinnings and implications of the pedagogy that participants are exploring. The virtual gathering known as a listserv must also be a safe place for teachers to discuss concerns and the focus must be pertinent to classroom activity. Administrators "listening in" on discussions can certainly affect the course of teacher conversations.

Listservs are one kind of network service that supports ongoing discussion among a large number of people via e-mail. These can provide a conduit for ongoing professional development for teachers who can participate as their individual schedules permit. Over time, CoVis has established a number of listservs to serve the needs of cooperating teachers. These fall into two broad categories:

Topic Driven Listservs: These talk forums focus on a particular content area:

The Water CIA Listserv
The Land Use Management CIA Listserv
The Weather CIA Listserv
The Soil CIA Listserv
The Global Warming CIA Listserv

Community Based Listservs: These talk forums are designed to accommodate the concerns of a particular segment of the CoVis Community:

Covis-announce —> all CoVis community members
Covis-teachers —> all CoVis teachers
Earth —> CoVis teachers grades 9 - 12
Ozone —> CoVis teachers grades 6 - 9
Windy-city —> Chicago CoVis teachers
Tech-talk —> CoVis technical coordinators

In our experience, topic driven listservs have proven to be the most beneficial and prolific. Only about six informational announcements, such as the schedule for school-based workshops, were posted to Windy-city. In comparison, the global warming listserv has passed on more than 500 messages exploring substantive challenges to the implementation of the curriculum in particular school settings.

A salient feature of these discussions is an explicit link to immediate classroom activity. That is, the teacher can use the information or knowledge gained through listserv participation immediately in her or his classroom. While the perceived utility is immediate professional development around a particular content, the project pedagogy, as well as the technology, ultimately unfolds on several levels. The following excerpts of Listserv activity highlight the strength in this type of teacher discourse for the purpose of supporting and guiding sustainable changes in teacher practice.

It is important for teachers adopting innovations such as CoVis to keep perspective. Teachers in schools will face difficulties associated with the change process and a listserv can provide support during the challenging phases of appropriation. Understandably, project work often takes more time than the novice project-based teacher plans. This first listserv excerpt features CoVis teachers encouraging one another to persist while experiencing the proverbial "time crunch."

Dear John,
I am in the same situation as you are. I won't get to the point in
time to use the mentors but I am doing what I can as a class exercise. I'm finding that there is a lot of value in it so far. I sure would
like to hear about your progress. I haven't contributed to this dialog much because I was afraid that our not being up to speed
would detract from the groups that were going full steam ahead. In
hind sight I think I was wrong.
Keep plugging!! Mary

Another common hurdle is facilitating (versus directing) student
work. Student project work represents a significant shift from the his-
toric didactic model of teaching and learning. The next excerpt is an example of teachers refining one anothers' practice in the highly
unpredictable project-based classroom.

Tom said:
Having done a good job of building the models, my students have
drawn a blank when it came time to interpret the basis for differences in insolation. They cannot picture what is meant by matching
the white disc to the equator to judge the relative amount of the
available energy that went to each hemisphere. How can I help
them see?

Anne responded:
I had a similar experience... I handled it by drawing a circle and a
nearby diameter (perpendicular to a reference line connecting the
centers) on a piece of graph paper. I made the circle the same diameter as the ball and disc of the model. The equatorial line was
drawn 23 degrees from the reference line. In this way, the circle
could represent the ball, and the near end of the equator was
matched to the diameter line by a construction parallel to the reference line. Then the same circle could be the disc, with the construction coming back to mark a chord of the circle parallel to the
reference line. It is easier to do it or show it than to describe it. By
counting little boxes inside the respective regions, the students determined that at the solstice, one hemisphere got 75% and the other
25% of what the beam from the sun was carrying.

Notably, this interaction implies that students, as well as teachers,
need to be supported through this change in schooling. New ideas represent another challenge shared by teachers and students alike. In a project-based classroom, often in the absence of a textbook, there is a
continual need for new and unique ideas. In the next excerpt, a teacher
divulges an innovative and highly technical activity and his pedagogi-

cal motivations for the lesson, providing a powerful development experience for his colleagues on the listserv.

> Greetings!
> This morning I gave the following cryptically stated tasks to the class. This followed their manual graphing of a subset of CO2 data, and some discussion of the "Wouldn't it be nice if ..." variety to prepare for spreadsheets. This was their first look at a spreadsheet — in a gee whiz context as they watched the various applications hand off to one another.
>
> [] "Startup" launches Netscape aimed at CoVis home page if net connected
> [] clicking Desktop brings Finder Icon to upper right of screen
> [] double-clicking Hypercard Icon Alias on desktop starts Excel tutorial.
> [] "Index" button and "Charts" selection starts today's lesson
> [] follow the lesson from "Charts" thru "Chart Wizard"
> [] return to Netscape, GW-CIA, art SYLK for Mauna Loa data
> [] make several graphs (i.e. charts) of this data
>
> In this way, I have this class group in the pool at the shallow end, and my colleague is ready to do something similar tomorrow. By making BOLD certain words in this ritual, I made the basis for a short quiz with which to start off the next class meeting.

Since global warming is a topic with which few K-12 teachers have had in-depth experience, detailed concrete procedural electronic messages such as the one above above help to support participating teachers and their students through a complex terrain. The CoVis version of the global warming project, "A Global Warming Summit," calls for the analysis of visualizations; several visualization activities are provided in the program. To guide students though the activities, teachers must understand the tool. The CoVis project also incorporates the analysis of complicated data sets (e.g., the Mauna Loa data that was accessed when art SYLK was selected) stored on the CoVis Web Server, to be downloaded into a spreadsheet, a task that requires a great deal of technological facility. In addition to providing guidance to participating teachers and their students, the excerpt above also highlighted the need for a common language among CoVis community members.

While new ideas are always in demand, all of them do not have to originate from CoVis Community members. On the listservs, the teachers have begun to act as a clearinghouse or quality filter for activities that they have discovered. The next two postings are samples of teachers sharing and critiquing classroom resources.

> Example 1:
> There is an article that would be very good for the one side of the controversy that was presented in the "Greenhouse Conspiracy" video. If someone who is just starting did not have access to that video, this article would be a nice alternative. It is, at least, a really readable summary of information that would serve as good teacher background. The article comes from a book called "The True State of the Planet" edited by Ronald Bailey. This is a collection of essays by environmental researchers ". . . in a major challenge to the environmental movement." The article is "Global Warming: Messy Models, Decent Data and Pointless Policy" by Robert C. Balling, Jr. I have a copy of the book if anyone is interested. —Barb

> Example 2:
> Check this out: www.ciesin.org
> 2 CDs can be ordered on line...FREE ;-)
> They are good products!

As the above examples indicate, most online professional development has been reactive. Recently, however, several teachers have become proactive about development. In the following message, a teacher initiates professional development with his colleagues.

> Greetings and good morning from Hometown USA. Just a couple of things I need to tell you:

> The American Meteorological Society (AMS) is a professional scientific organization. It is the "NEA" of anyone who does anything Wx related. "Project Atmosphere" is the educational program of the AMS. These modules represent their commitment to pre-college education. The guides are not hand-outs, you cannot send for them, they are only available through workshops. The intent is to prepare teachers to use them next day. They are not written by teachers, rather leading atmospheric scientists, who are also great educators. The information is scientifically accurate. There is much time spent over choosing proper wording to make some complex concepts clear. The guides are not meant to merely reproduce for your students, but to give you more confidence in your preparation. They are written for you, the teacher. AMS trusts your abilities to present them in the best fashion to your students. The really interesting part of this to me is conducting a long distance workshop. I believe the reading in this module is straightforward, let me know what you think. Please feel free to contact me if you have questions. Best regards, Brad

The final message below illustrates the many meaningful opportunties for enhanced technical capacity that listservs can provide. This excerpt is prototypical of a communication from a teacher seeking technical support.

> Hi Guys,
> It is me again with another technical problem. I have Netscape at home. This is not a problem, this is good since I can do my CoVis cramming at night. However, for the last couple of days a strange occurrence has been happening. When I go into the CoVis homepage, I click on the GeoSciences Webserver stuff and I get a message that there is no data. On the bottom it says something like Error Zero something. I get into the teacher's lounge by doing a search and it comes up. But then I try to do a search for the projects (for the soil) and the page comes up, but most of the activities say under construction...Can this problem be fixed...Jane

A CoVis teacher helped Jane resolve this technological "glitch." There are limits, however, to this type of support as a means of sustaining curricula supported by technology.

CoVis teacher virtual communities have proven to be a potent path for extending the classroom. Via the listservs, teachers have notified one another of interesting professional pursuits such as accessing the National Oceanic and Atmospheric Administration (NOAA) Library and obtaining grant money. The listservs have served as a powerful medium for community announcements, supporting interactions such as the co-tailoring of suggested CoVis activities. And, listservs have had a profound and immediate impact on daily teacher work in CoVis classrooms. Notably, both types of interaction have contributed to a classroom climate more reflective of the National Research Council's (1996) science education standards.

While virtual communities of students have not yet been broadly successful, school networking can offer students additional rare opportunities to reach outside the school. With the help of their teachers, students can establish and maintain relationships with adults outside the classroom for a variety of curriculum-related purposes. These relationships, which may involve a small number of students working with an adult, can be as brief and simple as an e-mail exchange with the authors of a Web resource to clarify points or offer feedback, or as long-term and complex as a research partnership between students and a professional volunteer who offers guidance and feedback on student work. The second type of online relationship, modeled on the traditional concept of a mentoring relationship, is known as "telementoring."

THE IDEA OF TELEMENTORING

As you may know, mentoring is a very old idea. It goes back thousands of years to the epic poem, the *Odyssey* (Homer 1961), in which Odysseus' son Telemachus is counseled by a wise old sea captain named Mentor (actually the goddess Athena in disguise) about coping with his father's long absence since the Trojan war. Today, many mentoring programs bring adult professionals to classrooms on a regular basis (Educational Development Center 1994) or bring students into laboratories or other adult workplaces periodically (Waltner 1992). Unfortunately, these programs have not become widespread, partly because they disrupt the work routines of the volunteers.

For some time, there has been an interest in using the Internet to support ongoing relationships among adult experts in a variety of fields and K-12 students at school. Telementoring has always been one of the core ideas behind the CoVis Project but, at an early stage, we took the "if-you-build-it-they-will-come" attitude. That is, we hoped that if we put high-speed networks into schools, it would be so convenient for teachers and students to communicate with adults outside the school that it would simply happen. To a limited extent it did. For instance, in the first year of the project, a group of freshmen at Evanston Township High School, with no help from their teacher or CoVis staff, got in touch with a seismologist in Japan and corresponded about his work for a short time. However, while this was appreciated by the teacher and generated some enthusiasm, it proved to be an isolated incident.

Today, a number of projects are underway to foster telementoring activity on a regular basis (Harris 1996, Neils and Durkin 1997), in addition to our own (O'Neill, Wagner, and Gomez 1996). These projects vary in their goals and approaches, but share a few general assertions.

First, our experience has shown that quite a few well-educated adults are willing to volunteer their time to mentor students online. Census data show that, in general, the likelihood that a person will volunteer rises with level of education (Hayghe 1991). Volunteer telementors do not need to be Nobel prize winners, however, in order to be of tremendous help. We have had significant success recruiting telementors from local companies and government agencies. Generally, it is best to capitalize on the existing relationships between the school and

159

community, but telementoring can offer a way to begin or renew relationships as well.

Organizing telementoring is not as simple as finding willing volunteers. While one might think that outside experts could enrich almost any curriculum, we have found that standard freestanding curriculum provides little opportunity to develop relationships with telementors. If the curriculum is implemented with telementoring as an add-on, volunteers are likely to be placed in the position of helping students interpret their textbooks, an activity for which they are unlikely to volunteer more than once.

In addition, telementoring generally benefits longer term curricula. Because of the delays involved in exchanging e-mail, a two or three-week unit provides little time for students to learn much from a telementor. Despite its immediacy, videoconferencing is not necessarily a better way to support telementoring. While it may be more "personal," videoconferencing also requires significant coordination efforts to get everyone in front of the camera at the same time. Although compelling, videoconferencing may not be practical for frequent use.

A TELEMENTORING RELATIONSHIP

In one CoVis classroom where telementoring occurs frequently, students are given a high degree of autonomy in deciding what they would like to research over a period of roughly seven weeks. They may choose topics ranging from avalanches to volcanoes and address an enormous array of research questions within their chosen topics. At times, this freedom can seem like a mixed blessing to students, since their first (or second, or third) ideas may not be workable given the resources known to them and their teacher, the time available to them, and their knowledge of the field. In these circumstances, a well-matched telementor can help students to sharpen the focus of their research by using professional knowledge to help students obtain and analyze data that would otherwise not be available.

In the last quarter of the 1995/96 school year, one team of students decided to do a research project on earthquakes and was "matched" by their teacher with a graduate student in Geology. We'll refer to her as Mandy. The following excerpts from her e-mail exchanges with the earthquakes team illustrate some of the kinds of support, both intellectual and emotional, that can be provided by a telementor:

Date: Thu, 2 May 1996
Dear Mandy,

We are juniors at Lakeside High School. We are participating in a group project involving earthquakes. Your help would be greatly appreciated. Our project is due on May 17.

Yours Truly,
Marilyn and Robert

Date: Sat, 4 May 1996
Dear Marilyn and Robert,

Hello and welcome! Glad to hear from you. I'm really excited about working with you on this project.

>Our project is due on May 17.

Whew! Tight timeline, but I'm sure we can make it. My help is at your disposal. What aspect of earthquakes are you interested in? We first need to define the question/info that best grabs your interest, and then we can formulate a "research attack" plan for the project.

Draft a few ideas down on paper, then e-mail me back with the info. Once we have a good topic, we can hit the ground running.

If you're short on ideas, grab the local paper or the *Tribune*, or news magazines like *Time*, *Newsweek*, or even *Discovery*. With the recent earthquake in the Pacific northwest, I'm sure the media has cooked up a few articles with cool graphics.

Date: Thu, 9 May 1996
Dear Mandy,

I'm sorry about not really corresponding with you as much as I should... I'm starting to get nervous about not completing much on our project so far. The following is the exact question we are researching: Where and why do the largest earthquakes occur? Please write back. Thanx.

Your friend,
Robert

At this point in the exchange, Mandy sent Robert and Marilyn a long message suggesting a four-step process to complete their project. Robert was so impressed with this message that he expressed concern over the amount of time that Mandy was taking away from her job to help out with his project. Mandy responded:

Date: Tue, 14 May 1996

>It's me, Robert. I want you to know that I did get your rather large
>message sent on Friday. It will be very helpful.

>Thank you very much. Our new due-date is Monday, May 20,
>instead of Friday.

All right! Deadline extensions are always a great feeling. Together
we'll make sure to make the best of it!

As to the "four step plan," the approach is really that simple. And if
you hit a stumbling block, just e-mail (or in a last ditch effort as the
deadline nears and you don't have computer access . . . call) because I have a small confession to make . . . I already know the answer to your thesis question. The steps I outlined last week are the
exact same steps I put my undergraduates through to answer the
same question within a 50 minute lab. They have it easier since I
provide all the necessary references; you have to find them on your
own.

E-mail a quick research summary the next time you get on the computer; that way I know where you are and can drop suggestions to
make sure your time isn't lost on unimportant sidetracks.

Another confession . . . it doesn't take me that long to write these
letters, so please don't worry about that. After being face to face
with a computer since I was six, I've been typing at 90+ words per
minute since junior high. And also please don't worry about my fi-
nals and job because it's also my "job" to help you through as
much of the research snarls that I can for your project. I'm a teacher
here at the university, and I make myself available to my students
anytime during the day, except after Letterman has read the Top
Ten :-)

If you want me to read your paper before you turn it in, just attach
it to an e-mail message and I'll review it and e-mail back suggestions.

Talk to you tomorrow, Robert — Mandy

Getting this kind of personal attention doesn't necessarily mean
that student projects will be successful. The work is still up to them. Student ideas can often come closer to realizing their potential with an expert helping them handle the "snarls," as Mandy puts it.

TELEMENTORING CHALLENGES

In our early experiences orchestrating telementoring for high
school and middle school science students, we and our collaborators

identified a number of challenges that could prevent telementoring from serving as a practical component of project-based science teaching.

To be successful, telementoring should demand no net effort on the teacher's part. That is, if teachers are to see the worth of orchestrating telementoring, any required effort should be offset by a reduction in the workload that would be required to achieve the same quality of outcomes in student project work.

Telementoring requires teacher work in the following areas:

- Finding suitable volunteers
- Communicating with volunteers about student needs for guidance and support, and expected student project work
- Maintaining suitable records regarding mentor-student "matches"
- Managing communication between students and mentors

Because the available volunteer force for telementoring is not infinite, the long-term success of telementoring depends on providing volunteers with a satisfying experience. Interviews with volunteer telementors have shown that most of them appreciate being able to focus their efforts on a few students at a time. This allows them to see the effect of their efforts most clearly and limits the potential for time demands to get out of control. Ideally, volunteers should be asked to work with only one small group of students at a time, and should be introduced to another group immediately after the preceding project has ended.

Even when student access to e-mail is reliable, communications between student and mentor can be unreliable. One or two students may monopolize a mentor's attention, leaving his or her project partners "out of the loop." This becomes a problem when the primary contact is absent from school, leaving her or his teammates unable to communicate with their mentor. These problems led O'Neill and others on the CoVis team to develop a service that might alleviate some of these difficulties. The CoVis Mentor Database is a World-Wide Web service modeled on the work of one innovative CoVis teacher, Rory Wagner of New Trier High School in Winnetka, Illinois, extending his approach to other school settings.

THE COVIS MENTOR DATABASE

First and foremost, the CoVis Mentor Database provides a convenient means for teachers to solicit help from a central pool of volunteers.

The time-demanding process of recruiting telementors can be taken from teachers' shoulders, leaving in their hands control over the selection of volunteers for particular projects and student teams. At the same time, the system protects mentors from being deluged with requests by ensuring that they are "checked out" of the mentor pool while working with a student team. Finally, the Mentor Database helps teachers and students manage e-mail communications with telementors in a reliable fashion that keeps everyone involved.

Figure 7.1 shows a small piece of the Mentor Database system. This menu was generated for a CoVis teacher running a telementored project with matches between 18 volunteer mentors and 18 teams of students in his classes. As you can see, the program provides access to facilities for recruiting additional volunteers from the pool, releases

FIGURE 7.1
The Mentor Database: a teacher's personal options menu.

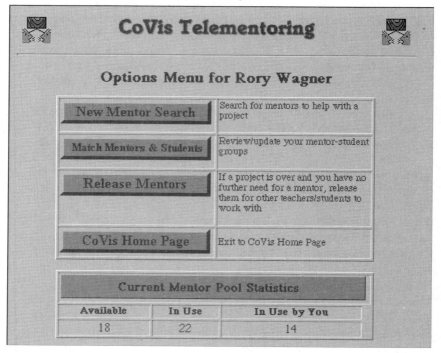

telementors at the end of a project, and changes or updates information on the identity of telementors working with specific students.

In the settings where we have helped orchestrate telementoring, each student is given an individual e-mail account. This is very useful, but can lead to members of student project teams inadvertently being left out of e-mail exchanges with their telementors. To avoid this, the Mentor Database contains a mail routing mechanism that allows telementors to send messages to all members of their assigned project teams through a central address (Figure 7.2). Likewise, students send e-mail to a central address where it is forwarded to their team mentor and copied back to each of the other team members (Figure 7.3). Teachers also can choose to be copied on the e-mail exchanges.

FIGURE 7.2

The Mentor Database routes e-mail from a telementor to the members of a student research team.

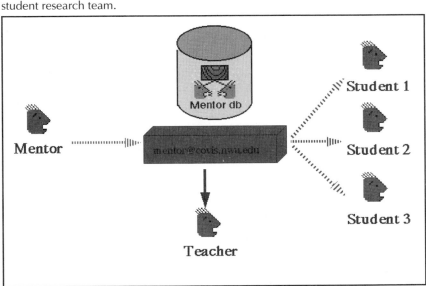

With this service in place, absenteeism and absent-mindedness cannot interfere with a team's telementoring relationship, and teachers can have easy access to student exchanges with telementors as needed. This organizational aid allows more attention to be focused on telementoring activity, rather than on logistics.

FIGURE 7.3

The Mentor Database routes e-mail from a telementor to teammates and their assigned telementor.

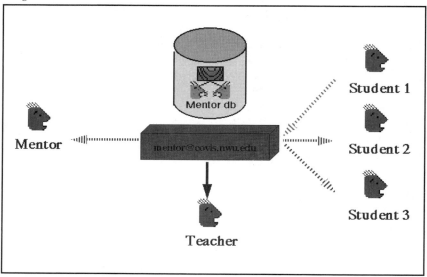

We believe that services developed to support and extend existing innovative teaching practices, like the Mentor Database, will become increasingly important to school networking in the next decade.

SUMMARY

Throughout this chapter, we have said that the focus of attention in school networking should be on *what teachers and students do with the technology.* Network use should support engaged learning on the part of students and their teachers, and it can do this in a variety of ways.

One of the most important functions that computer networks can serve for schools is the formation of a community. Working toward common goals, teachers can give and receive professional development via networked communities. Cross-classroom communities of students require more carefully crafted conditions to succeed.

Telementoring can lead students to meaningful contact with worlds of professional practice outside the school. Telementoring relationships can help students shatter stereotypes of the working world and can facilitate project work in ways that take maximum advantage of the freedoms provided by a project-based curriculum.

In all cases where we have witnessed success in school networking, school communities have accepted student and teacher participation in new relationships as key to teaching and learning. Without this fundamental recognition, the effective integration of networking into school life is either difficult or impossible. Consensus also is essential to invest in ongoing technical support services and professional development for teachers. If community leaders expect their investment to justify itself in learning outcomes, they cannot simply buy computers and hook them up to the Internet.

At the most fundamental level, our message is that network resources cannot be effective as simple replacements for textbook materials. Their best use is in the context of challenging problems—what we call projects. In this context, both teachers and students can find ways to make networking a part of their ongoing learning activities. Without this kind of integration, the Internet will be just another in a long series of technologies that did not find a home in schools. We believe that partnerships among creative teachers, administrators, and university researchers, such as those we have tried to build with CoVis, are leading to a body of knowledge that will support the effective integration of networking into the lives of school communities.

REFERENCES

American Association for the Advancement of Science. (1990). *Science for All Americans: Project 2061*. New York: Oxford University Press.

American Association for the Advancement of Science. (1993). *Benchmarks for Science Literacy*. New York: Oxford University Press.

Ball, D.L., and S.M. Wilson. (1997). "Helping Teachers Meet the Standards: New Challenges for Teaching Educators." *The Elementary School Journal* 97,2: 121-138.

Cuban, L. (1986). *Teachers and Machines: The Classroom Use of Technology since 1920*. New York: Teachers College Press.

Educational Development Center. (1994). *Industry Volunteers in the Classroom: Freeing Teachers' Time for Professional Development*. Newtonville, Mass.: author.

Edelson, D.C., R.D. Pea, and L.M. Gomez. (1996). "Constructivism in the Collaboratory." In *Constructivist Learning Environments: Cases Studies in Instructional Design*, edited by B.G. Wilson. Englewood Cliffs, N.J.: Educational Technology Publications.

Elmore, R., and S. Fuhrman. (1994). "Governing Curriculum: Changing Patterns in Policy, Politics, and Practice." In *The Governance of Curriculum: 1994 Yearbook of the Association for Supervision and Curriculum Development*, edited by R. Elmore and S. Fuhrman. Alexandria, Va.: ASCD.

Gomez, L.M., B.J. Fishman, and R.D. Pea. (In press). "The CoVis Project: Building A Large Scale Science Education Testbed." *Special Issue on Telecommunication in Education. Interactive Learning Environments*. Interactive Learning Environments.

Harris, J.B. (1996). *The Electronic Emissary*. A Web site located at http://www.tapr.org/emissary/ .

Hayghe, H.V. (February 1991). "Volunteers in the U.S.: Who Donates the Time?" *Monthly Labor Review* 114, 2: 17-23.

Homer. (1961). *The Odyssey*. R. Fitzgerald, trans., Garden City, N.Y.: Doubleday, Inc.

Hunter, B. (October 1993). "NSF's Networked Testbeds Inform Innovation in Science Education." *T.H.E. Journal* 21, 3: 96-99.

Lave, J., and E. Wegner. (1991). *Situated Learning: Legitimate Peripheral Participation*. Cambridge: Cambridge University Press.

Lento, E.M. (1996). "CoVis InterSchool Activities: An Outreach Aimed at Building a Community of Learners." In *International Conference on the Learning Sciences*, edited by D.C. Edelson and E.A. Domeshek. Evanston, Ill.: Association for the Advancement of Computing in Education.

National Council of Teachers of Mathematics. (1989). *Curriculum and Evaluation Standards for School Mathematics*. Reston, Va.: NCTM.

National Council of Teachers of Mathematics. (1991). *Professional Standards for Teaching Mathematics*. Reston, Va.: NCTM.

National Research Council. (1996). *National Science Education Standards*. Washington, D.C.: National Academy Press.

Neils, D., and S. Durkin. (1997). The HP E-mail Mentor Program. A Web site located at http://mentor.external.hp.com/ .

O'Neill, D.K., R. Wagner, and L.M. Gomez. (1996). "Online Mentors: Experimenting in Science Class." *Educational Leadership* 54, 3: 39-42.

Pea, R.D. (1993). "The Collaborative Visualization Project." *Communications of the ACM* 36, 5: 60-63.

Pea, R.D., and L.M. Gomez. (1992). "Distributed Multimedia Learning Environments: Why and How?" *Interactive Learning Environments* 2, 2: 73-109.

Schank, R.C., and M.Y. Jona. (1991). "Empowering the Student: New Perspectives on the Design of Teaching Systems." *The Journal of the Learning Sciences* 1, 1: 7-35.

Shrader, G.W., L.M. Gomez, E.M. Lento, and R. Pea. (1997). "Inventing Intervention: Cases from CoVis," *AERA*. Chicago, Ill.: American Educational Research Association.

Waltner, J.C., and S. Bernard. (March 1992). "Learning from Scientists at Work." *Educational Leadership* 49, 6: 48-52.

Part IV

Education in the 21st Century: Another Vision

8

Teaching and Learning in the Educational Communities of the Future

MARGARET RIEL

"Education is not preparation for life, it is life itself."
—*John Dewey*

The year is 2005. You are a member of a Quality Review Panel that is meeting with staff and students to evaluate the elementary program at Central Community School.

The school is unique in its emphasis on Learning Communities, groups of students and teachers who stay together for several years

Acknowledgments: Special thanks to all of the great teachers and leaders I have worked with over the years, especially Bud Mehan.

and move through a series of Learning Centers, working with additional teachers to develop learning experiences.

The teachers in this school have new roles, responsibilities, and opportunities for professional employment in positions that, in the past, would have meant leaving teaching. The teacher model incorporates four key characteristics:

1. Paraprofessionals are used as Learning Guides to provide supervision for students working independently or in small groups.

2. Three professional strands are available for teachers:

   - *Community Teacher* with emphasis in assessment and evaluations,
   - *Center Teacher* with emphasis in writing, literature, and humanities,
   - *Center Teacher* with emphasis in problem solving, math, and science.

3. Teachers follow a career path from *Entry* to *Mentor* to *Master* teacher.

4. Teachers are engaged in professional work, both inside and outside of the classroom.

THE HISTORY OF SCHOOL REFORM AT CENTRAL COMMUNITY SCHOOL

The initial meeting of the Quality Review Panel and the School Planning Team has just begun. Barb Milner and Nancy Broyles are Co-Principals and Master teachers at Central. Ben Barrel is a member of the Curriculum Committee at the State Department of Education and a Master teacher at Central. Josie Rowe is part of the district's Superintendent team and a Master teacher at Central.

Let's listen to Barb describe the history and rationale for setting up a Charter District model.

BARB MILNER (CO-PRINCIPAL):

By the end of the 20th century, it was clear that schools designed on the "industrial model" to transmit knowledge were no longer serving students, teachers, or our communities. But it was hard to find models for change. There had been more than one "education president," and many "education governors." Some of these leaders believed that technology was the answer.[1] They tried to "infuse the school" with advanced technology, hoping students' skills would dramatically improve. To their disappointment, these efforts resulted in no significant gains in academic achievement.[2] Real educational change required modifying the relationships among teachers, learners, information, and experience.[3]

As you know, early attempts at changing these relationships were mostly isolated. For example, the charter schools initiatives in Minnesota, California, and other states led to some limited success in educational innovation.[4] In these schools, teachers, parents, and community members developed plans for individual schools free from state or district regulations. But these efforts divorced the school from valuable district, state, and national services. The Star Schools initiative in the early 1990s helped science teachers produce action plans for science education, but these innovations were not well integrated with other aspects of students' learning. Privatizing public education was marginally successfully when the public school children came from relatively privileged backgrounds. But these schools did not provide the promised "quick fix" to help students from less privileged backgrounds make educational advances. They often concentrated on low-level skills and preparation for standardized tests. These isolated attempts were neither cost-effective nor efficient in providing quality education to all children.[5]

---

[1]For more on the way current reform efforts are supported by exemplary uses of technology:

Means, B., ed. (1994). *Technology and Education Reform: The Reality Behind the Promise*. San Francisco: Jossey-Bass.

Riel, M. (1995). "Educational Change in a Technology-Rich Environment." *Journals of Research on Computers in Education* 26, 4: 452-474.

[2]One of the most dramatic efforts of infusing schools with technology is the "Apple Classrooms of Tomorrow" project. The extensive research on student achievement in these classrooms shows that students were able to learn to use a complex set of tools without any loss of school achievement. This research failed to show how an infusion of technology would answer the problems faced by schools, however. For more information:

Dwyer, D. (1994). "Apple Classrooms of Tomorrow: What We've Learned." *Educational Leadership* 51, 7: 4–10.

[3]Many of the school reform initiatives suggest that the failure of schools is directly related to the existing power relationships in schools. For more information:

Sarason, S.B. (1990). *The Predictable Failure of Educational Reform*. San Francisco: Jossey-Bass.

Sarason, S.B. (1982). *Culture of the School and Problem of Change*. Boston: Allyn and Bacon.

[4]For more on charter school initiatives and their progress across the United States, see Charter School Research at http://csr.syr.edu, The Center for Education Reform at http://edreform.com/press/ wkbkpr.htm, and United States Charter Schools at http://www.uscharterschools.org

[5]The current experiment, Education Alternatives Inc. (EAI), has not succeeded in raising test scores of students in eight Baltimore schools, despite dedicating 30 minutes a day to math and reading drills

In the late 1990s, the rapid growth of the national information infrastructure pushed teachers to accept new responsibilities. Before long, teachers were overwhelmed with electronic mail and conferences on every topic. We wasted too much of our most valuable educational resources—teacher time and student learning time—on undefined explorations and surfing the Internet.

As we approached the 21st century, we knew that a revolutionary plan for changing education was necessary. That revolutionary change came when we understood that we needed to create schools where *change was an ongoing process* rather than an end state. Once we accepted this idea, we knew we would have to change the way teachers spend their day. And once we got started, we realized that this would only be possible if we changed our entire district.

We want to give you a brief overview of this change. It has been only five years since we initiated our new plan, although we began planning in the mid-1990s. Before the shift, we kept trying to discover the right mix of interpersonal and intellectual skills to define our conception of the "ideal" teacher. Some of us supported school site management plans, with teachers as curriculum experts and school leaders. Others, excited about Internet projects, wanted telecomputing to be central. Experts on different learning styles wanted us to integrate new assessment programs. And then there were teachers who had "had enough" of every social problem being dumped at the classroom door. They were tired of being asked to work at the pace of a hospital emergency room doctor without support, while being held accountable for all failures. They didn't want another meeting on any subject!

Our initial designs overwhelmed even the most dedicated teachers. A school that relied on "super" teachers was unrealistic. We tried to make time for collaborative work, reflection on teaching, project-based learning, and professional development. Our efforts to make more time were about as effective as holding bake sales to pay off the national deficit. So, we took a different approach and decided to develop a range of teaching positions.

---

similar to those used in the tests. Recently, the U.S. Department of Education concluded that EAI is not providing special education students needed services in their mainstreaming efforts. There are similar concerns that money allocated for disadvantaged students is not being used for this purpose.

The Edison Project has set higher educational goals with a longer school day and a longer school year, but it has not demonstrated that it can reach its goals in a cost-effective way.

For more information on the issue of school privatization, watch for a new book by U.S. News and World Report senior editor Thomas Toch.

The system we envisioned would recognize achievement and provide opportunities for people with different talents to play a role in education. One of the most difficult constraints, however, was a very lean school budget.

BEN BARREL (MASTER TEACHER):

Our vision required collaboration, as well as individual initiative. Teachers and students, information and ideas, could not remain insulated and isolated in classrooms. The changes you see today came from increased partnerships among teachers, students, librarians, museum curators, publishers, developers, scientists, and researchers—both near and distant and at all levels of school leadership. These interactions changed this school.[6]

We knew that we could not ask a teacher to do any more without changing the dimensions of the job. We were stretched too thin. We needed a system where a teacher's expertise in working with students was rewarded and respected. But we also wanted a system where the rewards for good teaching *did not result in leaving the classroom.*

The Charter School District Initiative provided the perfect vehicle to test our ideas. I had been doing grade-level team teaching for a number of years, and the idea for Learning Centers evolved from our work. At first I teamed with two other teachers. I was involved in a Math Forum,[7] another teacher was a part of PLANET,[8] and a third teacher set up some ties to local artists. Initially, we worked together, with funds for a long-term substitute teacher. This arrangement evolved into Learning Centers with Learning Guides.

---

[6]For case studies of change that occurs when school administrators move toward transformational leadership patterns:

Leithwood, K.A., and R. Steinbach. "Indicators of Transformational Leadership in the Every-day Problem Solving of School Administrators." *Journal of Personnel Evaluation in Education* 4, 3: 221-244.

For a wider sense of leadership provided through electronic communities:

Ruopp, R., S. Gal, B. Drayton, and M. Pfister. (1993). *LabNet: Toward a Community of Practice.* Hillsdale, N.J.: Lawrence Erlbaum Associates.

[7]The Mathematics Learning Forums provide a unique experience for elementary and middle school teachers to reflect on and refine their mathematics teaching practices through online seminars (http://www.edc.org:80/CCT/mlf/MLF.html).

[8]PLANET (People Linking Across NETworks) was a 1992 project coordinated by I*EARN to involve students around the world in preserving the rainforests. Here PLANET refers to projects such as Global Lab (http://www.terc. edu/projects/at_globallab.html), Globe (http://www.globe.gov/) and I*EARN (http://www.iearn. org/iearn).

JOSIE ROWE (CO-SUPERINTENDENT):

Let me give you an overview of our program. The Learning Centers are arranged to allow for different forms of activity. Students are grouped into cross-age learning communities when they leave the primary center. A Learning Guide and Community teacher stays with each learning community. In some ways, each learning community is a minischool. Students will remain in the same community for three years, but the group will evolve each year as older students leave and younger students join.

Learning Guides are paraprofessionals who help students learn. They do not have all of the added responsibility of teachers. They are not expected to develop curriculum, plan lessons, or create student reports. Learning Guides supervise and facilitate independent and group work by students. Because they stay with the same community of students as the students move through the Learning Centers, they know the students well and create a consistent set of expectations for appropriate Center behavior.

As you will see when you visit the Centers, we encourage students to take responsibility for their projects and activities. While students are working under the supervision of Learning Guides, teachers can work with smaller groups. Some demonstration or performance lessons, however, are designed for the whole Learning Center, a community of about 85 students.

While Learning Guides were the only completely new position created in our district plan, all other positions from teacher to superintendent were significantly altered. I was an Assistant Superintendent at the time we began the process of change. I had been missing the classroom from the moment I left it years before, and had even considered leaving my district position to return to teaching. When the teacher teams made their recommendations for reform, they proposed that all administrators teach. The teams expected resistance to this idea but, to their surprise, they found the administrators to be receptive because they enjoy teaching. Administrative duties now are spread among four Superintendents, each of whom is a Master teacher. In this new model, the administrators work closely with all of the teachers, helping to create and manage the culture of the learning community.[9] We also serve as Resource teachers to the Learning Center.

---

[9]For more on the administrator's role in creating and managing collaborative cultures, see the following articles in *Educational Leadership* 49, 5: *(continued on next page)*

NANCY BROYLES (CO-PRINCIPAL):

The Center curriculum is based on the new *California Frameworks for Theme-Based Instruction*.[10] Ben and some of our district Mentor teachers were on the state committees that developed these new curriculum plans. We are proud of our participation. By working outside of the school, our teachers have developed expertise in important areas, which enriches their teaching and rewards the district.

In the Learning Centers, students are placed into cross-age groups. We moved away from age grouping because students who did not do as well as their agemates gave up trying to learn. Student interest makes it possible for kids of different ages to work together as partners. We emphasize participation and accomplishments, rather than competition and comparisons. Cross-age grouping benefits both younger and older students.

Our learning communities move to a new Center after a 12-week term (5-year-olds remain in the Early Childhood Center all year). Our school schedule (Figure 8.1) shows how student communities move through the Centers. Currently, the students are just returning from our first session break.

All student work is directed toward a two day Center exhibition.[11] The whole community looks forward to these exhibits. They are heralded in the local papers and, just like parades or fairs, these events bring a strong feeling of community investment and pride. Local businesses provide resources and business partners join their students to see the end result of their educational help. These events are public portfolios of student work and the help provided by our community. The students are motivated to do well because their friends, neighbors, and online partners will see their work. Parents *see* what takes place in their school, and they are encouraged to evaluate what they see. I wish you could be here for an exhibition.

Fullan, M.G. (February 1992). "Visions That Blind." pp. 9-20.

Hagstrom, D. (February 1992). "Alaska's Discovery School." pp. 23-26.

Schmuck, P. (February 1992) "Educating the New Generation of Superintendents." pp. 66-71.

[10]These nonexistent documents would be the natural extension of the excellent curriculum frameworks developed in California. Many of the current frameworks celebrate a theme-based structure for learning.

[11]These school exhibitions help make the school the center of the community and learning a valued activity. Students contribute to the community by creating these evolving museums.

The term "exhibition" comes from T. Sizer. (1992). *Horace's School.* Boston, Mass.: Houghton Mifflin. This book has influenced many of my ideas on school reform.

FIGURE 8.1

Central School Schedule
2005-2006

Sep. 5–9	**Learning Community Orientation Week**
	Student skill assessment

Sep. 12–Dec. 16. **Term 1 (12 weeks)**
Sep. 12 Term 1 begins
Oct. 10 Columbus Day
Oct. 24–28 Half Term Break (one week)
Nov. 24–25 Thanksgiving Break
Dec. 9 Term 1 ends
Dec. 11–Jan. 2 Term Break (2 weeks), one week holiday
Dec. 10, 12 Exhibition Days
Total Center Instruction Days = 57 days

Jan. 3–Mar. 30 **Term 2 (12 weeks)**
Jan. 3 Term 2 begins
Jan. 16 Martin Luther King Day
Feb. 13–17 Half Term Break (one week)
Mar. 30 Term 2 ends
Apr. 4–14 Term Break (2 weeks)
April 1, 3 Exhibition Days
Total Center Instruction Days = 58 days

Apr. 17–July 14 **Term 3 (12 weeks)**
Apr. 17 Term 3 begins
May 29–June 2 Term Break (one week)
July 4–5 Independence Break
July 14 Term 3 ends
July 15, 17 Exhibition Days
Total Center Instruction Days = 58

July 18–20 School Reflection and End of Year Activities

School year:
   173 days of Center Instruction
     5 days of Orientation and Assessment
     6 days of Student Exhibitions
     3 days of Reflection & End of Year
   ——————————————————
   186 days of school for students

FIGURE 8.1—*(continued)*

Central School Schedule 2005-2006			
Learning Centers \ Terms	**Term 1** **Sep–Dec**	**Term 2** **Jan–Mar**	**Term 3** **Apr–July**
Entry Program			
Tadpole Center		–L.C. K all year–	
Primary Program			
The Lands Learning Center	L.C. P-1	L.C. P-2	L.C. P-3
The People Learning Center	L.C. P-2	L.C. P-3	L.C. P-1
Our Imagination Learning Center	L.C. P-3	L.C. P-1	L.C. P-2
Intermediate Program			
The Oceans Learning Center	L.C. I-1	L.C. I-2	L.C. I-3
Time Machine Learning Center	L.C. I-2	L.C. I-3	L.C. I-1
Inner & Outer Space Learning Center	L.C. I-3	L.C. I-1	L.C. I-2
	L.C. - Learning Community		

Now let's talk a bit about the changes in teaching. Our teachers specialize in either subjects or students. Our curriculum experts focus on embedding important skills and content in theme-based projects. Each Center has a Curriculum Coordinator for the humanities/language arts/social sciences strand and another one for the science/math strand. The arts and technology are integrated into both strands. These curriculum experts coordinate the local and distant resources for designing Center activities.

Community teachers focus on assessing student learning and addressing the special needs of their learning community. Working with Center teachers, they develop a rich set of strategies to help students understand and master the content. Learning Guides stay with the same community of students for three years, moving with them through the Centers. They bring a strong knowledge of student skills and interests to collaborative planning.

Resource teachers provide special work in a particular subject area or for a particular group, for example, bilingual or technology resources. Planning the Learning Center environment means coordination of expertise in academic disciplines, knowledge of the student community, and integration of resources both local and distant.

Now it's time to see how this works in practice. School is about to start.

THE OCEANS LEARNING CENTER

At the Oceans Learning Center (illustrated in Figure 8.2), student groups of different sizes are collecting, talking, and working before the bell rings. Members of the Review Panel move around the Center talking to Michael (a student), Center teachers Noel Phillips and Marilyn Quinsay, Community teacher Dave Brott, and Learning Guide Carl Side. The Panel also encounters the work of Computer Resource teacher Mary Stanley and Distant Resource Teacher Dr. Noorg.

FIGURE 8.2
Three traditional classrooms converted to a Learning Center.

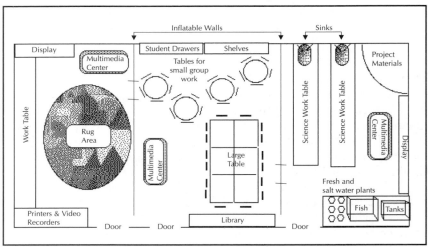

CARL SIDE (LEARNING GUIDE):

Welcome to the Oceans Center! Please look around. I open the Center as soon as I arrive and the kids join me to check mail or work on their projects. Some kids are experimenting with different ways to convert salt water to fresh water. Next to the aquariums, plants are getting different amounts of salt water. Another student team is trying to figure out what properties make it possible for a plant to live in salt water and what happens to plants as the amount of salt in the water changes. That's why some of those plants don't look so great.

These experiments are supervised by Dr. Hugo from the University. See that group of eight students on the right? They are doing the first part of a genetics experiment that will be continued all year by each of the communities.

In front, Tama and Vincent's group is working on a play they wrote. They are directing the younger kids and are coming in early to practice. Other students are sitting at the tables with small computers unplugged from a central charging unit.

A student looks up from his powerpaper computer to talk with a panel member.

MICHAEL (CENTER STUDENT):

Michael shows off the graphic interface.

We get to pick a sea creature or plant and design our habitats. See, I am a shark, and this is my computer habitat. I keep my personal mail on that rocky ledge. Project messages are over here. During Center time, my personal mailbox won't open. I have to read mail before or after school or during our free interaction times. See, I am sharing game hints with Kia in Alaska. On other Center computers, we have might have offices, or a home, or a car as our private space, but in here we have habitats.

I work with one of the Resource teachers, a biologist at the San Elijo Lagoon. He and the others are creating preserves for the California least tern and the western snowy plover. Look, here are their pictures. My friend Rio and I used binoculars and observed these birds over the break. See, we sent a message to Dr. Cooper recording our observations, but he hasn't written back yet. More birds are coming now that their nests have been restored. We are studying wetlands, oceans, and lagoons—you know, water, with kids in other places.

Mr. Phillips, the Center teacher in charge of the humanities/language/ arts strand, enters a few minutes after the bell and talks with members of the Review Panel.

181

Noel Phillips (Center Teacher):

Hello. Welcome to our Center. I hope you have seen some student projects. Ask Tera's group to show you their multimedia display of the effect of the moon on the tides. They are doing a great job. They can also show you what would happen to the earth if the moon wasn't there. It is impressive.

Today, we're going to have one of our "big ideas" discussions. The students know that they will soon see whales migrating down the coast. The question is, "Why do whales migrate instead of hibernate like bears?" This was Ellie's question.

Students have been asked to bring their hypotheses about why whales migrate, when they migrate, what factors would increase or decrease the whale migration, and why they don't hibernate. Students have had time to explore the topic, talk with parents, and try to find resources online in NetWorld, or from print or people resources. Then we share what we learned. The younger kids often ask questions that push all of us to really understand the issue. The goal is to help students understand their reality. The National Teacher Online Resource List can help us if we get stuck on something. You probably know about it. Companies or businesses donate a few hours of employee time to respond to teacher questions.[12]

If you will excuse me, the students and I need to get started. You are welcome to come and listen or to visit the other Center activities. You need to move away from the yellow line, however, because I am going to pull down the optional wall so our talk does not disturb others.

Mr. Phillips flips a wall switch. There is a mechanical whir, and something that looks like a carpet roll drops slowly, unwinding from the ceiling. Like a large projection screen, it unrolls until it reaches the floor and snaps. It begins to inflate slowly, creating a rigid wall with a small doorway.

As the discussion begins on the other side of the wall, students are collecting small packs from one of the closets, talking about who will take what. Some kids are arguing about nets, who gets the Batiquitos Lagoon CD guides, and which microsensors are needed. Center teacher

---

[12]Many projects are working to find ways to connect subject matter experts to schools as resources. For example, Hewlett Packard provides release time so that employees are available to answer questions. For examples see:

Riel, M. (1997). *Transportation for the Mind: A Webtour.* http://www.iearn.org/iearn/webtour

Marilyn Quinsay arrives and is introduced to the Panel as the Center math/science/design coordinator. She talks to the students.

Marilyn Quinsay (Center Teacher):

Panel members, it's too bad that you don't have time to join us on our field trip, but I hope that you enjoy your visit.

Students, I assume you have your data recorders, any microsensors you need, and sketch pads. Your group should have a camera, binoculars, and guides. The community leaders should have the data recorders, and the youngest member takes the binoculars.

Approximately 16 students leave the room in small groups. Their departure leaves about 35 kids working in the now smaller Center. The Learning Guide is talking.

Carl Side (Learning Guide):

You just met our two Ocean Center Curriculum Coordinators. Let me show you around.

The room to the right is our lab. This central area has mostly tables and chairs. The discussion room is now hidden by the wall. Teachers can decide which space is best for the lessons they teach. Inflatable walls make it easy to divide the space. Whiteboards that connect to computers make it possible for students to print notes off the boards.

If we have the large group lesson, we use all of the tables and the rug area. If some students are not participating in the lesson, we can wall off the science lab area and they can work with me. The three multimedia computers can be moved wherever they are needed. These powerpaper computers have a group interface replacing the old desktop of personal computers. Each student has their own area and there are protected public spaces.

Quality Review Panelist:

What are the rest of the students doing?

Carl Side (Learning Guide):

Different things. These kids over here are creating their own designs for desalination. And this group is examining a colony of fairy shrimp, a species that has recently made a dramatic comeback now that we are preserving more of the wetlands. They are following the work of scientists involved in restoring the Batiquitos and San Elijo Lagoons. Some students are working on individual learning contracts, for example, by practicing for a math "24 Game"[13] tournament, which will be part of the exhibition. Playing the game develops mental math skills.

Oh, perfect, here comes Dave Brott, he can answer your questions.

DAVE BROTT (COMMUNITY TEACHER):

Dave gives a quick overview of the Center activities for the day. We listen in on the discussion of student assessment.

Assessment is what concerns most people when they see kids of different ages involved in group projects. We spent a good deal of time talking about why and what we assess until we produced a different *process* of assessment.[14]

The functions of student assessment are complex, and some functions conflicted with our goal of promoting lifelong learning. We create multi-age groupings to avoid tracking students for success or failure at very early ages; low grades can be very destructive. We find that performance, like creating museum exhibits that the community enjoys, provides more intrinsic motivation. We try to encourage a sense of self improvement through learning that we hope will become a lifelong habit. We don't use assessment to sort students according to their "intellectual skill."

Traditional assessment often tested students' memory for content information. It was an easy, but inaccurate, measure. Now we use the intersection of four measures to assess student learning: self-assessment, community comments, teacher evaluation, and national school standardized tests.

Let me explain. During every session, the students reflect on their work, selecting the best for the exhibition. They compare the goals they set for themselves with their accomplishments. Then they set new goals. The first form of evaluation is the students' written reflection on their accomplishments and success in reaching their goals.

---

[13]An innovative math game that helps students see and use number patterns to solve puzzles of increasing difficulty. From Suntex International, Easton, Pa. (610) 253-5255.

[14]For more information on the functions of grading:
Kohn, A. (1994). "Grading: The Issue Is Not How But Why." *Educational Leadership* 52, 2: 38-41.

The exhibition provides a time for parents and community members to see what students have accomplished. Students participate in tournaments, games, plays, and demonstrations. Parents can see how their child's work compares with that of other children. The exhibition gives students the chance to teach their parents. We ask our visitors to comment on what they see in the Center and to compare it to their expectations for learning. These Center assessments often provide a view into the work accomplished outside of school, in homes, and in the community.

The third measure is a process report from the teachers. Computer technology plays an important role by providing an efficient way for our team of teachers to make, store, and share observations about students. Using the security of microchips on these pocket assistants (handheld computers), we can make quick notes that are automatically added to student observation files.

For example, suppose a student is using the ruler and calculator with ease: finding the length, converting it to scale, and explaining it to a younger student. This observation can be reduced to a small set of codes related to the activity and, using a pocket assistant, any teacher or guide can record the observations in a few seconds.

It is important to make student observations as they happen because memory fades quickly. We create a system of benchmark codes for different aspects of tasks from academic to interpersonal issues. Comments can be made about a group, and copies will be added automatically to each student file. Filter programs can organize these observations. In the end, student profiles can be formed from the discrete observations of many different people in many different settings.

An advantage of this system is that any of us can note patterns among the comments. For example, if I notice that we write more comments about either boys or girls in one area, I alert others so we are more aware of this. In the past, at report card time, some kids just slipped through the system because they escaped the notice of overworked teachers. Now, every week a printout identifies students who have not been noted and we refocus attention.

We compare process reports with student self-assessments each session. If they match, then the student is aware of his or her learning and is likely to have appropriate goals set for the next term. If they don't match, it is time for a parent/teacher/student conference to arrive at a common understanding of expectations in a learning community. Students who are doing well earn the freedom to explore areas of personal interest. In some ways, students earn their intellectual freedom. Giving students more responsibility for their learning helps change students. We have many more gifted students than we did in the past.

School assessment takes place in the first part of September when we compare our students with others on the National Standards Assessment Tasks.[15] Our students score very well here, as the Learning Center structure helps them apply knowledge learned in one setting across many other settings. The Center teachers use these scores to identify areas of concentration; I use them to help students set goals. You will be able to see these scores later in the office. But now you might want to watch what is happening over at the science tables while I check with Mr. Phillips.

> *Mary Stanley, the Computer Resource teacher, enters the room and sets up the teleconference with Dr. Noorg, one of the Distant Resource teachers helping students with the saltwater marshes project.*
>
> *At the other end of the room, the big ideas discussion is over. Mr. Phillips organizes students into small groups at the round tables, provides some instructions to Carl, the Learning Guide, and leaves. A Resource teacher enters to help the students who will be writing their reports in Spanish.*

AT THE DISTRICT/SCHOOL OFFICES

> *After school, we move to a group discussion taking place in the school offices. The topic is the career of teaching and how it has changed.*
>
> *Here we find Co-Superintendent Josie Rowe, Master teacher Ben Barrel, Community teacher Michel Lickte, Co-Principal Nancy Broyles, Mentor Community teacher Hernando Borja, and Mentor Center teacher Mary Stanley.*
>
> *We are listening to a member of the Superintendent's team.*

---

[15]These do not exist now, but are a reasonable projection from the current debate and work on National Standards. For more information:

National Council on Educational Standards and Testing. (1992). *Raising Standards for American Education*. Washington, D.C.: U.S. Government Printing Office.

Josie Rowe (Co-Superintendent):

Now we have time to talk about the changes in the career path of teachers. Four critical components make our plan unique. The first is our use of paraprofessional Learning Guides. The second is teacher specialization in either instructional design or learning assessment. The third is the career progress from Entry to Master teacher, and the fourth is the combination of outside resources and public funding.

Learning Guides are paraprofessional positions. They need to have two years of college, a guide certification or a B.A., and good skills in working with and motivating students. Learning Guides work from September to mid-July. During the half-term breaks, they have meetings and record-keeping tasks, but they do not work for the two-week periods between sessions. Guides open and close the Centers and are in the Centers or on the playground seven hours a day with a 45-minute lunch and a 15-minute break. They do not have to prepare lessons, write report cards, or work on weekends.

Quality Review Panelist:

How do you react to the criticism that you are de-skilling the teacher's job? If you keep increasing the time kids spend with Learning Guides, won't students suffer?

Josie Rowe:

Yes, this does worry us, and we have spent many hours discussing this very issue. But we try to look at the whole picture. We wanted a system that included those who want to work with kids as soon as possible, but that also provided a system of rewards and a career ladder for those who had more education and expertise.

We need to attract the most talented men and women into the teaching field. Many teachers in other school districts have less skill than our Learning Guides, who work with students all year. We are trying to *increase* the level of skill by keeping talented teachers and not losing them to other careers. Because job opportunities for women continue to expand, it is important to create incentives to attract the level of teachers that we want in leadership roles in education.

Remember that Learning Guides are not teachers. They *supervise learning*. Without the teachers, there would be no learning to supervise.

QUALITY REVIEW PANELIST:

You already explained about the difference between curriculum designers and learning experts. Is this what you mean by a career ladder?

JOSIE ROWE:

No, these areas of expertise are all equivalents. Teachers move through three levels with step increases in each level. Entry teachers are beginning teachers. Most have full credentials, but they can be hired with a provisional credential and finish their credential work while teaching. Entry teachers are expected to spend five or six hours a day teaching students in the Center, either as Center or Community teachers. Entry teachers are paid for time spent with students, but there is an expectation that the time between sessions and during the summer is used to develop an area of expertise.

Learning Guides and Entry teachers differ in their commitment to the educational community. Beginning teachers are expected to plan and develop ties in the professional community that will lead to research or development. Learning Guides are not expected to work after school or over the summer.

During the first five years of teaching, Entry teachers have almost a full year of professional development time and flexible control over their work. They can work in the school office complex (it is open all summer), at a resource center or library, or at home. In the normal career path, peer review for tenure comes in the fifth year. Entry teachers are evaluated in terms of their teaching skills, their expertise in an area of choice, and their education community service. The advancement to a Mentor teacher requires productive use of this time.

We believe it takes a teacher three to four years of teaching to develop a style. Entry teachers begin as either Community teachers or Center teachers. Once Entry teachers have demonstrated good teaching skills, they are free to develop an area of expertise that will eventually lead to professional opportunities. We provide time and encouragement for our teachers to pursue intellectual challenges outside of the Center. Because we did not have funds to pay teachers an increasingly higher salary for teaching, we made it possible for them essentially to split a teaching position with other work in the educational community. We give teachers *time* to pursue intellectual challenges that will make them better teachers.

QUALITY REVIEW PANELIST:

What counts as "an area of expertise," and how do teachers decide what to do in their professional development time?

JOSIE ROWE:

That's a good question, and some Entry teachers find making that choice difficult. We want a model that encourages teachers to be self-directed learners. Of course, the options are constrained by economic realities and regional opportunities. The goal is to have an area of interest evolve into contractual work. If you decide to become a specialist in an area in which there is little need, it is going to be more difficult to find work in this area. On the other hand, grant money for environmental science or bilingual expertise might make these choices more attractive.

Mentor teacher positions are very different from traditional teaching positions. Mentor teachers are paid a slightly higher rate for classroom contact hours. The advancement to this level is a shift in the *amount of time spent* in the classroom. The expectation is that they teach about four hours a day or two thirds of the year. The rest of their time is devoted to their area of expertise—for example, consulting contracts, district resource positions, foundations and government grants, or university research. Mentor teachers can write grants or take jobs for up to 50% of their time, similar to the way a university professor might do this.

If an Entry teacher develops an area of expertise early and is awarded a grant or receives a contract, he or she can ask to be reviewed for Mentor status after two or more years of teaching. At the other end, Entry teachers must develop an area of expertise within seven years, or their contract will not be renewed. They can, if they wish, however, continue as a Learning Guide. Basically, we are saying that teachers are professional learners who want the intellectual stimulation that comes from following personal interests.[16] We have taken a strong stance in

---

[16]The professional development of teachers requires that they take an active role in learning new ways of teaching. This is more likely to happen if professional development is linked to career advancement in a chosen area of expertise.

For more on the multiple factors in professionalizing teaching:

Fireston, W., and B. Bader. (1992). *Redesigning Teaching: Professionalism or Bureaucracy?* Albany, N.Y.: SUNY Press.

this district. We don't think someone can be a good teacher if he or she is not learning.

Josie continues with a description of Mentor teachers.

A Mentor teacher has nearly half a year to work on other contracts, considering session breaks and the summer months. Our contracts and grants office must approve all of these work arrangements, but provides an open-ended salary for teachers based on achievement. Each of our teachers can choose how hard they want to work. Some work year-round using the term breaks to pursue exciting projects. Their salaries are much higher than they would have been in the past. Our district benefits from these arrangements in three ways:

1. Most important, our teachers are intellectually engaged in educational issues that often enrich Center teaching.
2. The outside employment covers office and other overhead expenses that support our office complex.
3. We rarely lose our best teachers to jobs outside of the classroom.

Our district has one of the best records in the nation for pulling in grant money. Some of our teachers are partially funded by grants—in fact, you might have noticed the group in the Oceans Center working with the vernal pool fairy and tadpole shrimp. Their work is part of Center teacher Noel Phillips's grant from the Wildlife Federation. I think some of the highest paid Mentor teachers have contracts with Web publishers to maintain online learning environments or create net-courses.

I've said enough about Mentor teachers, so I will give Ben a chance to tell you how Mentor teachers progress to Master teachers. He might want to address the issue of travel; he has a 50% contract with a curriculum committee at the State Department of Education.

BEN BARREL (MASTER TEACHER):

Travel is not a problem, as most of my work is done online and meetings are held at conferences that I regularly attend. But let me describe the Master teacher position.

After five years as a Mentor teacher, a teacher can request or be recommended for a peer review for advancement to Master teacher. Some teachers may not be ready after five years, and that is fine. There is no pressure for all Mentor teachers to be Master teachers. Being a Master teacher is a way to reduce teaching responsibilities to provide more time to pursue leadership roles in a wide range of educational settings.

You have to be a Master teacher to be a member of the Principal or Superintendent teams. But Master teachers don't have to be administrators. Because of the way we started, most Master teachers currently have either Principal or Superintendent positions. But this year that will start to change. For example, Marilyn Quinsay is up for review. She has developed an international reputation as one of the leading developers of multimedia programs and wants more time for this work.

In the past, teachers such as Marilyn would have left teaching for corporate positions, which provide prestige and financial rewards. We give teachers the option to develop expertise and stay connected with students. That is what I like about our plan. But I do have a concern: I am worried that if all teachers stay in education and become Master teachers, the work in the Center could become too fragmented.

QUALITY REVIEW PANELIST:

How does this system compare in cost to the more traditional plan of having one teacher for 30 kids? I can see that there are some savings with Learning Guides, but how many teachers do you have, and what is the price tag of your payroll?

Josie uses charts to make the comparisons, demonstrating that the current configuration represents about a 5% increase from the traditional model. We drop in at the end of this discussion.

JOSIE ROWE:

We now have seven Learning Guides (one for each Center), four Entry teachers, 12 Mentor teachers, and four Master teachers. The Center time for Mentors (two thirds) and Master teachers (one third) is an average, and in practice it differs for specific teachers. This gives us, counting Learning Guides, the equivalent of more than two additional full-time positions. Teacher-student ratios are not too meaningful, as we have many Resource teachers and students are in groups of different sizes all day. The 5% increase in the school budget is not significant given all the positive changes.

Next, the Review Panel meets with the Community Advisory Board to hear changes in the relationship of the school to the community.

We now listen to the teachers as they make their closing comments to the panel. They are describing the benefits of the changes in the teacher's roles and responsibilities.

MICHEL LICKTE (COMMUNITY TEACHER):

The most significant difference from the past is that we have time—time to think, time to reflect, time for collaboration with others making the important decisions that set the stage for learning. Most of us had an area of expertise before these changes, but we had to develop it while teaching full time, and we rarely received recognition or encouragement. Being able to retreat to the office and make professional contacts during business hours—this is a rare opportunity for teachers. The changes have encouraged an entrepreneurial sense to professional development, which many of us find very rewarding.

JOSIE ROWE (CO-SUPERINTENDENT):

An important difference is that we can support one another informally. If I have a meeting that is scheduled for a time when I am teaching, I can check with one of the Center teachers and trade times or days. With more people comes much more flexibility. I remember my days as a classroom teacher when you couldn't go to the bathroom without causing staffing problems.

NANCY BROYLES (CO-PRINCIPAL):

Having a Principal team has helped us make tough decisions. This is my second year. This shifting responsibility within a partnership keeps us from either changing things too drastically or becoming too fixed in a single way to accomplish a task.

QUALITY REVIEW PANELIST:

How would you characterize the most significant change in your charter district?

HERNANDO BORJA (MENTOR COMMUNITY TEACHER):

For me, it is becoming part of a vibrant learning community at the school, in the local area, and across the world. The collaboration is intellectually satisfying. We are all proud of what the students and teachers are accomplishing. The rewards are collective rewards. In the past, there was always a bit of competition among teachers about who was the "best" teacher at a grade level, who had the "best" classroom. Parent requests caused conflict. In our new arrangement, teachers as well as students work and learn from each other. The multi-age communities are working very well; kids are more supportive in helping one another learn and teachers are more willing to help one another. We have always known that teaching is one of the best forms of learning, but it was much harder to arrange for it to happen naturally in traditional classrooms. In the Centers, *teaching and learning* are part of almost every interaction.

The other part is the shift in the relationships among teachers, principals, and superintendents. The decisions that affect our schools and our work as educators are made by us in the Teacher Senate. We all ask ourselves what we can do to improve education, and we all have a say in the answer. The design of this school district is *our design*, and that is what makes it so powerful.[17]

BEN BARREL (MASTER TEACHER):

Well, the teachers here are alive with passionate interests, and they have *time* and support to pursue them. When they teach, they teach from what they are learning. No one is bored.

QUALITY REVIEW PANELIST:

How would you evaluate the role of technology in the changes that have taken place?

---

[17]For more on the school as a community with self-management by professional teachers:
Sergiovanni, T.G. (1992). *Moral Leadership: Getting to the Heart of School Improvement*. San Francisco: Jossey-Bass.

Mary Stanley (Mentor Center Teacher):

As Central's Technology Resource Teacher, I can respond to that.

The tools that we have, and acquire each year, are incredible. They are tools we use to accomplish important educational goals. In some ways, we no longer think about the role of the technology as separate from the activities. Ties to Networld have helped us create a vibrant global and local educational community.

The ability to work in groups with people across the globe is providing new perspectives on all issues. Everything from Teacher Senate decisions to student group projects are facilitated by our communication tools. I can say, without a doubt, that the rich network of human resources is the most significant technological advancement we have. We have made the transition from the information age to the communication age. We no longer teach disconnected information bits. We help students participate in communities of learners creating their connected ideas.[18]

CONCLUSION

What forms of technology are central to this charter district model? I have intentionally focused on the roles of teachers and learners because education is an interactive, social process. Ideas are connected to the people who construct them, who value them, who use them, who preserve them, and who share them. These people together constitute a "community of learning." And technology is both a reflection and a production of this community.

Early school technology—slate and slateboards—narrowly defined the learning community as the teacher and students present in the classroom. Today's classroom is a complex community of thousands of people: writers, publishers, artists, photographers, actors, educators, producers, and programmers, all using technology to participate, often in limited ways, in day-to-day classroom activities. By extension of this process, the technology of tomorrow will make it possible for even more people, from more distant places, to play more central roles in classroom learning.[19]

---

[18]For more on this idea, see:

M. Riel. (1997). "Transportation for the Mind." http://www.iearn.org/webtour/

[19]Riel, M. (1997). "Learning Spaces in the Networlds of Tomorrow." http//www.iearn.org/webtour/2/

I have described my vision of the future, therefore, in terms of the changes in the learning community in this model of reflexive teaching and learning. Students teach and learn from one another and from their local and global communities. Teachers teach and learn from one another and from their participation in these larger educational communities. To me, technology is the tool that will extend the reach of our ideas and participation, not a mechanism that will dehumanize education.

Author's note: This chapter is taken from a longer paper, "Pacifica: A Learning Community of the Future."

For a more detailed description of learning spaces in networlds of tomorrow, you may want to look at my Web tours, http://www.iearn.org/iearn/webtour/

Part V

Implementing Educational Technology "Tomorrow Morning"

9

The Scaling-Up Process for Technology-Based Educational Innovations

CHRIS DEDE

As the previous chapters in this Yearbook document, new technology-based models of teaching and learning have the power to dramatically improve educational outcomes. Still, much work is needed to enhance the design of the educational tools this Yearbook describes. Also, dialogue among all stakeholders in education is necessary to refine our visions of learning environments for the 21st century knowledge-based society. In this chapter, the discussion focuses on scaling-up the scattered, successful "islands of innovation" empowered by instructional technology into universal improvements in schooling.

Undertaking systemic reform (sustained large-scale simultaneous innovation in curriculum, pedagogy, assessment, professional development, administration, incentives, and partnerships for learning among schools, businesses, homes, and community settings) requires policies and practices different than those that support pilot projects for small-scale educational improvement. Systemic reform involves moving from using special external resources to reconfiguring existing budgets to free up money for innovation. Change strategies that are effective when pioneered by leaders in educational innovation must be modified to be implemented in a powerful form by typical educators.

Technology-based innovations offer special challenges and opportunities in this scaling-up process. Certainly, the authors and editors of this Yearbook believe that systemic reform is not possible without using the full power of high-performance computing and communications to enhance the reshaping of schools. Yet the cost of technology, its rapid evolution, and the special knowledge and skills required of its users pose substantial barriers to effective use. In this chapter, these issues have been framed as six questions that school boards, taxpayers, educators, business groups, politicians, and parents are asking about implementing large-scale, technology-based educational innovations. After each question, I respond to the related issues it raises. Collectively, these answers outline a strategy for scaling-up, leveraging the power of technology while minimizing its intrinsic challenges.

1. *How can schools afford to purchase enough multimedia-capable, Internet-connected computers so that a classroom machine always is available for every two to three students?*

Giving all students continuous access to multimedia-capable, Internet-connected computers currently is quite fashionable. For politicians, the Internet in every classroom has become the modern equivalent of the promised "chicken in every pot." Communities urge everyone to provide volunteer support for NetDays to wire the schools. Information technology vendors are offering special programs to encourage massive educational purchases. States are setting aside substantial amounts of money for building information infrastructures dedicated to instructional use.

As an educational technologist, I am more dismayed than delighted by the way this enthusiasm about the Internet is being expressed. Some of my nervousness about this initiative comes from the "first generation" thinking about information technology that underlies these visions. Multimedia-capable, Internet-connected computers are seen by many as magical devices, silver bullets to solve the problems of schools. Teachers and administrators who use new media are assumed to be automatically more effective than those who do not. Classroom computers are envisioned as a technology comparable to fire: just by sitting near these devices, students get a benefit from them, as knowledge and skills radiate from the monitors into their minds.

Yet decades of experience with technological innovations based on first generation thinking have demonstrated that this viewpoint is misguided. Classroom computers that are acquired as panaceas end up as doorstops. As discussed later, information technology is a cost-effective investment only in the context of systemic reform. Unless other simultaneous innovations in pedagogy, curriculum, assessment, and school organization are coupled to the use of instructional technology, the time and effort expended on implementing these devices produces few improvements in educational outcomes—and reinforces many educators' cynicism about fads based on magical machines.

I feel additional concern about attempts to supply every student with continuous access to high-performance computing and communications because of the likely cost of this massive investment. Depending on the assumptions made about the technological capabilities involved, estimates of the financial resources needed for such an information infrastructure vary (Coley, Cradler, and Engel 1997). Extrapolating the most detailed cost model (McKinsey & Company 1995) to one multimedia-capable, Internet-connected computer for every two to three students yields a price tag of about $94 billion of initial investment and $28 billion per year in ongoing costs, a financial commitment that would drain schools of all discretionary funding for at least a decade.

For several reasons, this is an impractical approach for improving education. First, putting this money into computers and cables is too large an investment in just one part of the infrastructure improvements that many schools desperately need. Buildings are falling apart, furnishings are dilapidated, playgrounds need repair, and asbestos must be removed. Otherwise, the machines themselves will cease to function as their context deteriorates.

Also, substantial funding is needed for other types of innovations required to make instructional hardware effective, such as standards-based curricular materials for the World Wide Web and alternative kinds of pedagogy based on partnerships between teachers and tools. (The McKinsey cost estimates do include some funding for content development and staff training, but in my judgment too little to enable effective technology integration and systemic reform.) If most of the money goes into new media, little funding is available for the new messages and meanings that those devices could empower.

Second, without substantial and extended professional development in the innovative models of teaching and learning that instructional technology makes affordable and sustainable, many educators will not use these devices to their full potential. "Second generation" thinking in educational technology does not see computers as magic, but does make the mistake of focusing on automation as their fundamental purpose. Computers are envisioned as ways to empower "teaching by telling" and "learning by listening," serving only as a fire hose to spray information from the Internet into learners' minds. Even without educational technology, however, classrooms are already drowning in data, and an overcrowded curriculum puts students and teachers on the brink of intellectual indigestion. Adding additional information, even when coated with multimedia bells and whistles, is likely to worsen rather than improve educational settings. Professional development needs are more complex than increasing educators' technical literacy (e.g., training in how to use Web browsers). The issue is building teachers' knowledge and skills in the alternative types of pedagogy and content described in the rest of this Yearbook, and such an increase in human capabilities requires substantial funding that will be unavailable if almost all resources are put into hardware.

Third, the continuing costs of maintaining and upgrading a massive infusion of school-based technology are prohibitive. High-performance computing and communications require high tech skills to keep operational and will become obsolete in five to seven years as information technology continues its rapid advance. Yet taxpayers now see computers as similar to blackboards: buy them once, and they are inexpensively in place for the lifetime of the school. School boards rapidly become restive at sizable yearly expenditures for technology maintenance and telecommunications usage—especially if, several months after installation, standardized test scores (unsurprisingly) have not yet dramatically risen—and will become apoplectic if another substantial sum to replace obsolete equipment is required only a few years after an initial huge expenditure. For all these reasons, investing a huge amount of money in information infrastructures for schools is impractical and invites a later backlash against educational technology as yet another failed fad.

I would go further, however, and argue that we should not make such an investment even if the technology fairy were to leave $100 billion under our virtual pillows, no strings attached. Kids continuously working on machines with teachers wandering around coaching the confused is the wrong model for the classroom of the future; I wince when I see those types of vendor commercials. In that situation—just as in classrooms with no technology—too much instructional activity tends to center on presentation and motivation, building a foundation of ideas and skills as well as some context for why students should care. Yet this temporary interest and readiness to master curricular material rapidly fades when no time is left for reflection and application, as teachers and students move on to the next required topic in the overcrowded curriculum, desperately trying to meet all the standards and prepare for the test.

The research described in this Yearbook documents that helping students make sense out of something they have assimilated, but do not yet understand, is crucial for inducing learning that is retained and generalized. Reflective discussion of shared experiences from multiple perspectives is essential in learners' converting information into knowledge, as well as in students' mastering the collaborative creation of meaning and purpose. Some of these interpretative and expressive activities are enhanced by educational devices, but many are best conducted via face-to-face interaction, without the intervening filter and mask of computer-mediated communication.

What if, instead, much of the presentation and motivation that is foundational for learning occurred outside of classroom settings, via information technologies that are part of home and workplace and community contexts? Students would arrive at school already imbued with some background and motivation, ripe for the types of guided inquiry this Yearbook describes, ready for interpretation and collaborative construction of knowledge. People are spending lots of money on devices purchased for entertainment and information services: televisions, videotape players, computers, Web TV, video games. Many of these technologies are astonishingly powerful and inexpensive; for example, the Nintendo 64 machine available now for a couple hundred dollars is the equivalent of a several hundred thousand dollar graphics supercomputer a decade ago. What if these devices—many ubiquitous in rich and poor homes, urban and rural areas—were also used for educational purposes, even though not acquired for that reason? By removing from classroom settings some of the burden of presenting material and inducing motivation, learning activities that use the technology infrastructure outside of schools would reduce the amount of money needed for adequate levels of classroom-based technology. Such a strategy also enables teachers to focus on students' interpretation and expressive articulation without feeling obligated to use technology in every step of the process.

Such a model of distributed learning involves orchestrating educational activities among classrooms, workplaces, homes, and community settings (Dede 1996). This pedagogical strategy models for students that learning is integral to all aspects of life—not just schooling—and that people adept at learning are fluent in using many types of information tools scattered throughout our everyday context. Such an educational approach also can build partnerships for learning between teachers and families; this is important because parental involvement is certainly one of the most powerful levers in increasing any student's educational performance.

In other words, unless systemic reform in education is conducted with one boundary of the system around the school and another boundary around the society, its affordability and sustainability are doubtful. As a bridge across these boundaries, new media can play a vital role in facilitating this bi-level approach to large-scale educational innovation. For example, video game players are the only interactive devices widely available in poor households, and they provide a sophisticated but inexpensive computational platform for learning—if we develop better content than the mindless follies of SuperMario™ or the grim dystopias of Doom™. My research in virtual reality illustrates how multisensory, immersive virtual environments could make learning complex scientific concepts on computational platforms as commonplace as next decade's video games (http://www.virtual.gmu.edu).

Most of the chapters in this Yearbook describe various models for distributed learning. The Schools for Thought initiative (Chapter 5-Williams et al.) involves building communities of learners that include many human resources outside of schools. The Union City project (Chapter 6-Honey, Carrigg, and Hawkins) uses parental involvement as a lever for increasing educational outcomes and also encourages students to use their technical skills in the service of community organizations. In Chapter 7, Lento, O'Neill, and Gomez describe the way the CoVis project enables students to work in partnership with scientists, collaborating across distance to collect and interpret data. The visionary scenarios from Riel (Chapter 8) and from Kozma and Schank (Chapter 1) picture future educational systems in which students and teachers learn using a seamless web of information technologies in and out of school.

While each of these strategies for distributed learning is somewhat different, the underlying message is clear. Districts can leverage their scarce resources for innovation, as well as implement more effective educational models, by using information devices outside of classrooms to create learning environments that complement computers and communications in schools. To instead saturate schools with information technology is both very expensive and less educationally effective.

2. *How can schools afford enough computers and telecommunications to sustain the new models of teaching and learning that this Yearbook describes?*

Educational improvement based on distributed learning—using information technologies external to school settings to enable increased interpretive and expressive activities in classrooms—does not mean that schools won't need a substantial amount of computers and communications technology. To empower the types of project-based learning through guided inquiry described in the Yearbook chapters, students must have access to sophisticated information devices in schools. Even if this is accomplished via notebook computers and wireless networks moved from class to class as required, with pupils also spending significant amounts of time learning without the aid of technology, districts must allocate more money to purchasing, maintaining, and upgrading computers and telecommunications than has historically been true.

Where will educators find the funds for equipment, software, technical staff, ongoing telecommunications services, professional development—the myriad of costs associated with a sophisticated information infrastructure? In the past, this money has come largely from special external sources: grants, community donations, bond initiatives. To be sustainable over the long run, however, resources for technology must come from reallocating existing budgets by reducing other types of expenditures. Of course, such shifts in financing are resisted by those groups whose resources are cut, and district administrators and school boards have been reluctant to take on the political challenges of changing how money is spent. An easy way to kill educational innovations is to declare that of course they will be implemented—as long as no existing activities must be curtailed to fund new approaches. Such an approach to institutional evolution is one reason why, if Rip Van Winkle awoke today, he would recognize almost nothing in modern society—except schools.

Educational organizations are unique, however, in demanding that technology implementation must be accomplished via add-on funding. Every other type of societal institution (e.g., factories, hospitals, retail outlets, banks) recognizes that the power of information devices stems in part from their ability to reconfigure employee roles and organizational functioning. These establishments use the power of technology to alter their standard practices, so that the cost of computers and communications is funded by improvements in effectiveness within the organization, by doing more with less. If educators were to adopt this model—reallocating existing resources to fund technology implementation—what types of expenditures would drop so that existing funds could cover the costs of computers and communications?

First, schools that have adopted the inquiry-based models of pedagogy described in this Yearbook find that outlays on textbooks and other types of standardized instructional materials decrease. While these materials are a smaller part of districts' budgets than salaries or physical plants, they nonetheless cost a significant amount of money. When students collect their own data, draw down information across the Internet, and interact with a larger pool of experts than teachers and textbooks, fewer commercial presentational resources are required—especially if learners draw on topical data flowing through information sources outside of schools. Moreover, covering a few concepts in depth rather than surveying many ideas superficially reduces the amount of pre-packaged information educators must purchase.

A second way to reconfigure existing financial resources is to reduce the staff involved in data entry operations. Educators are inundated with recordkeeping work, and one of the most debilitating aspects of this work is the continuous re-entry of identical information on different forms. Businesses have saved substantial amounts of money by altering routine information processes so that data are entered only once, then automatically flow across the entire organization to every useful destination. Were educators to adopt these already proven models for cost-efficient information management, the amount of time and staff required for data entry functions would decrease markedly, freeing funding for instruction-related uses of technology.

Third, and on a more fundamental level, teaching is more efficient and effective with the types of technology-based curriculum and pedagogy this Yearbook describes. At present, substantial re-teaching of knowledge and skills is required; presentational material flows into students' minds, is retained just long enough to be used on a test, and then is forgotten. Class sizes are typically between 25 and 40—somewhat too large for effective project-based learning, yet small given that lectures work as well for several hundred students as for several dozen. The scheduling of class periods is too short, limiting teachers and students to fragmentary presentational and practice activities. Teachers all have comparable roles with similar pay structures—unlike other societal organizations, which have complementary staff roles with a mix of skill levels and salaries. The visions presented by Kozma and Schank and by Riel depict how altered configurations of human resources, instructional modalities, and organizational structures could result in greater effectiveness for comparable costs—even with the acquisition of substantial school-based technology.

In the commercial sector, these types of institutional shifts too often result in layoffs. The coming wave of retirements among educators, however, gives districts a window of opportunity to accomplish structural changes without major adverse effects on employees. Over the next decade, large numbers of "baby-boom" educators will leave the profession, and a staged process of organizational restructuring could occur in parallel with those retirements. Coordinating technology expenditures as an integral part of that larger framework for institutional evolution is vital in districts' planning to afford computers and communications.

3. How can many educators uninterested in or phobic about computers and communications be induced to adopt new technology-based models of teaching and learning?

Thus far, most educators who use technology to implement the alternative types of pedagogy and curriculum this Yearbook describes are *pioneers:* people who see continuous change and growth as an integral part of their profession and who are willing to swim against the tide of conventional operating procedures, often at considerable personal cost. To achieve large-scale shifts in standard educational practices, however, many more teachers must alter their pedagogical approaches; and schools' management, institutional structure, and relationship to the community must change in fundamental ways. This requires that *settlers* (people who appreciate stability and do not want heroic efforts to become an everyday requirement) must be convinced to make the leap to a different mode of professional activity—with the understanding that, once they have mastered these new approaches, their daily work will be sustainable without extraordinary exertion. How can a critical mass of educators in a district be induced simultaneously to make such a shift?

Studies of innovation in other types of institutions indicate that successful change is always bottom-up, middle-out, and top-down. The driver for bottom-up innovation in a district is the children. Typically, students are joyful and committed when they are given the opportunity to learn by doing, to engage in collaborative construction of knowledge, and to experience mentoring relationships. That these types of instruction are accomplished via educational technology will excite some kids, while others will be indifferent—but all will appreciate the opportunity to move beyond learning by listening. Educators can draw enormous strength and purpose from watching the eager response of their students to classroom situations similar to those depicted in this Yearbook. Often, teachers have shifted from pioneers to settlers because they were worn down by the unceasing grind of motivating students to master uninteresting, fragmented topics; and administrators have undergone a similar loss of enthusiasm by being inundated with paperwork rather than serving as instructional coordinators. The professional commitment that kids' enthusiasm can re-inspire is a powerful driver of bottom-up change.

The source of middle-out change is a district's pioneers. Many teachers entered the profession because they love students of a certain age and want to help them grow—or love their subject matter and want to share its beauty and richness. Often, these teachers feel alienated because the straightjacket of traditional instruction and school organization walls them away from meaningful relationships with their students and their subject. Similarly, many administrators want to serve as leaders and facilitators, but are forced by conventional managerial practices into being bureaucrats and bosses. Middle-out change is empowered when educators who have given up hope of achieving their professional dreams see pioneer colleagues using technology to succeed in those goals—and realize that, if everyone made a similar commitment, no one would have to make continual personal sacrifices to achieve this vision.

The lever for top-down innovation is the community served by the district. Educators want respect—yet teaching has fallen from a revered profession to a much lower status. The relationship between educators and their community is seldom seen as a partnership; instead, teachers and administrators often feel isolated, forced to perform a difficult task with inadequate resources. Parents, the business sector, and taxpayers bitterly debate the purpose of schools and sometimes attempt to micro-manage their operation. In contrast, when homes, classrooms, workplaces, and community settings are linked via new media to achieve distributed learning, much more positive interactions emerge between schools and society. As the chapters in this Yearbook describe, educators can move from isolation to collaboration with the community, from a position of low esteem to a respected role in orchestrating children's learning across a spectrum of settings. This shift in status is a powerful driver for innovation.

To activate these bottom-up, middle-out, and top-down forces for improvement, educators must take the lead in developing a shared vision for systemic reform, distributed learning, and sophisticated use of technology. The Yearbook chapters suggest various strategies for where to begin. Making such a commitment to large-scale educational innovation is not only the right thing to do, but is increasingly essential to educators' professional integrity.

In many ways, physicians working in health maintenance organizations (HMOs) face challenges similar to teachers and administrators working in today's schools. These doctors are responsible for the well-being of their patients, but work within administrative structures that restrict their decision-making capabilities, that are focused on saving money at least as much as on combating illness, and that do not provide the latest technology or much time and resources for professional development. Yet we expect those physicians to do whatever it takes—fight the system for what the patient needs, spend personal time mastering the latest medical advances and technologies—to help those whom they serve. To do otherwise would be malpractice, a betrayal of trust, a breach of ethics as a professional.

Given the advances in information technology that are reshaping the knowledge students need and the ways educators can help them learn, we need to accept a professional obligation—despite current institutional constraints—to do whatever it takes to change traditional instructional practices so that a generation of children is truly prepared for the 21st century.

4. How do we prove to communities that new, technology-based models of teaching and learning are better than current instructional approaches?

Few communities are willing to "take on faith" the types of educational innovations discussed in this Yearbook. Many people are uneasy about whether conventional instruction and traditional testing are developing and assessing the types of knowledge and skills children need for their future. However, most parents and taxpayers feel that the current system worked for them and do not want to substitute something radically different unless new methods are proven to be superior. What types of evidence can educators offer communities that innovative, technology-based models of teaching and learning are so much better—given what our society needs in the 21st century—that the substantial cost and effort of systemic reform is more than worth the trouble?

Research documents that new, technology-based pedagogical strategies result in at least four kinds of improvements in educational outcomes. Some of these gains are easy to communicate to the community; others are difficult—but together they constitute a body of evidence that can convince most people. These four types of improvements are listed below, in sequence from the most readily documented to the hardest to demonstrate.

Increased learner motivation. As discussed throughout this Yearbook, students are very excited when exposed to learning experiences that go beyond information assimilation and teaching by telling. Guided inquiry, project-based collaboration, and mentoring relationships all evoke increased learner motivation, manifested via readily observable indicators such as better attendance, higher concentration, and greater time on task. All of these not only correlate with increased educational performance, but also are in stark contrast to the attitudes parents and taxpayers formed about most of their schooling. Documenting to communities that students care about what they are learning and are working hard to achieve complex goals is not difficult, given the ubiquity of videotape players and camcorders. Student-produced videos that show learners engaged and excited are intriguing to parents and taxpayers, who may not fully understand what is happening in the classroom, but are impressed by student behavior divergent from their own memories and likely to result in better learning outcomes. Too often, educators take little advantage of this easy way to open a dialogue about instructional improvement with the community.

Advanced topics mastered. Whatever else they believe about the purposes of schooling, parents want their children to have a prosperous lifestyle and know that this necessitates mastering advanced concepts. In the 21st century, being a successful worker and an informed citizen will require the sophisticated knowledge delineated in the national curriculum standards, especially in the sciences and mathematics. The Yearbook chapters describe how using information technology can help students not only to learn these difficult concepts, but also to master the learning-how-to-learn skills needed to keep their capabilities current in a rapidly evolving economy. When shown that technology-based instructional strategies enable teaching sophisticated ideas not now part of the conventional curriculum, more complex than the items on current standardized tests, and harder than what they learned in school, parents and taxpayers are impressed.

Students acting as experts do. Developing in learners the ability to use problem-solving processes similar to those of experts is challenging, but provides powerful evidence that students are gaining the skills they will need to succeed in the 21st century. One of the most striking features of a classroom based on the instructional models this Yearbook describes is that learners are behaving as do teams of scientists, mathematicians, designers, or other kinds of expert problem solvers. Pupils' activities in these learning environments mirror the analytic, interpretive, creative, and expressive uses of information tools increasingly characteristic of sophisticated workplace settings. When parents and taxpayers see students perform complex tasks and create intricate products, they are impressed by the similarity between the recent evolution of their own workplaces and the skills children are developing.

Better outcomes on standardized tests. The most difficult type of evidence to provide for the superiority of new, technology-based instructional models is what communities first demand: higher scores on conventional measures of achievement. Standardized tests are designed to assess only a narrow range of knowledge, and the other three types of improvements just discussed fall largely outside the scope of what they measure. A major challenge for educational assessment is to develop methods that measure a wider range of skills than paper-and-pencil, multiple-choice tests—without bogging educators down in complex, time-consuming, and potentially unreliable performance evaluations. Research shows that students' outcomes on conventional achievement tests rise when the educational innovations discussed in this Yearbook are implemented, but this does not occur immediately, as teachers and learners must first master these new models of pedagogy. To succeed in systemic reform, educators must prepare communities for the fact that test scores will not instantly rise and that other, complementary, types of improvements less easy to report quantitatively are better short-range measures of improvement.

Overall, the single most effective means of convincing parents, the business community, and taxpayers that technology-based models of teaching are superior to conventional instructional approaches is to involve them in students' education. Through distributed learning approaches that build partnerships between schools and society, communities have ample opportunities to observe the types of evidence discussed above, as well as to further enhance students' educational outcomes.

5. How can educational technology increase equity rather than widen current gaps between the "haves" and "have-nots?"

Implemented within a larger context of systemic reform, emerging information technologies can produce the dramatic improvements in learning outcomes this Yearbook describes. But won't such educational usage of computers and communications widen inequities in our society? However ample the access to technology that students have in schools, learners differ greatly in the number and sophistication of information devices in their homes and communities. Isn't all this effort simply making education better for the *haves*, potentially worsening our society's pathological gaps in income and power? Certainly, new media such as Web TV are dropping in price, and almost all homes have video games, television, and videotape players—but won't the rich always have more information devices of greater power than the poor, skewing the advantages of distributed learning and increasing inequality?

From an historical perspective, innovative information technologies at first widen inequities within civilization, because initial access to the differential advantage they bring is restricted to the few who can afford the substantial expense of this increased power. As emerging media mature, drop in price, and are widely adopted, however, the ultimate effect of information technology is to make society more egalitarian. For example, the world of universal telephone service is a more equitable environment than was the world of messenger boys and telegraph offices. The challenge for current educational policy is to minimize the period during which the gap between the haves and have-nots widens, rapidly moving to a maturity of usage and a universality of access that promotes increased equity.

At present, most of society's attempts to decrease the widened inequalities that new educational technologies could create are centered on access and literacy. In schools that serve disadvantaged and at-risk populations, extra efforts are made to increase the amount of available computers and communications technology. Similarly, educators and learners in have-not situations are given special training to ensure that they are literate in information tools, such as Web browsers. To compensate for more home-based technology in affluent areas, many feel that our best strategy is providing teachers and students in low socioeconomic status areas with additional technology to "level the playing field" (Coley, Cradler, and Engel 1997).

Although a good place to begin, this approach to educational equity is inadequate unless taken beyond access and literacy to address issues of content and services. The online materials and types of assistance that learners and teachers can access must reflect the needs and interests of diverse and at-risk students. For example, I can take homeless people to the public library and show them how to use a Web browser to download images of Impressionist paintings at the Louvre, but this experience is not likely to motivate or impress them, since it does not speak to their primary needs. Similarly, emerging graphical interfaces such as Microsoft Windows™ enhance many users' capabilities, but adversely affect learners with reduced eyesight who cannot effectively manipulate the visual features of these interfaces.

As Behrmann's chapter on assistive technologies discusses, the real issue in equity is empowerment—tailoring information technology to enable dispossessed groups to achieve their goals. For example, I worked with a local team of politicians to explore the implications of information technology for improving public services. They were excited about using community-based information terminals to offer improved access to health care, welfare, education, and other social services for the immigrant and minority populations they served. When I began to describe how online communication tools could help these groups to increase their participation in voting and to form coalitions for political action, however, the elected representatives immediately lost interest. To truly achieve educational equity, working collaboratively with have-not populations is vital in developing content and services tailored to their needs and designed to build on their strengths and agendas. Otherwise, improving access and literacy will fall short of the success for all students essential to America's prosperity in the 21st century.

6. If we use technology well, what should we expect as "typical" student performance?

If we were to implement systemic reform based on new strategies for learning through sophisticated technology, research suggests that "typical" students might do as well as "exemplary" learners do now. Our expectations for what pupils can accomplish are far too low, largely because standard educational processes are obsolete given the progression of information technology, insights into the nature of learning, and shifts in the educational outcomes society needs. In many ways, we live in the "Dark Ages" of schooling—restrained from making rapid advances toward increased instructional effectiveness by outmoded ideas, ritual, and tradition.

Setting our sights higher and using better metrics to measure progress are vital to successful innovation. For example, many people are intrigued by results from the Third International Mathematics and Science Study (TIMSS), which show the United States well behind nations such as Singapore and Japan on math and science outcomes from a globally developed achievement test. Crusaders are implementing reforms to ensure that our students do much better on this test. Our goal, however, should not be to exceed the level of Singapore on an assessment instrument that, as described earlier, measures only a fraction of what students need to know for their future prosperity—and, moreover, incorporates a diluted definition of educational quality negotiated across many countries with very different populations and national goals.

Others advocate using a standards-based curriculum as the touchstone for educational effectiveness, and reformers are centering state and national judgments of educational worth on this measure. Certainly, the National Council of Teachers of Mathematics (NCTM) standards are a major improvement over the hodgepodge math curriculum that existed before their inception, as are the American Association for the Advancement of Science (AAAS) standards and similar efforts in other fields. But our metric for students' success should not simply be whether they learn the math that mathematicians think is important, the science that scientists believe is vital, and so on. Being a productive worker and citizen involves much more than having an adequate background in each field of knowledge. Integrating these concepts and skills and being a lifelong learner with the self-worth, discipline, and motivation to apply this knowledge is of paramount importance—yet not captured by discipline-based standards alone.

New forms of pedagogy also are no "philosopher's stone" that can make golden each educational experience for every learner. Some argue that, if only all classrooms were based on constructivist learning or situated cognition or individualized tutoring or multimedia presentations or integrated learning systems or whatever pedagogical panacea, every student would succeed. However, learning is a very complex and idiosyncratic process that requires, for each pupil, a repertoire of many different types of instruction orchestrated together. In other words, no test, no curriculum, and no instructional strategy in itself can guarantee educational quality—even though our current approach to determining schools' worth is based on these inadequate measures. Instead, we need new standards for a knowledge-based society that combine all

214

these metrics for success and that are based on much higher levels of "typical" student outcomes.

The educational strategies in this Yearbook illustrate a large group of successful technology-based innovations with the common characteristic that learners exceed everyone's expectations for what is possible. Second graders do 5th grade work; 9th graders outscore 12th grade students. What would those 9th graders be accomplishing if, from kindergarten on, they had continuous access to our best tools, curriculum, and pedagogy? Would they be the equivalent of college sophomores? We are selling short a generation by expecting less and by orienting our curriculum, instruction, and tests accordingly.

CONCLUSION

My responses to the six questions above sketch a conceptual framework for thinking about the process of scaling-up from islands of innovation to widespread shifts in standard educational practices. These answers illustrate that technology-based systemic reform is difficult in part because our ways of thinking about implementation are often flawed. Large-scale educational innovation will never be easy, but it can be less difficult if we go beyond our implicit assumptions about learning, technology, equity, schooling, and society. The ideas in this Yearbook do not present a blueprint for universal educational improvement—no one yet has such a recipe—but do illumine both insightful visions and "tomorrow morning" strategies for accomplishing them. Understanding the scaling-up process is vital for making such strategies affordable, generalizable, and sustainable. By balancing investments in advanced technology and standardized tests with investments in sophisticated curriculum, assessment, and educators—in and out of school—we can successfully prepare children for the tremendous challenges of the 21st century.

REFERENCES

Coley, R.J., J. Cradler, and P.K. Engel. (1997). *Computers and Classrooms: The Status of Technology in U.S. Schools*. Princeton, N.J.: Educational Testing Service.

Dede, C. (1996). "Emerging Technologies and Distributed Learning." *American Journal of Distance Education* 10, 2: 4-36.

McKinsey & Company. (1995). *Connecting K-12 Schools to the Information Superhighway*. Palo Alto, Calif.: McKinsey & Company.

About the Editor

Chris Dede is Professor of Education and Information Technology at George Mason University, Mail Stop 4B3, 4400 University Drive, Fairfax, Va. 22030. He has served as a Senior Program Director at the National Science Foundation, a Visiting Scientist at MIT and at NASA, and a Policy Fellow at the National Institute of Education. His research interests include technology forecasting and assessment, emerging technologies for learning, and leadership in educational innovation. Phone: (703) 993-2019. Fax: (703) 993-2013. E-mail: cdede@gmu.edu. URL: http://www.virtual.gmu.edu/

About the Authors

Michael Behrmann is Professor of Education and Director of the Center for Human disAbilities at George Mason University, 4400 University Drive, MS 1F, Fairfax, Va. 22026, USA. His research and training interests are focused upon instructional technology and assistive technology for individuals with mild to severe disabilities. Phone: (703) 993-3670. Fax: (703) 993-3681. E-mail: mbehrmann@gmu.edu

Phyllis Blumenfeld is Professor of Education, Educational Studies Program, School of Education, University of Michigan, 610 E. University Avenue, Ann Arbor, Mich. 48109-1359. She is the author of papers on project-based science, classroom tasks, inquiry learning, and enhancing thoughtfulness. Her research interests are motivation, learning, and instruction in classrooms. Phone: (313) 763-6101. Fax: (313) 763-1368. E-mail: blumenfe@umich.edu

John D. Bransford is Centennial Professor of Psychology and Education and Co-Director of the Learning Technology Center, Vanderbilt University, Box 45, Peabody College, Nashville, Tenn. 37203. His research interests include cognition, problem solving, learning, and technology. Phone: (615) 322-8070, (615) 343-7556. E-mail: bransfjd@ctrvax.vanderbilt.edu

Melinda H. Bray is Research Associate at the Learning Technology Center, Vanderbilt University, Box 45, Peabody College, Nashville, Tenn. 37203. Phone: (615) 343-1642. Fax: (615) 343-7556. E-mail: braymh@ctrvax.vanderbilt.edu

Katherine L. Burgess is Research Associate at the Learning Technology Center, Vanderbilt University, Box 45, Peabody College, Nashville, Tenn. 37203. Her principal interest is the application of cognitive theory to the design of technology-based instructional materials. Phone: (615) 322-8070. Fax: (615) 343-7556. E-mail: burgeskl@ctrvax.vanderbilt.edu

Fred Carigg is the Executive Director for Academic Programs in Union City, New Jersey. His responsibilities include the supervison of the development and implementation of curriculum for all programs, Pre-K through Adult Education, including the integration of technology into the curriculum. Previously, he served as District Supervisor of Bilingual/ESL programs. Phone: (201) 348-5671. Fax: (201) 330-1736. E-mail: fcarrigg@union-city.k12.nj.us

Susan R. Goldman is Co-Director of the Learning Technology Center and Professor of Psychology at Vanderbilt University, Box 45, Peabody College, Nashville, Tenn. 37203. Her research interests focus on strategies for learning from text and integrated media, problem-solving skills, new forms of assessment, and uses of technology for educational reform. Phone: (615) 322-8070. Fax: (615) 343-7556. E-mail: Susan.R.Goldman@vanderbilt.edu

Louis M. Gomez is Associate Professor of Learning Sciences and Electrical/Computer Sciences, Northwestern University, 2115 North Campus Drive, Evanston, Ill. 60208. He is the Principal Investigator of the CoVis Project and the Co-Director of the NSF-sponsored Center for Technologies in Urban Schools. He is interested in the way curriculum and technology can serve to bridge communities of practice in schools with communities of practice beyond schools. Phone: (847) 467-2821. Fax: (847) 491-8999. E-mail: l-gomez@nwu.edu

Mark Guzdial is Assistant Professor in the College of Computing (M/S 0280) at the Georgia Institute of Technology, 801 Atlantic Drive, Atlanta, Ga. 30332. Phone: (404) 894-5618. Fax: (404) 853-0673. E-mail: guzdial@cc.gatech.edu

Jan Hawkins is the Director of the Center for Children and Technology of the Education Development Center, Inc. Previously, she directed the national Center for Technology in Education, where she focused on the design of technology-enhanced classrooms and curricula and new approaches for assessing student learning. She also has directed work on gender issues in relation to technologies, the integration of technologies into learning environments for students with hearing impairments, and technology enhancement for museums. Phone: (212) 807-4208. Fax: (212) 633-8804. E-mail: jhawkins@edc.org

Margaret Honey is Deputy Director of the Education Development Center's Center for Children and Technology. Previously, she served as Associate Director of the national OERI-funded Center for Technology in Education and has served as co-chair of Harvard University's "Leadership and the New Technologies" summer institute. She has focused her research and development interests on the role of telecommunications technologies in education. Phone: (212) 807-4209. Fax: (212) 633-8804. E-mail: mhoney@tristram.edc.org

Robert Kozma is Principal Scientist at the Center for Technology in Learning, SRI International, 333 Ravenswood Avenue, Menlo Park, Ca. 94025. His research interests include media theory, policy issues related to educational technology, the impact of technology on cognition, and the application of advanced technology to improve teaching and learning, particularly in the sciences. Phone: (650) 859-3997. Fax: (650) 859-2861. E-mail: rkozma@unix.sri.com

Joseph Krajcik is Associate Professor of Science Education, Educational Studies Program, School of Education, University of Michigan, 610 E. University Avenue, Ann Arbor, Mich. 48109-1359. His research interests focus on re-engineering science classrooms so that students engage in solving authentic, ill-structured problems through inquiry and the use of computing and communication technologies. He is an author of papers on project-based science, inquiry learning, and the use of technology. Phone: (313) 647-0597. Fax: (313) 763-1368. E-mail: krajcik@umich.edu

Eileen M. Lento is Assistant Professor of Research in the Learning Sciences, Northwestern University, 2115 North Campus Drive, Evanston, Ill. 60208. Currently, she serves as the Learning Through Collaborative Visualization (CoVis) Project Manager. Prior to accepting this position, she headed teacher and curriculum development for the CoVis Project. Her research interests include teacher change, school improvement planning, and educational asssessment and evaluation. Phone: (847) 467-2824. Fax: (847) 491-8999. E-mail: lento@nwu.edu

Ronald Marx (Ph.D. Stanford University) is Professor of Education and Chair of the Educational Studies Program at the University of Michigan. He has conducted classroom-based experimental and observational research focusing on how classrooms can be sites for learning that is highly motivated and cognitively engaging. In the late 1980s, he conducted policy research in British Columbia that led to substantial reform of the province's schools. Recently, he has been working with computer scientists, science educators, and educational psychologists to enhance science education and develop teacher professional development models to sustain long term change in science education.

D. Kevin O'Neill is McDonnell Postdoctoral Fellow at the Ontario Institute for Studies in Education of the University of Toronto (OISE/UT), 252 Bloor Street West, Toronto, Ontario, Canada M5S 1V6. He recently completed his doctorate in Learning Sciences at Northwestern University. As a graduate, he worked on the development of software and activities for science learning. Currently, he is continuing his research and development efforts in telementoring. Phone: (416) 923-6641. Fax: (416) 926-4725. E-mail: dko@acm.org

Margaret Riel is the Associate Director of the Center for Collaborative Research in Education at the University of California, Irvine, 2001 Berkeley Place, Irvine, Ca. 92697-5500. Phone: (714) 824-1230. Fax: (714) 824-2965. In addition, she is Director of InterLearn, 943 San Dieguito Drive, Encinitas, Ca. 92024. Phone: (619) 943-1314. She has designed models of learning with interactive technology and writes on both the current (*Transportation for the Mind*) and future (*Learning Spaces in the Networlds of Tomorrow*) uses of the Internet in school learning. Her online office is found at http://www.iearn.org/circles/riel.html/

Patricia Schank is Research Scientist at the Center for Technology in Learning, SRI International, 333 Ravenswood Avenue, Menlo Park, Ca. 94025. Her main interests are in the design, development, and evaluation of computer-mediated learning environments, especially multi-user environments and simulation technology in science education. Phone: (650) 859-3934. Fax: (650) 859-2861. E-mail: schank@unix.sri.com

Elliot Soloway is Professor of Electrical Engineering and Computer Sciences and Professor of Education, University of Michigan, 146 ATL, Ann Arbor, Mich. 48109-2122. His research interest is the use of technology in education. He is an author on numerous articles on the use of computational and telecommunication technologies in the classroom and the author of "Artificial Intelligence and Learning." His research interests include developing software that takes into consideration the unique needs of learners. Phone: (313) 936-1562. Fax: (313) 763-1260. E-mail: soloway@umich.edu

Susan M. Williams is Senior Research Associate at the Learning Technology Center, Vanderbilt University, Box 45, Peabody College, Nashville, Tenn. 37203. Her research interests focus on students' learning as it occurs during complex problem solving. Much of her work involves the design of problem-based curricula and technology that supports collaborative problem solving. Phone: (615) 322-8070. Fax: (615) 343-7556. E-mail: williams@ctrvax.vanderbilt.edu

ASCD 1997-98
Board of Directors

Diann Gathright, ScholAR, Little Rock, Arkansas
Kolene Granger, Washington County Schools, St. George, Utah
Lou Howell, Urbandale Community School District, Urbandale, Iowa
Lisbeth Johnson, Walnut Valley Unified Schools, Walnut, California
Leon Levesque, Maine School Administrative District No. 16, Hallowell, Maine
Patricia H. Marshall, Jefferson County Board of Education, Louisville, Kentucky
Francine Mayfield, Clark County School District, Las Vegas, Nevada
Saundra McCray, District of Columbia Public Schools, Washington, D.C.
Marie Meyer, Thornton Fractional Area Educational Cooperative, Calumet City, Illinois
Michaelene Meyer, Elkhorn Public Schools, Elkhorn, Nebraska
Ronald R. Musoleno, Parkland School District, Allentown, Pennsylvania
Thomas J. O'Rourke, DeKalb County School System, Decatur, Georgia
Denrick T. Richardson, Deninoo School, Fort Resolution, Northwest Territories, Canada
Sarah Booth Riss, Riverview Gardens School District, St. Louis, Missouri
Douglas G. Schermer, Briggs Elementary School, Maquoketa, Iowa
Barbara Warner-Tracy, Susan B. Anthony School, Sacramento, California
Peyton Williams, Jr., Georgia Department of Education, Atlanta, Georgia
Jill D. Wilson, Riverland Elementary School, Ft. Lauderdale, Florida
Ellen Wolf, Walla Walla School District, Walla Walla, Washington
Thomas V. Zandoli, Yaquina View Elementary School, Newport, Oregon

Affiliate Presidents

Alabama: Peggy H. Connell, Talladega County Board of Education, Talladega
Alaska: Mary Starrs Armstrong, Juneau School District, Juneau
Alberta: Julie Prest, Calgary
Arizona: John G. Mansour, Ottawa University, Phoenix
Arkansas: Andrew Tolbert, Pine Bluff High School, Pine Bluff
British Columbia: Bruce Mills, Terry Fox Elementary School, Abbotsford
California: Mary Beall, San Diego County Office of Education, San Diego
Colorado: Peg Portscheller, Lake County School District, Leadville
Connecticut: Marie E. Diamond, North Haven Public Schools, North Haven
Curacao: Adrie Bloem
Delaware: Catherine Gilbertson, Polytech High School, Woodside
District of Columbia: Paula K. Boone, Seabrook
Florida: Simone P. Hebert, Hollywood
Georgia: Jay R. Wucher, Fulton County Schools, Atlanta
Germany: Elise Henderson
Hawaii: Ermile Hargrove, Honolulu
Hong Kong: Angela Cheung
Idaho: Jewell Hoopes, Dean Goodsell Primary School, Shelley
Illinois: Cheryl W. Kopecky, Elmhurst Unit School District 205, Elmhurst

Indiana: Nancy Moller, Anderson University, Anderson
Iowa: Dorothy A. Engstrom, Council Bluffs Community Schools, Council Bluffs
Israel: Tali Friedman, Levinsky College, Moshav Bnei Zion
Japan: Paul Raschke, St. Mary's International School, Tokyo
Kansas: Richard Flores, Oakley USD 274, Oakley
Kentucky: Wayne Starnes, Dayton Independent Schools, Dayton
Louisiana: Lindsey Moore, George Washingon Carver Junior-Senior High School, New Orleans
Maine: Beatrice McGarvey, Portland Public Schools, Portland
Manitoba: Linda Thorlakson, Assiniborne South School District, Winnipeg
Maryland: JoAnne L. Carter, Maryland State Department of Education, Baltimore
Massachusetts: David Troughton, North Reading Public School, North Reading
Michigan: Roxanne DeWeerd, Hudsonville Public Schools, Hudsonville
Minnesota: Mark Youngstrom, Vandais Heights
Mississippi: C. E. Craft, McComb School District, McComb
Missouri: Mary A. Laffey, Oakland Middle School, Columbia
Montana: Joanne Erickson, Havre
Nebraska: Craig Kautz, Hastings Public Schools, Hastings
Netherlands: Ingrid Smit
Nevada: David Wilson, Las Vegas
New Hampshire: Leo P. Corriveau, Fall Mountain Regional School District, Charlestown
New Jersey: Christine A. Kane, Clinton Township Board of Education, Annandale
New Mexico: Chris Milyard, Tombaugh Elementary School, Las Cruces
New York: John Gangemi, Nassau BOCES, Westbury
North Carolina: Jane C. King, Kings Mountain District Schools, Kings Mountain
North Dakota: Karen Nelson, Hettinger
Northwest Territories: Marge Osted, Harry Camsell School, Hay River
Ohio: Michael D. Ross, Warren County Office of Education, Lebanon
Oklahoma: Wayne Beam, Myers Elementary School, Yukon
Ontario: Carolyn Bennett, Nipissing University, North Bay
Oregon: David Nuss, Gervais School District # 1, Gervais
Pennsylvania: Lawrence Palko, Schuylkill IU #29, Mar Lin
Puerto Rico: Maria I. Ortiz, San Lorenzo
Rhode Island: William R. Fasano, Tiverton High School, Tiverton
Singapore: Kam Kum Wone, Ministry of Education
South Carolina: Michael M. Turner, Horry County School District, Conway
South Dakota: Grace Christianson, Lennox School District, Lennox
Spain: Irene Conway, Colegio Hispano Norteamericano, Valencia
St. Maarten: Velda James, St. Maarten Academy, Philipsburg
Tennessee: Gordon Stone, Brighton

Texas: June Hogue, Lubbock Independent School District, Lubbock
Trinidad & Tobago: Jennifer Lavia
United Kingdom: Sue Raven, Cambridgeshire
Utah: Shauna Carl, Salt Lake City
Vermont: Judith M. Ouellette, Westford School, Westford
Virgin Islands: Dolores T. Clendinen, St. Thomas
Virginia: J. Richard Lewis, Yorktown
Washington: Amy Bragdon, Centennial Middle School, Spokane
West Virginia: Lydia McCue, Putnam County Schools, Winfield
Wisconsin: Nancy Gurrie, Cudahy School District, Cudahy
Wyoming: Rick Staldine, Campbell County School District, Gillette

ASCD Review Council

Chair: Quincy Harrigan, Insular Department of Education, Philipsburg, St.
    Maarten, Netherlands Antilles
Corrine Hill, Educational Consultant, Salt Lake City, Utah
Maryann Johnson, Bella Vista, Arizona
Arthur Steller, Kingston City School District, Kingston New York
Sandra Gray Wegner, S. W. Missouri State University, Springfield

ASCD Headquarters Staff

Gene R. Carter, *Executive Director*
Diane Berreth, *Deputy Executive Director*
Frank Betts, *Associate Executive Director*
Melody Ridgeway, *Assistant Executive Director*
Doug Soffer, *Assistant Executive Director*
Mikki Terry, *Assistant Executive Director*

Holly Abrams
Diana Allen
Barry Amis
Joanne Arnold
Eva Barsin
Vickie Bell
Jennifer Beun
Steve Blaufeld
Gary Bloom
Cecilia Boamah
Meltonya Booze
Maritza Bourque
Dana Bowser
Joan Brandt
Dorothy Brown
Beverly Buckner
Colette Burgess
Angela Caesar
Kathryn Carswell
Sally Chapman
John Checkley
Katherine Checkley
Raiza Chernault
Sandra Claxton
Judi Connelly
Misty Copeland
Andrea Corsillo
Agnes Crawford
Sandi Cumberland
Marcia D'Arcangelo
Michael Davis
Jay DeFranco
Keith Demmons
Becky DeRigge
Michael DeVries
Stephanie Dunn
Shiela Ellison
Don Ernst
Olivia Evans
Honor Fede
Kathie Felix
Gillian Fitzpatrick
Harriett Forster
John Franklin
Christine Fuscellaro
LaKiesha Gayden

Troy Gooden
Nora Gyuk
Dorothy Haines
Joan Montgomery Halford
Charles Halverson
Susan Hlesciak Hall
Vicki Hancock
Nancy Harrell
John Henderson
Helené Hodges
Davene Holland
Julie Houtz
Angela Howard
Debbie Howerton
Todd Johnson
Jo Ann Jones
Mary Jones
Teola Jones
Pamela Karwasinski
Leslie Kiernan
Crystal Knight-Lee
Tamara Larson
Angelika Machi
John Mackie
Indu Madan
Gina Major
Larry Mann
Helen Marquez
J'Anna McCaleb
Jan McCool
Michelle McKinley
Clara Meredith
Ron Miletta
Frances Mindel
Nancy Modrak
Kenny Moir
Karen Monaco
Margaret Murphy
Dina Murray
Charwin Nah
Christie Nelson
Mary Beth Nielsen
KayLani Noble
John O'Neil
Margaret Oosterman
Jayne Osgood

Millie Outten
Diane Parker
Kelvin Parnell
Mark Cantor Paster
Margini Patel
Elisa Perodin
Terrence Petty
Carolyn Pool
Ruby Powell
Tina Prack
Pam Price
Judy Rixey
Erik Robelen
Rita Roberts
Gayle Rockwell
Carly Rothman
Jeff Rupp
Jamie Sawatzky
Marge Scherer
Jan Schmidt
Beth Schweinefuss
Timothy Scott
Bob Shannon
Katherine Sibert
Darcie Simpson
Tracey Smith
Valerie Sprague
Karen Steirer
Brian Sullivan
Michelle Tarr
Beth Taylor
Carol Tell
Jocelyn Thomas
Janis Tomlinson
Judy Walter
Tisha Ware
Gena Randall
Karen Rasmussen
Hope Redwine
Vivian West
Kay Whittington
Linda Wilkey
Helena Williams
Melissa Williamson
Scott Willis
Carolyn Wojcik